NEO−SEGREGATION NARRATIVES

BRIAN NORMAN

NEO–SEGREGATION NARRATIVES

Jim Crow in Post–Civil Rights

American Literature

The University of Georgia Press ▸ Athens and London

Publication of this book was made possible in part by the
David L. Kalstone Memorial Fund of the Rutgers University
English Department.

Designed by Mindy Basinger Hill
Set in 10.5/13.5 Adobe Caslon Pro

Printed digitally in the United States of America

Library of Congress Cataloging-in-Publication Data
Norman, Brian, 1977–
Neo–segregation narratives : Jim Crow in post–civil rights
American literature / Brian Norman.
        p.   cm.
Includes bibliographical references and index.
ISBN-13: 978-0-8203-3596-4 (hardcover : alk. paper)
ISBN-10: 0-8203-3596-7 (hardcover : alk. paper)
ISBN-13: 978-0-8203-3597-1 (pbk. : alk. paper)
ISBN-10: 0-8203-3597-5 (pbk. : alk. paper)
1. American literature—African American authors—History and
criticism. 2. American literature—20th century—History and
criticism. 3. African Americans in literature. 4. Segregation in
literature. 5. Race discrimination in literature. I. Title.
PS153.N5N65 2010
810.9'896073—dc22   2010005969

British Library Cataloging-in-Publication Data available

CONTENTS

ILLUSTRATIONS

ACKNOWLEDGMENTS

I am awed by the vigor, generosity, and intelligence of friends and colleagues at each stage of the research and writing process.

I was privileged to finish the bulk of this manuscript while in residence at the Center for the Humanities at Wesleyan University. I am grateful for the friendship and intellectual acumen of the director, Jill Morawski, and my fellow Fellows for lengthy and challenging conversations. As I was finishing this book, I joined the English Department at Loyola University Maryland. There I found a terrific bunch of colleagues, students, and new friends. I also continue to profit from the richness of the Rutgers diaspora, especially fellow citizens Hillary Chute and Channette Romero, and my mentors Marianne DeKoven and Cheryl Wall, whose guidance, wisdom, and downright niceness are such gifts.

I am indebted to Nancy Grayson and the readers at the University of Georgia Press, whose encouragement and thoughtful suggestions helped me hone my scope and aim. I also thank everyone else involved with the project at the University of Georgia Press, especially Jon Davies, John McLeod, Beth Snead, and Kay Kodner for her thoughtful copy-editing. A special issue of *African American Review* (*AAR*) and related volume on "Representing Segregation" laid crucial groundwork. The review's former editor Joycelyn Moody took a chance on me and I hope to have earned her enthusiastic support. I am also happy to have worked with Aileen Keenan, Piper Kendrix Williams, Elizabeth Abel, Trudier Harris, Shawn Michelle Smith, and all the contributors. Audiences for early versions of this work were helpful, especially at the American Literature Association, Wesleyan University, Rutgers University, Idaho State University, and the Modern Language Association; for the latter, I thank Leigh Anne Duck for the invitation and Hortense Spillers for her comments. JoSann Lien provided superb graduate research assistance. I also thank *Canadian Review of American Studies* for publishing an earlier version of chapter 4.

I am grateful for a research fellowship and accommodations at the Center for the Humanities at Wesleyan University, a summer research grant from the dean's office at Loyola University Maryland, a research fellowship from the Idaho Humanities Council, and a grant from the Humanities/Social Sciences Research Committee at Idaho State University.

As always, I thank my partner, Greg Nicholl, who allows me to spend a bit more time at my desk or in the library than I should. That makes coming home to him all the sweeter.

NEO−SEGREGATION NARRATIVES

JIM CROW THEN

The Emergence of
Neo–Segregation Narratives

Contemporary America is drawn to segregation's artifacts: "Whites Only" signs, mammy cookie jars, blackface performances, lynching photographs, civil rights placards—that is, when they are encased in plexiglass, displayed as collectibles, or cropped neatly in glossy coffee-table books.[1] We look on these images with dread, which is staved off only by faith in overarching narratives of racial progress. Thus these artifacts become what civil rights writer James Baldwin deemed "irrelevant monuments." David Leeming reports, "In Atlanta [Baldwin] visited the monument to Martin Luther King—a monument 'as absolutely irrelevant as the Lincoln Memorial.' Making monuments was 'one of the ways the Western world has learned . . . to outwit history [and] time—to make a life and a death irrelevant. . . . There's nothing one can do with a monument.'"[2] So today, when Whoopi Goldberg proudly displays her "Wall of Shame" of mammies, coons, and Jim Crow signs, post–civil rights American subjects can gaze with curiosity and contempt, accepting their admission ticket to a newer, more enlightened era.[3] We deputize ourselves as watchful guardians of the backdoor lest Jim Crow Jr. and his goons come knocking. Then we put our children to bed with a picture book that recalls the journey to school integration in order to recite a national narrative of racial progress that need no longer end at the Oval Office in an avowedly postrace era.[4]

Jim Crow nevertheless creeps in despite our vigilance. He makes anachronistic appearances, such as self-conscious showings in the guise of "entertainment"—the donning of blackface by actors Ted Danson or Sarah Silverman or by characters in Spike Lee's satiric film *Bamboozled* (2000). Or he may appear in more insidious ways, as a threat—such as when nooses are tacked on doors at Ivy League institutions or hung from a tree (which occurred in Jena, Louisiana, in a notorious incident in fall 2007). That is why David Pilgrim, curator of the Jim Crow Museum of Racist Memorabilia, resists "thick naïveté about America's past" by opting for a therapeutic "belief that open, honest, even painful discussions about race are necessary to avoid yesterday's mistakes." Such racial progress narratives inevitably accompany Jim Crow today. We gawk in fascination and fear, inexplicably drawn into his gravitational field while we are also resistant, attracted and repulsed, committed anew to keeping him in his place. Segregation now stands as an era to which we must not return yet to which we are ever in danger of returning. So we perpetually seek reassuring signs that Jim Crow is indeed dead.

Today's writers rarely offer comforting tonics of Jim Crow's demise, however. They take on the racial kudzu, as Alice Walker describes such work in her 1973 essay "Choosing to Stay at Home: Ten Years after the March on Washington." She writes, "It is sometimes hard to eat here because of those memories, but in Mississippi (as in the rest of America) racism is like that local creeping kudzu vine that swallows whole forests and abandoned houses; if you don't keep pulling up the roots it will grow back faster than you can destroy it."[5] Post–civil rights writers draw on Jim Crow to tell us as much about our present as our past. For example, Ernest J. Gaines returns to 1940s Louisiana for his acclaimed 1993 novel *A Lesson before Dying*. In the novel, a poor, uneducated young black man finds himself on death row for his role in a liquor store robbery as an innocent bystander. The defense attorney perpetuates the dehumanization of African Americans under Jim Crow in his unsuccessful argument that executing the young man is unnecessary because it would be equivalent to executing a hog. In response, his grandmother, Miss Emma, asks Grant, a local schoolteacher, to teach her grandson to reject white society's view and die as a man. Grant initially resists the request because he wants desperately to leave the South, knowing that manhood and dignity are unavailable to him in such a place.[6] It is easy to see the repulsion and lure the Jim Crow South poses for Gaines himself, since it carries both an unavoidable history of racial terror and despair as well as stories of racial survival and kinship. Despite his reluctance, Grant is pulled deeper and deeper into that black community. There he finds redemption and strength in locations of abjection and subjection, signified by the death-row cell for the novel's characters and the Jim Crow South for Gaines and his national readership. The occasion of *A Lesson before Dying*'s National Book Award presented a stark contrast between the dehumanization of the novel's subjects in the 1940s and the lionization of its author in the 1990s. The novel's selection for Oprah Winfrey's Book Club in 1997 helped secure its place in the American imagination as a celebrated testament to black resistance and dignity.

Gaines's title begs a question: What are the lessons for a post–civil rights readership, an era in which segregation is no longer the law of the land yet Jim Crow's legacy persists, albeit in different and more subtle forms? How does a tale of Jim Crow degradation *then* create a narrative of pride *now*? Renee Romano and Leigh Raiford argue, "While contemporary civil rights movement memorialization espouses a necessarily antiracist perspective, such monuments, museums, streets, and the like both tend to adhere to grand historical narratives of the movement and eschew much discussion of contemporary racial issues."[7] In the literary realm, however, writers return to the time of compulsory race segregation and its attendant racial horrors precisely to address contemporary concerns about racial injustice and its history. Larger questions emerge: When writers such as Toni Morrison and Colson Whitehead join Gaines to excavate that era, how do we read such stories through the layers of history and narratives we tell ourselves of Jim Crow's supposed death? Are we disinterring him, or was he buried prematurely? What do we do with lessons culled by writers of that era such as Charles Chesnutt, William Faulkner, Richard Wright, and Ann Petry? Now, in a self-consciously multicultural era that commemorates the heady gains of the civil rights movement, what lingering concerns and anxieties can stories of Jim Crow address? And is Jim Crow up to the challenge?

This book considers a selection of such stories and argues that they point to a "neo–segregation narrative" tradition. Neo–segregation narratives are contemporary fictional accounts, often historiographic, of Jim Crow. The authors that I will highlight here write from a post–civil rights era and its inclusive, multicultural sensibilities while their characters inhabit the terrain of compulsory race segregation. Writers draw on the perceived clarity of that period to highlight and explain more elusive systems of racial disenfranchisement and division after the end of de jure segregation. I insist on *perceived* clarity, because the actual experiences were as varied and complex as in any other era. Because neo–segregation narratives seek to expose systems of exclusion and disenfranchisement today, they upset dominant national narratives of achieved equality and Jim Crow's passing. The "neo" in the term is debatable, but it marks the shift in the horizon of expectations around race segregation before and after the civil rights movement. Segregation may still be a fact of life, but it no longer has overt legal sanction. Debates about the nature and morality of racial segregation are now largely settled, and people generally agree that Jim Crow segregation was wrong, artificial, and indefensible, even if underlying assumptions or patterns persist.

I use the term "Jim Crow" as a convenient, albeit slippery, shorthand for the history of compulsory race segregation in America. Segregation profoundly shaped the lives of everyone, African Americans in particular, in the late nineteenth and twentieth centuries, and it informs how we think about group identity in the United States today. Segregation comprises a diverse set of cultural practices, ethnic experiences, historical conditions, political ideologies, municipal planning schemes, and de facto social systems, though it is primarily associated with the Jim Crow South and bookended by the court cases *Plessy v. Ferguson* (1896) and *Brown v. Board of Education of Topeka* (1954). The origin of the term "Jim Crow" is tricky because Jim Crow himself made his historical debut in Tim Rice's minstrel shows in the urban north in the 1830s and 1840s, which built on earlier lore cycles.[8] But in contemporary parlance, "Jim Crow" typically describes a loose series of post-Reconstruction phenomena that codified the bright line between black and white in intricate legal and cultural codes in the South. Such lines were later dismantled in sundry desegregation efforts leading to, embodying, and continuing what we call the U.S. civil rights movement. W. E. B. Du Bois famously announced that the twentieth century's defining problem was the color line in *The Souls of Black Folk* (1903). The term "Jim Crow" captures many of the core experiences, attitudes, and practices associated with that color line. In this same vein, I use the term "civil rights" as useful and slippery shorthand for the time between that first major national desegregation victory in 1954 and passage of the 1964 Civil Rights Act. It was then widely possible to conceive of de jure segregation as a relic. The major task shifted to ferreting out segregation's de facto guises, or reconsidering the merits of self-segregation. Still, Jacqueline Dowd Hall warns against overly relying on these signposts in what she dubs the *short civil rights movement* to argue for a *long civil rights movement*.[9]

The chapters in this book discuss pairs of exemplary texts to illuminate key aspects of neo–segregation narratives as well as to sketch the emergence and development of that tradition. The pairings point to five overarching concerns: genre, gender, blackface minstrelsy, ethnicity, and literary history. These entry points also tap into key political and philosophical debates, such as the value of segregated spaces, the tension between black feminism and

Black Power, black complicity in racist cultures, cultural appropriation by way of multicultural inclusion, and ambivalence toward integration ideals. In the first chapter, "Jim Crow Jr.," I discuss the transition from segregation narratives to both the neo–segregation and neo–slave narrative traditions. I consider Lorraine Hansberry's revisions to her iconic play *A Raisin in the Sun* (1959) for a screenplay, which she took as an opportunity to respond to vexing criticisms of her depiction of segregation. Hansberry's transitional case reflects some of the new challenges of representing segregation amid key civil rights desegregation successes. Those challenges shifted considerably by 1970 when Morrison returned to the time of compulsory race segregation in *The Bluest Eye*, which receives less attention than *Beloved* (1987) and thereby signals how the neo–segregation narrative generally is less famous than its fraternal twin, the neo–slave narrative. In the second chapter, "Jim Crow Returns, Jim Crow Remains," I then consider how neo–segregation narratives engage questions of gender, especially long-standing debates between black feminism and masculinist visions of Black Power, of which David Bradley's *The Chaneysville Incident* (1981) and Alice Walker's *The Color Purple* (1982) are high-stakes epicenters. The third chapter, "Jim Too," considers post–civil rights concerns about racial complicity and self-segregation within a notorious tradition now seen as beyond the pale: blackface minstrelsy. I look at the curious role of black blackface performers in Wesley Brown's *Darktown Strutters* (1994), which joins higher-profile depictions, such as in Spike Lee's satiric Hollywood film *Bamboozled* (2000). Brown's playful post–civil rights sensibilities cast Jim Crow as a celebrated model of inclusive separatism, opting for neither integration nor self-segregation. He counterintuitively positions a black minstrel named Jim Crow as a figure of racial pride and Black Power.

Jim Crow experiences and lessons touch Americans from all backgrounds, so as a fourth entry point in the chapter "Jim Crow in Idaho," I consider Jim Crow in white and multiethnic literature. Writers often look to African American experiences of Jim Crow as a reference point to make sense of racialized division among and within other minority groups, even those with little apparent connection to African American culture. I pair American Indian writer Sherman Alexie's depiction of blues legend Robert Johnson in *Reservation Blues* (1995) with a lesser-known novel of the settlement of the interior West in white writer Tom Spanbauer's *The Man Who Fell in Love with the Moon* (1991). Far removed from core African American literary traditions, these texts provide another angle onto the narrative power of Jim Crow in the multiethnic imagination, showing how he can lend moral clarity to other forms of racial division, though this inevitably triggers concerns about cultural appropriation. I then turn to matters of literary history and post–civil rights ambivalence toward integration ideals in chapter 5, "Jim Crow Faulkner," where I discuss playwright Suzan-Lori Parks's masterful and playful revision of William Faulkner's *As I Lay Dying* (1930) in her first novel *Getting Mother's Body* (2003). Parks's novel concerns a poor black family in rural Texas on the eve of the 1963 March on Washington for Jobs and Freedom. The novel turns away from federal politics and toward an integrated literary history to tell the story of a black community living under Jim Crow whose members never make it to the nation's capital or into its history books.

Finally, in the epilogue, I venture into the political and cultural arena to return to the question of a postrace era and the enduring relevance of the neo–segregation narrative, such as Colson Whitehead's *The Intuitionist* (1999). I consider telling examples of Jim Crow's appearances in presidential speeches, political cartoons, activist politics, crime records, museums, and other corners of contemporary American culture. I propose the concept of *temporal dysphoria* to explain the effect of seeing images of Jim Crow *today* when dominant cultural narratives suggest he should be *then*.

This study does not include an exhaustive survey of the literature that could be called "neo–segregation narratives" or related works. Instead, I sketch the outlines of a tradition. Rich examples of neo–segregation narratives abound, but the line that connects them in literary history is not yet fully visible. Such a project is doubly compounded because there is no bright line between pre– and post–civil rights eras, a lack that the "neo" in these terms exploits and belies. However, I mention other key texts for which the examples might stand and arrange chapters roughly by publication date to suggest chronological development. My primary aim is to identify core concerns, dilemmas, and tropes of the neo–segregation narrative tradition and to speculate on the cultural work such a tradition performs. It is up to future scholars to debate which texts do and do not belong in the tradition, as well as to respond to the key ideas presented here. My focus is on what brings post–civil rights authors to return to the Jim Crow era armed with historiographic designs on the one hand and contemporary concerns on the other.

I have chosen pairings that would engender the most interesting discussion about a particular aspect of Jim Crow in post–civil rights American literature, especially African American literature. Some of the exemplars are quite famous, such as *The Color Purple*; some are underread, such as *Darktown Strutters*; and a few are candidates for future classics, such as *Getting Mother's Body*. Other texts are interestingly obscure, as is the case with *The Man Who Fell in Love with the Moon*, which I chose over a more famous instance of white representations of Jim Crow experiences, such as Philip Roth's contemporary passing narrative *The Human Stain* (2000). Such direct and high-profile representations of Jim Crow segregation by white authors raise fairly common questions about appropriation and problematic constructions of whiteness. This approach leads inevitably to John Howard Griffin's notorious account of his experiment to cross the color line from white to black in *Black Like Me* (1961). The consciously multiethnic projects by Alexie and Spanbauer, on the other hand, deliberately and playfully bring Jim Crow out of the familiar terrain of the black-and-white South, though Jim Crow brings that baggage with him. With such multiethnic examples, I can trace the long shadow Jim Crow casts on the post–civil rights literary imagination.

The key to this work, then, is a focus primarily on African American literary traditions and discussion of representations of Jim Crow from white and ethnic minority writers as offshoots. Some scholars, influenced by whiteness studies and comparative ethnic studies, might prefer a more balanced approach to the subject, perhaps concerned that Jim Crow segregation should be framed more as a national issue than a black one. I agree, especially following Du Bois's early insistence that we shift our discourse away from the Negro problem and toward the problem of the color line. Still, it is important to place African American writers at the center of this tradition because neo–segregation narratives return to, control, and rewrite the script of Jim Crow, which historically defined black people as its object.

Interestingly, the majority of writers discussed here do not hail from the South, yet the South figures prominently in their narratives. For some scholars, this may point to a deficiency in the study, especially given the exciting flurry in recent scholarship on the construction of the idea of the South and southern cultures.[10] But my sampling accurately reflects the gravitational pull the South holds in the post–civil rights image of Jim Crow. Whereas southern writers are at the center of the segregation narrative tradition, more often than not the Jim Crow South becomes an imagined place to which neo–segregation narrative writers return, even if their own origins or present locations lie elsewhere. Further, as the segregation narrative evolves in a post–civil rights era, the distinction between North and South becomes less important than that between de jure and de facto modes of segregation. In fact, many neo–segregation narratives purposefully deemphasize North-South distinctions or position the distinction as a relic of a bygone era. The shadow of the Jim Crow South looms large in the post–civil rights multiethnic literary imagination so that it frames other forms of race segregation and ethnic division in the West and urban north.

Many alternate angles remain largely unexplored. I could have considered African American writers' depictions of whiteness under segregation and civil rights, from Baldwin's polemical play *Blues for Mister Charlie* (1964) to Stephen Carter's mystery novel *New England White* (2007). Or I could have traced post–civil rights trajectories of key segregation narrative authors, such as Wright and the increasingly transnational and pan-Africanist scope in his later work, or Gwendolyn Brooks's noted turn toward cultural nationalism in the 1970s. I could have traced post–civil rights depictions of key segregation figures, such as Booker T. Washington in Randall Kenan's "This Far; Or, a Body in Motion" from *Let the Dead Bury Their Dead* (1992). Another approach would be to look beyond literary arenas to trace Jim Crow culture in the present. That work is well underway by others, such as in Elizabeth Abel's examination of the enduring social life of segregation signs, Kimberly Wallace-Sanders's history of the mammy figure, and Bill Brown's and Kenneth Goings's work on black collectibles and their post–civil rights lives.

My concentration here is on narrative forms, especially the novel, which deserves some explanation. Writers have returned to Jim Crow via other genres, such as poetry from Brooks and Rita Dove; drama from August Wilson and Parks; scads of memoirs and autobiographical essays following Baldwin and Audre Lorde; nonfiction from writers such as Caroll Parrott Blue; academic reflections from Trudier Harris, Houston Baker, and others; and a treasure trove of oral history projects. Why, then, is the novel the go-to vehicle more often than not? The historiographic mode fits especially well in the novel form and allows writers to address not only experiences of the segregation era but also how the stories we tell about Jim Crow inform what it means to live in a post–civil rights era or, later, a postrace era.

The Segregation Narrative

The neo–segregation narrative tradition that this book traces implicitly depends and draws on segregation narratives. What does that tradition look like? We now universally recognize the genre of a "slave narrative," but we have only just begun to identify a "segregation narrative." Scholars from various corners of American and African American literary studies took on that work in a recent special issue of *African American Review* on "Representing Segregation" (2008) and a volume that followed, *Representing Segregation: Toward an Aesthetics of Living Jim Crow, and Other Forms of Racial Division* (2010), both edited by Piper Kendrix Williams and myself. We asked: Have the pervasive experiences of racial division in the late nineteenth- and early twentieth-century United States given rise to a distinct literary tradition or set of aesthetic practices? In response, scholars drew on decades of work on individual segregation narratives to map a literary terrain that extends from Chesnutt's post-Reconstruction South to Brooks's urban north as well as transnational and comparative projects by James Weldon Johnson and Wright in his later work. In her afterword, Cheryl Wall notes, "The concept of race as a fixed identity, visible in its marking and permanent in its effect, was the premise on which Jim Crow rested. If on the one hand . . . these writers reject that premise, they remind us as well how pervasive the system was and how impenetrable to change it seemed."[11] While segregation narratives attempted to revise America's racial script, neo–segregation narratives continue that effort in revising Jim Crow's history.

Identifying a segregation narrative tradition is necessarily speculative and ambitious. Nonetheless, Wall insists that "we must vigilantly analyze the strategies of representation that these historical conditions produced and provoked."[12] Ultimately, the tradition comprises multiregional and multiera literary representations of U.S. racial segregation, with African American literature and the Jim Crow South at the center. Attitudes about segregation and integration shift over time; so too, do strategies for depicting race segregation. Whether protesting, rejecting, or perhaps even reaffirming segregation, writers have responded to U.S. race segregation in diverse literary projects. They grapple with how to represent the experiences, systems, and ideologies of race segregation, without necessarily reinscribing its underlying white supremacism. Some writers, of course, sought to do just that, most notoriously in the case of Thomas Dixon's literary chronicles of the early

Ku Klux Klan,[13] which inspired D. W. Griffith's *The Birth of a Nation* (1915), and also perhaps in the case of some of Booker T. Washington's writings.

A full account of the segregation narrative is outside the scope of this study, but scholarship is far enough along to identify the literary tradition, assumptions, and tropes on which neo–segregation narratives draw. Wright's famous essay "The Ethics of Living Jim Crow" (1937) is an instructive entry point because it dramatizes his "Jim Crow education."[14] As he matured into adulthood and took on employment, Wright notes, "[i]t was no longer brutally cruel, but subtly cruel. Here I learned to lie, to steal, to dissemble. I learned to play that dual role which every Negro must play if he wants to eat and live."[15] He signals not only what it means to be a colored citizen under Jim Crow but also the tactics, ingenuity, and acrobatics required to represent that experience. Wright chronicles what happens when representative figures like Bigger Thomas or Big Boy cross color lines, be they de jure or de facto. Other writers play Wright's dual role through different techniques: Chesnutt's learned narrator relaying Uncle Remus tales, Du Bois's invitation to join him on the Jim Crow car at the turn of the twentieth century, or Hansberry's cramped Chicago apartment at the tail end of de jure segregation in *A Raisin in the Sun* (1959). Some of these strategies are closely identified with specific genres, such as the passing narrative and its efforts to fix or unfix identity through characters of ambiguous racial origins, most notably Clare Kendry in Nella Larsen's *Passing* (1929) and Joe Christmas in Faulkner's *Light in August* (1932). Some strategies are tied to specific political philosophies, such as miscegenation as a cure to the nation's race problems in Reconstruction romances by Lydia Maria Child and George Schuyler's proto–science fiction. Other tropes are more diffuse, including a focus on movement between differently raced locations in domestic migration narratives, such as Baldwin's first novel *Go Tell It on the Mountain* (1953), and cross-national narratives, as in James Weldon Johnson's use of Latin America in *The Autobiography of an Ex-Colored Man* (1912) and *Along the Way* (1933).[16]

Together, these examples point to a shared set of strategies for how to represent segregation, including three defining traits of segregation narratives: a cartography of racial division, an aesthetics of fear, and crucial scenes of cross-racial contact. First, in the opening lines of Wright's essay we see a prime example of a writer's creation of symbolic geographies to reveal how segregation shapes spaces in society: "My first lesson in how to live as a Negro came when I was quite small. We were living in Arkansas. Our house stood behind the railroad tracks. Its skimpy yard was paved with black cinders. Nothing green ever grew in that yard. The only touch of green we could see was far away, beyond the tracks, over where the white folk lived."[17] Wright underscores how space is organized by color in segregated societies, even at the level of foliage. James Tyner argues, "The imposition of Black Codes following emancipation, for example, and the later Jim Crow laws were attempts to fix the meaning of space, reflecting a hegemonic cultural norm (white supremacy, for example). Spaces in this sense were color-coded and imbued with particular racial meanings."[18] Farrah Jasmine Griffin suggests that segregationist violence is written into the soil of the South itself, as we see in the haunting antilynching song "Strange Fruit,"[19] though much the same can be said of Petry's *The Street* (1946), set in Harlem. These color palettes demarcate segregation's lines in any location, including the North and the South, but also between public and private spaces, zones of confinement or mobility, and areas of the known and unknown. Characters chart the intricate landscape of segregation and the narratives then hinge on the ability to read those maps, or to understand what happens when segregation encroaches on seemingly safe spaces, as Gershun Avilez argues about black domestic spaces in Brooks's *Maud Martha* (1953) and Frank London Brown's *Trumbull Park* (1959). By the time of the post–civil rights era, a shared map of segregation emerges. Eve Dunbar detects in Wright's later, international work an effort to construct segregation as a time and region unto itself.

Second, once a segregation narrative establishes a cartography of racial division, it highlights the dangers of not obeying its dividing lines. Sometimes the consequences are as stark as racially motivated violence, and sometimes they are more subtle, as in psychological narratives of racial alienation, for example, in Du Bois's essay "Of Our Spiritual Strivings." The result is an aesthetics of fear that ascribes value to those who dare to cross heavily policed racial lines. In Wright's "Big Boy Leaves Home" (1936), we see Big Boy's loss of innocence, from the moment he encroaches on white private property to swim in an edenic pond through the ensuing accidental murder of a white soldier and the lynching of Bobo, one of Big Boy's adolescent friends. Or we experience the psychological terror of the three African American women passing as white in the drawing room of the unsuspecting bigot John Bellew in Larsen's *Passing*. Children are especially prominent because they exhibit so clearly the cognitive process of learning to navigate segregated space. The underside of an aesthetics of fear is one of safety, as explored by Anne

Rice in her study of Angelina Weld Grimké's representation of a lynching in Valdosta, Georgia.

Third, the aesthetics of fear and safety come to a head in scenes of cross-racial contact. Often these scenes are central and severe, as in lynching narratives. Other times they are pivotal points in narratives far removed from the color line and set deep within black or white communities. The best example is Zora Neale Hurston's *Their Eyes Were Watching God* (1937), which takes place primarily in the all-black incorporated town of Eatonville, Florida. Janie belatedly learns at age six that she is black when she can't initially recognize herself among a sea of white faces in a photograph of her classmates. Such crossings are typically among black and white characters, but scenes of contact between minority groups or different nationalities can serve similar purposes, such as analogies between African American and immigrant experiences or transnational comparisons, which Pauline Hopkins employs with Ethiopia in *Of One Blood* (1903) and Ida B. Wells deploys in her transnational antilynching work.[20]

As these shared strategies turn into tropes and conventions, neo–segregation narratives focus on the mechanics of telling stories of Jim Crow. Neo–segregation narratives veer from real-time realist or naturalist modes in favor of more historiographic forays, often exhibiting a more playful sensibility, though the stakes remain just as high. This is not surprising because the postmodern moment casts history itself as a narrative. The Parks/Faulkner pairing is a crucial measure of the relation between literature and history, especially their relative abilities to speak to the full register of black concerns and experiences following civil rights gains. Still, representational desires remain strong because Jim Crow narratives matter well beyond literary arenas. That is why many writers take pains to offer thoughtful portrayals of key segregation figures. A good example is the long tradition of telling Emmett Till's infamous story in literature.[21] Starting shortly after the 1955 racially motivated murder, key black writers retold Till's story, including Brooks, Baldwin, Lorde, Ishmael Reed, Bebe Moore Campbell, and many others, including a key allusion in *Darktown Strutters*. Christopher Metress explains, the "court of literature" is better equipped to deliver the justice denied to Till in the legal arena.[22]

There is also a strand of the segregation narrative tradition that appears once Jim Crow is no longer the law of the land. Contemplating Du Bois's famous announcement of the color line, Patricia Hill Collins argues, "In contrast, the problem of the twenty-first century seems to be the seeming *absence* of a color line. Formal legal discrimination has been outlawed, yet contemporary social practices produce virtually identical racial hierarchies as those described by Du Bois."[23] Neo–segregation narratives insist that the color line remains relevant in a post–Jim Crow era. As neo–segregation narratives take on such contemporary concerns as the merits and limits of integration, self-segregation, multiculturalism, legislative reform, and the prospect of a truly postrace era, they must choose whether to position the color line as central or to put it on the outer horizon of their narratives. And they must choose whether to take up the black culture–directed legacy of segregation writers such as Hurston and Langston Hughes or to take up the legacy of cross-racial plots and integration-minded fiction of such writers as Wright, Schuyler, and early Baldwin, as in Thulani Davis's *1959* (1992), Nanci Kincaid's *Crossing Blood* (1992), and Elizabeth Cox's *Night Talk* (1997).

Ultimately, neo–segregation narratives arise at the moment when segregation is perceived as having a past, even if it has not fully passed. That is why Trudier Harris insists on the term "attempted desegregation" so that we do not prematurely declare success for a movement's aims when its historical period is perceived as over. She writes, "It is indeed a small historical circle that transforms seeming gains into losses, seeming advances into steps backward. . . . I emphasize 'attempted' because the reality never measured up to expectation, and I emphasize 'desegregation' because this country has never been, nor do I ever expect it will be, truly, fully, irrevocably *integrated*."[24] As de jure transitioned to de facto segregation, neo–segregation narratives have adopted bitemporal fields of vision as a way to reflect, swap, and undermine the relationship between nominal equality and lived inequality.

Harris alerts us to a key problem in these works: identifying a distinct literary tradition could itself be accused of prematurely announcing the end of segregation, in direct contradiction to the aims of neo–segregation narratives. That is one reason why I open with a study of Hansberry's film adaptation of *A Raisin in the Sun*, a late segregation narrative that foresees the arrival of successful integration struggles and the problems such struggles may not yet address. Hansberry's play remains wildly popular, including recent Broadway revivals and a 2008 ABC television special starring Phylicia Rashad and Sean P. Diddy Combs. Such revivals tend to underscore the play's classic status, which sits well with contemporary audiences ready to note evidence of progress between then and now. Neo–segregation narratives, on the other hand, embody Hansberry's original designs: tell a story of segregation that brings the past to bear on the present and segregation's shifting manifestations, just as Mama learned to adapt the lessons of her southern origins to her current dilemmas in the urban north.

Neo–Segregation Narratives in American Literary and Cultural Studies

This book joins scholarly conversations about the segregation narrative and segregation's role in the contemporary literary imagination. Scholars have explored the legacies of key practices associated with segregation, such as rape and lynching.[25] For instance, Jacqueline Goldsby explores the cultural logic of lynching and finds that "formalist aesthetics allow us to situate lynching as an historical phenomenon more decisively than we might ordinarily expect" (284). Because lynching could happen anywhere, anytime, by anyone, and against any black person, Goldsby argues, "[l]ynching's cultural logic reveals the stakes of our fixation on the extremities of the practice, as does literature that grapples with its dynamics, both of which free us to imagine lynching's history as broadly as it demands."[26] Goldsby strikingly concludes that the heightened spectacle of lynching masks more pervasive and subtle "social deaths" of black Americans that do not look like lynching. That is why literary depictions are so important: to connect or disconnect (depending on the book's politics) the spectacular deaths of lynching victims with more mundane forms of disenfranchisement. For instance, Jean Toomer's *Cane* (1923) "stages lynching's passage from being a literal threat to a malaise that infuses the whole of American institutions from the cane fields of Georgia to the university metropolis of Chicago."[27] Scholars have also done important work on how post–civil rights writers work through key segregation-era concerns that persist, such as Suzanne Jones's study of "race mixing" in post-1960s southern literature.

Literary critics discuss segregation as historical context, but they only rarely and recently use the term to describe the literature itself.[28] As a result, we do not yet appreciate Jim Crow's full literary impact.[29] Historians identify a culture of segregation, such as Grace Elizabeth Hale's examination of the construction of whiteness and Glenda Gilmore's pathbreaking book on gender and Jim Crow as well as her work with fellow historians Jane Dailey and Bryant Simon on the collection *Jumpin' Jim Crow* (2000). Hale identifies segregation's central product as "whiteness," a silent racial identity that denies itself as such while serving as a reference point for that which is superior and inferior, central and marginal, exalted and abject. The time is ripe to offer a compelling case for how segregation also resonates throughout the literary imagination. The rewards are suggested by Jonathan Markovitz's study of lynching's impact on the contemporary political imagination in which he finds that the shadow of lynching grows larger just as lynching fades from everyday practice.

Before the *Representing Segregation* volumes, Leigh Anne Duck went furthest in theorizing a Jim Crow literary aesthetic in her book *The Nation's Region (2006)*. She considers the competing ideals of national citizenship in which race segregation appears, on first glance, out of step with, or perhaps even an anachronistic or vestigial practice among, national narratives of post–Civil War progress and inclusion. She finds that southern modernists such as Faulkner and Hurston pose the South as a region removed from the nation's present, apart but within. "In sum," Duck contends, "apartheid was enfolded into national law through an understanding of the South's cultural, political, and temporal discontinuity from the nation, although apartheid emerged in the United States long before the nation's most severe sectional conflict and irrespective of regional boundaries, and continued amid the increasing commonalities between the South and the larger nation."[30] If southern modernism imagined Jim Crow outside the modern liberal nation-state, Duck explains, "[t]his divergence was naturalized through popular aesthetic narratives that staged a distinct and organically hierarchical southern social order. Depictions of the region's slaveholding past—epitomized by the filmic and literary genres of 'plantation romance'—presented it less as an anomaly in a liberal nation than as a privileged site of a coherent and binding white culture."[31] So too, I think that post–civil rights narratives return to the nation's Jim Crow past in order to disrupt easy proclamations of a coherent and binding multiethnic culture where competing ideals of civic and pluralistic citizenship are no longer at war. While Duck favors the term "apartheid" to defamiliarize ideologies that came to be seen as natural, I frame this study through the term "Jim Crow" in order to flag the role of a particular historical and regional location in the nation's contemporary literary imagination, especially if Jim Crow appears outside the place and time he is expected to reside.[32]

This project is ambitious and draws on multiple critical approaches and goals, four of which stand out. First, in staking out a distinct literary tradition, I identify and value lineage in American literature, whether specific to a racial group, such as in Cheryl Wall's genealogical study of black women writers in *Worrying the Line* (2005), or to a set of racialized experiences, such as in Ashraf Rushdy's *Neo–Slave Narratives* and Deborah McDowell and Arnold Rampersad's now-classic collection *Slavery and the Literary Imagination* (1989). Second, given the central concerns of history, historiographic fiction, and African American relationships to U.S. history, I am indebted to Linda Hutcheon's work on history, fiction, and postmodernism; Henry Louis Gates, Jr.'s foundational concept of signifying in African American literature; and recent literary criticism along these lines, such as Keith Byerman's *Remembering the Past in Contemporary African American Fiction* (2005). Third, neo–segregation narratives operate at the junction of literature and law, so work on civic myths by scholars such as Rogers Smith, Brook Thomas, and Deak Nabers are influential. Last, I draw from critical geography and planning regarding racialized space, such as Katherine McKittrick and Clyde Woods's collection *Black Geographies and the Politics of Place* (2007), and literary studies that revise our understanding of Jim Crow regions and periods, such as Barbara McCaskill and Caroline Gebhard's *Post-Bellum, Pre-Harlem* (2006), in addition to Duck's and Suzanne Jones's work.

Throughout this book, I deliberately ask aesthetic questions about political matters. At least that is the perception of what it means to inquire into literary representations of rather ugly practices of racial violence, disenfranchisement, and segregation. In Russ Castronovo's provocative study of "beautiful democracy," he notes, "[t]he intrusion of aesthetic criteria into the political field is frequently met with alarm, anxiously read as a signature effect of fascism."[33] But, Castronovo contends, when we look at unbeautiful events such as strikes, mob violence, and seemingly disordered anarchic crowds, we start to see that the beautiful and the democratic have an interesting relation.[34] Castronovo revisits Du Bois's famous insistence on politically interested Negro art and explains, "At a time when some black intellectuals found safe harbor in the doctrine of art for art's sake, *The Crisis* as an agent of black print culture pushed a confrontational aesthetics that revalued traditional categories of 'the beautiful.'"[35] Castronovo thus considers what it means to aestheticize violence and find beauty in, say, spectacle lynching and antilynching laws.[36] For Du Bois, art need not follow party-line orthodoxy; rather, "What matters instead is that instrumentality of beauty and art for political confrontation."[37] In the postmodern moment, most agree that history is a narrative to be written and rewritten, not just a box of dead documents stored in a dark archive. Neo–segregation writers attempt in the literary realm to achieve democratic aims where democratic legal and political systems have fallen short.

The scholarship on segregation narratives builds on model efforts to identify a slave narrative, including the influential *Slavery and the Literary Imagination*, which in turn led to recognition of the neo–slave narrative. It is logical to look for a corollary neo–segregation narrative tradition. Why have we recognized the neo–slave narrative for decades, but not the neo–segregation narrative? The neo–slave narrative officially begins when we no longer have access to unmediated testimonial accounts of slavery. The neo–segregation narrative, on the other hand, has not come into sharp focus because there is not enough historical distance between the contemporary moment and the era of de jure race segregation. We have not yet reached consensus that the segregation era has come to a close and the last eyewitnesses are no longer accessible. Testimonial accounts of experiences under slavery are now taken by literary scholars to represent one undeniable system (even if the authorship of so many slave narratives is in question). Slavery, while varied in every plantation, region, and economy, seems relatively distinct compared to segregation, which encompasses a whole set of practices and institutions, of which Jim Crow is only one hypervisible part. Segregation, on the other hand, is much looser and not as easy to sum up beyond obvious examples such as whites-only lunch counters and drinking fountains. Part of a neo–segregation narrative's project is to demonstrate that Jim Crow may no longer be the law of the land but that racial segregation persists in different, seemingly more complex forms. Neo–segregation narratives, then, must nearly reject their "neo" status.

This suggests another way neo–segregation and neo–slave narratives differ: there is no clear origin moment or signal experience but rather a series of shifting cultural expectations and legal codes. There is also no corollary to William Styron's *The Confessions of Nat Turner* (1967), against which Rushdy positions the entire neo–slave narrative tradition as a refutation, arguing that Styron's novel is a master-text written from the vantage of the dominant culture even while masquerading as a neo–slave narrative.[38] Neo–segregation narratives do not tend to directly emulate, reject, or rewrite master texts; they respond instead to a loose set of circulating scripts about racial progress in the post–civil rights American imagination. Finally, the politics behind neo–segregation narratives are also not quite so clear because race segregation can be seen as the product of choice (racial separatism or self-segregation) and even empowerment (Black Power), whereas slavery is now universally seen as a bad thing.

▶ ▶ ▶

Segregation is a thing of the past; segregation persists. The civil rights movement was a grand success worthy of monuments and national holidays, but the movement is an ongoing project requiring constant vigilance. These core contradictions in American race relations infuse America's democratic project and the role of black people in it. When we encounter Jim Crow in historiographic fiction, his very legibility threatens our intellectual certainties that Jim Crow's remains are artifacts, dead objects from a bygone era. If characters map themselves onto segregation's terrain, they risk becoming one of Jim Crow's wooden dolls. But if we *don't* read ourselves against the terrain of the novel—because we believe Jim Crow no longer wields direct power—we become wooden dolls of a progress narrative that would bury Jim Crow alive.

In the post–civil rights era, the color line is seen simultaneously as a relic of a time that has officially passed but also as a foundation for celebrations of diversity and racial heritage. Thus we find new uses for a color line that persists once its legal apparatus has been stripped away. Mark M. Smith goes so far as to suggest that segregation has been embedded into our very senses so that we may not be able to experience the world otherwise. On the other hand, scholars also resist reinforcing the color line, such as in Paul Gilroy's provocative *Against Race* (2000) and Ross Posnock's contention that culture need not have a fixed color. Neo–segregation narratives attempt to both explain and thwart segregation's social life. Obviously, the literary realm is only one venue where such contradictions find footing. In his study of the science underpinning segregationist legal arguments, John P. Jackson, Jr. traces the rise and eclipse of the scientific community behind the case against *Brown v. Board of Education of Topeka*. "A James Gregor," Jackson explains about one scientist, "always claimed that he was acting to defend segregation not because of white fears, but because segregation was in the best interests of Negro children."[39] While the science behind segregationist ideology lost credibility and converts by the 1970s, we can see how easily segregation coexists with or even informs separatist ideologies of Black Power and self-determination. The neo–segregation narrative gauges ever-shifting attitudes toward the project of integration and the relative horrors or merits of race segregation. It remains to be seen how we will account for the persistence of the color line in a reputedly postrace era, a question I take up in the epilogue.

I have highlighted what we gain by identifying a distinct literary tradition that binds post–civil rights narratives that return to Jim Crow. But what do we risk? Beyond the potential for a premature declaration of segregation's end (embedded in the "neo"), another key risk is a leaky definition, a problem that dogs any attempt to label literary traditions. Representing segregation demands historiographic attention to social and legal codes but not necessarily a predetermined plot or narrative structure, as in slave narratives and their well-traveled paths toward freedom and the north or the relatively settled genre of the passing narrative. Still, in his study of racial passing among ethnic whites in American realist fiction, Steven Belluscio notes that scholars "have made conscious efforts to define passing as broadly as possible—even at the risk of vagueness—and thereby have expanded ever further our understanding of the act's implications."[40] As a particularly "generous" example, he cites Werner Sollors's definition in *Neither Black nor White yet Both* (1997): "the crossing of any line that divides social groups."[41] But merely crossing a social line is not necessarily passing per se, depending on how, whether, and by whom the passer will be detected. The category "segregation," more so than passing or lynching or minstrelsy, is better suited to the task of taking on the nation's history of racial division, whether legal or cultural.

Ultimately my study asks: Why the neo–segregation narrative? Along the way, I point to some concerns and anxieties, both political and literary, that contemporary writers engage when they revise the historical record and exploit Jim Crow's notoriety in the post–civil rights imagination. The UCLA Civil Rights Project reports that racial segregation is increasing in public schools today. Neo–segregation narratives return to Jim Crow and civil rights at a moment when many citizens and leaders yearn for—even promise—a break from the past in a so-called postracial era. Houston Baker baldly deems this turn "betrayal" as he accuses black intellectuals and political leaders of prematurely abandoning civil rights movement ideals. Contrary to socioeconomic ideals of fairness and equality, Baker contends, "[t]here is today a monumental divide between black intellectuals and the black majority."[42] Neo–segregation narratives have long engaged—and questioned—civil rights ideals, from time of the movement's earliest successes. Many literary figures, at least, remain engaged with debates about civil rights ideals of full equality, integration, and black self-worth. However, as Parks's novel illustrates, they may prefer the imaginative arena over legislative politics or even grassroots activism. The literary venue may better speak to the lives, frustrations, and dreams of those on the outer edges of the Jim Crow South who are least prone to share in the spoils of civil rights victories. Just as neo–slave narratives assert a cultural legacy long after the abolition of chattel slavery, neo–segregation narratives highlight Jim Crow's presence today and the unfinished work of civil rights desegregation movements. Neo–segregation narratives do not presume the end of segregation, even if Jim Crow's time is supposedly past.

CHAPTER 1

JIM CROW JR.

Lorraine Hansberry's Late Segregation
Revisions and Toni Morrison's
Early Post–Civil Rights Ambivalence

By the mid-twentieth century, Jim Crow codes, practices, locations, and ideologies were widespread and varied, which meant segregation narratives had to adapt and diversify. Richard Wright tracked Jim Crow's path not only into the urban north but also across the globe, while Ann Petry, Gwendolyn Brooks, James Baldwin, and Frank London Brown chronicled the communities that grew far from the Jim Crow South yet remained deeply marked by it. Some writers sought clean breaks from segregation aesthetics, such as LeRoi Jones / Amiri Baraka and other writers who would come to be associated with the Black Arts movement, while others sought to revise the Jim Crow script by rewriting conventional white genres with black characters at the center, such as Chester Himes's detective fiction. Still others enlisted Jim Crow in their versions of the Great American Novel, such as Ralph Ellison's *Invisible Man* (1952). The inviolable lines of race segregation were a fiction imposed on the traffic between citizens of varying colors, as Grace Elizabeth Hale demonstrates in her history of Jim Crow culture. As the black-and-white veneer of Jim Crow wore increasingly thin in the 1950s, there was a shift in the strategies, influence, and career trajectories of writers long associated with chronicling segregation. At the same time, there was a rise in younger writers taking on that challenge.

With her iconic portrait of segregation and desegregation in *A Raisin in the Sun* (1959), Lorraine Hansberry emerges at the salt point between segregation and neo–segregation narratives in the wake of civil rights successes. She thus stands as a transitional figure in a tradition that comes of age with Toni Morrison's *The Bluest Eye* in 1970. In the introduction, I assert that the "neo" in the term "neo–segregation narrative" marks a fundamental, if elusive, shift in the cultural, legal, and political transition from de jure to de facto segregation. It is worth recalling that the civil rights movement was not a finite event but a complex series of struggles, events, victories, and losses, some coordinated and many dispersed. We can identify a discrete movement after the fact and for the convenience of historical narrative, whether a long or short civil rights movement. So, too, the segregation narrative is a slippery and evolving tradition only visible in retrospect. The cases of Hansberry and Morrison capture a snapshot of that all-important but diffuse shift from the segregation to neo–segregation narrative.

In a 1951 essay, "How I Told My Child about Race," Margaret Walker writes, "Living as we do, deep in Dixie, facing every day not merely the question of race but the problems of Jim Crow or segregation, we have a tendency to build an unreal world of fantasy, to draw a charmed circle around us and within this circle to feel safe; to close our eyes to the bitter struggle, and to forget if possible all the ugliness of a world as near as our front door, and closer than the house across the street."[1] Writing three years before *Brown v. Board of Education of Topeka*, Walker dismantled the "fantasies" of domestic safety as the ugliness of segregation was at the threshold. Further, as a forebear of the neo–slave narrative, Walker positions Jim Crow's "unreal world" of stark lines between black and white to show how African Americans experienced slavery's lasting effects. Hansberry has a remarkably different approach. In the posthumously assembled *To Be Young, Gifted, and Black* (1970), Hansberry writes, "All travelers to my city should ride the elevated trains that race along the back ways of Chicago. The lives you can look into! . . . My people are poor. And they are tired. And they are determined to live."[2] Hansberry does not frame her discussion of racial injustice through the lens of slavery. She also figures domestic space and the streets of Chicago—especially when seen from the rear via public transportation—as sites of realism and triumphant struggle against Jim Crow's pervasiveness. Between these two discussions of segregation lie the civil rights movement and the transition from compulsory race segregation to uncannily similar de facto conditions. This post–civil rights era also witnessed key generational shifts in racial sensibilities, experiences, and historical markers. The Youngers' apartment not only provides a space of refuge and strength but also stages Jim Crow's incursion into the daily lives of one black family in Chicago.

Nonetheless, with her characters confined to the apartment, Hansberry risks confirming Walker's warning about "charmed circles" and literary palliatives. Thus *Raisin* inadvertently invites some of the notorious (mis)readings that accuse Hansberry of uncritically endorsing a middle-class American dream. That criticism was put forward by many key black writers, perhaps most vociferously by Amiri Baraka in his early responses to the work, which in turn led to subsequent efforts by Hansberry to reclaim the revolutionary thrust of her play.[3] Hansberry turned to the motion picture medium to get the Youngers out of their apartment and into the streets of segregated Chicago. In doing so, Hansberry manufactured a way for Walker's "fantasy" and "ugly" worlds to collide. My thesis is that Hansberry's revisions to her already wildly successful play in preparation for the big screen point to a more fully realized version of how she pictured segregation at the tail end of Jim Crow and on the cusp of key desegregation victories. Ultimately, Hansberry's unfilmed screenplay is particularly illustrative of the transition toward the neo–segregation narrative and *The Bluest Eye*, to which I turn at the end of this chapter. By placing the Breedloves' home in an old rented storefront, Morrison uncannily shares a strategy with Hansberry: put a poor black family's living room on public display. Beyond this specific commonality, Hansberry finds general kinship with post–civil rights, neo–segregation writers whose portraits of segregation are shaped primarily by experiences of de facto segregation, be it in the post–Jim Crow South or elsewhere.

On the Mundane and Therefore Devastating Nature of Race Segregation

Hansberry portrays with precision and ferocity the frustrations, joys, and dignity of a family living under racial segregation in the urban north, which the matriarch of the family understands through her experiences in the Jim Crow South. Genre poses a problem: the traditional stage allows spectators to enter the Younger apartment in what Robin Bernstein calls a "fishbowl" effect. She explains, "The fishbowl could sit comfortably, decoratively, on a shelf in a white household; white people could peer through the glass (which contained and controlled the exotics and simultaneously kept the white spectator safely separated from the creatures) and enjoy their collection."[4] The screenplay version, however, follows the Youngers outside the apartment to their work and leisure lives and especially to their new home in the all-white suburb Clybourne Park. In this way, we get a fuller picture of segregation in Chicago and the nation. In a directorial note, Hansberry describes the new neighborhood: "These are American homes where rather ordinary types and varieties of Americans live; but at the moment something sinister clings to them."[5] The screenplay better diagnoses the "something sinister" that underlies the Youngers' apartment and their lives outside it. With film technology, Hansberry could bring her audience onto the streets of Chicago, not unlike Du Bois's famous invitation to his (white, northern) readers to join him on the Jim Crow car. In the end, Hansberry's unfilmed screenplay (and perhaps its status as such) is a fuller picture of segregation that is prescient of the new challenges of representing racial segregation in a post–civil rights era.[6]

Raisin is one of the most famous American plays of the mid-twentieth century and it is read and performed across the United States in regional theaters, classrooms, libraries, bookstores, literary anthologies, and television. The success has long caused considerable debate in literary and political circles as *Raisin* serves as a cultural reference point for segregation. The play is a rather conventional three-act drama in which the death of the patriarch, Walter Younger, and the resulting $10,000 insurance check promise to fulfill the dreams of each Younger: a down payment on a house for Mama, which promises the familial stability also sought by Ruth; an entrepreneurial investment in a liquor store for Walter Lee, Jr.; and medical school tuition for Beneatha. In an early academic review, C. W. E. Bigsby describes the check as "a specious *deus ex machina*" because "it is only the money which makes it possible for [the Youngers] to challenge the system under which they have suffered."[7] Nonetheless, the ensuing feuding reflects ideological struggles over which and whose dream takes precedence, which provokes conflict among generations, genders, social statuses, family roles, racial ideologies, cultural customs, and the emergent politics of black pride. The entirety of the play takes place in the tiny apartment, which Ruth at one point describes as a "rat trap."[8] Hansberry writes, "Its furnishings are typical and undistinguished and their primary feature now is that they have clearly had to accommodate the living of too many people for too many years—and they are tired" (1.1). As Hansberry describes the weary people through their furniture, she borders on personification in a play otherwise committed to realism. Such descriptions risk dismissal as overly sentimental or symbolic to the point of oversimplification. This is true of other objects ripe for high school theme papers and allegorical readings, especially the sun-starved potted plant in the tenement window. These meaning-laden props point to a desire to get us out of the Youngers' apartment and into another medium, film.

Hansberry turns to the streets of Chicago as a setting for the Hollywood film more up to the task of representing this atmosphere of want and exhaustion. "The screenplay is not simply a cinematic translation of the play," critic Lisbeth Lipari contends, "but a moment of dialogic interaction in an ever-evolving context of public discourse."[9] Critics who address the unfilmed screenplay (there aren't many) emphasize the importance of the outside shots. "By taking the camera outside the Younger apartment in her script and following the adult characters in their normal daily lives," Margaret Wilkerson says, "Hansberry forces her audience to see the conditions and circumstances" that explain the decisions of each character. She adds, "The camera's eye would be irrefutable as it swept the panorama of Chicago and, by implication, America's major cities where the majority of African Americans reside."[10] Hansberry paves the way for literary representations of racial division after the dismantling of de jure segregation by carefully exploring the cultural attitudes and practices buttressing segregation's legal codes, attitudes, and practices that would persist. If southern segregation became a national concern in large part due to news media coverage of the civil rights movement and media-savvy activists appealing to sympathetic journalists, as Gene Roberts and Hank Klibanoff argue,[11] literature of that time helped the nation understand how southern Jim Crow and urban forms of race segregation belonged in the same narrative.

In the play, the Youngers inhabit one side of Walker's domestic threshold, allowing a family drama of internecine squabbles. The play contains stories of black migration to the urban north, struggles with poverty, debates about black beauty and revolutionary politics, and generational tensions. Then the ugly head of Jim Crow's northern cousin enters: Karl Lindner, a representative of the Clybourne Park Improvement Association. While making a "generous offer" to buy the house, at a small profit, he explains, "I want you to believe me when I tell you that race prejudice simply doesn't enter into it. It is a matter of the people of Clybourne Park believing, rightly or wrongly, as I say, that for the happiness of all concerned that our Negro families are happier when they live in their *own* communities" (2.3). The mundane depiction of race segregation captures the horrors of Jim Crow's northern manifestation in such seemingly benign packages as race restrictive covenants. This turn to the mundane represents a turn away from climactic scenes of the dangers of crossing or not crossing racial lines and toward pedestrian or domestic scenes of the psychology of race segregation and daily strategies for survival and dignity. *Raisin* breaks from the segregation narrative's penchant for harsh scenes of cross-racial contact and policing, as in the murders in Richard Wright's "Big Boy Leaves Home" (1936) and *Native Son* (1940), Charles Chesnutt's retelling of the 1898 Wilmington race riots in *The Marrow of Tradition* (1901), and even the depiction of lynching in Jean Toomer's experimental, modernist *Cane* (1923). Hansberry also reverses the drawing room scene in Nella Larsen's *Passing* (1929) in which Irene Redfield is an interloper in white bigot John Bellew's drawing room. Instead, as critic Jeanne-Marie Miller explains, Lindner "is an intruder in the family and the mouthpiece of white racism. He is presented as an ordinary man, and in that ordinariness lies danger, for he represents the common people.... Lindner is a forerunner of the hostility and potential violence that the Youngers will experience in their new neighborhood."[12] *Raisin*'s mundane depiction of segregation's machinations stresses Jim Crow's wiliness and adaptability because Lindner comes with a community-written policy, not a noose. Hansberry pushes us to ask: Why would a white community leader put a benign face on racism, wrapped in a paternalistic bow, saying it was to benefit "our Negroes"? Rejecting a caricatured white supremacism, Hansberry signals the ease with which de facto segregation takes hold as its de jure purveyors come knocking at the door clad in modest business suits and democratic talk, not in Klan hoods and spouting racial epithets.

With *Raisin*, Hansberry became a household name and eventually entered the canons of American drama, African American literature, and black feminist criticism. In his posthumous rumination "Sweet Lorraine" (1969), Baldwin writes, "We had that respect for each other which perhaps is only felt by people on the same side of the barricades, listening to the accumulating thunder of the hooves of horses and the heads of tanks."[13] Baldwin places Hansberry on one side of a contested segregation line—the moral side. With unmistakable imagery of civil rights protest, Baldwin disallows an easy commitment to integration that might de-emphasize ongoing desegregation struggles in a post–civil rights era and the case for self-segregation. In his introduction to the restored version of the play, Robert Nemiroff sums up *Raisin*'s impact: "Produced in 1959, the play presaged the revolution in black and women's consciousness—and the revolutionary ferment in Africa—that exploded in the years following the playwright's death in 1965 to ineradicably alter the social fabric and consciousness of the nation and the world."[14] Nemiroff is in good company as he positions Hansberry as prescient of the grand social movements just on the horizon, a Cassandra whose mainstream success led to misunderstandings of her rather revolutionary aesthetic.

In the shadow of *Raisin*'s success, scholars repudiate, correct, defend, or in some way set the record straight against distortion and disparagement. To Nemiroff's dismay, many reviewers and early academics "transformed the Youngers into an acceptably 'middle class' family."[15] This response took place despite what was in the play: a female-headed household, a cramped apartment in a poverty-stricken neighborhood, Beneatha's quasi-revolutionary politics, and the many digs at George Murchison, a caricature of black upward mobility. For Baldwin, reactions fell along racial lines because "black people recognized that house and all the people in it—the mother, the son, the daughter, and the daughter-in-law—and supplied the play with an interpretive element which could not be present in the minds of white people: a claustrophobic terror, created not only by their knowledge of the streets." He concludes, "I personally feel that it will demand a far less guilty and constricted people than the present-day Americans to be able to assess it at all."[16] Neo–segregation narratives insist that we have not yet reached a point that would allow Baldwin's honest assessment. Nonetheless, Hansberry herself attempted to marshal such an assessment with key modifications for the screen, three of which I will discuss to get at how Hansberry reframes her picture of segregation.

Hansberry Reframes Segregated Chicago

Hansberry had reservations about *Raisin* becoming a Hollywood film, but she ultimately opted to maintain control over the script. The screenplay contains new scenes that bring the Youngers into the city and revised dialogue that amplifies or extends social messages. Hansberry "longed for the chance to re-imagine her story in filmic terms," Steven Carter argues. "She was filled with ideas about how to take the Younger family into their community," which would "heighten . . . viewers' awareness of the Youngers' role as representatives of a large, embattled minority."[17] Carter points to Walter's relation to Lena: "Hansberry juxtaposes the scene of Lena on the bus looking at the house with a scene of Walter on another bus looking at a liquor store, highlighting the obvious clash of their dreams. Moreover, it is significant that Lena and Walter are each enclosed in a boxlike structure that is rapidly moving past the dream, a visual symbolism not possible on the stage."[18] These film adaptations point to Hansberry's evolving sense of how best to picture segregation in the mid-twentieth century. One of her new film directions provides an excellent clue: in a casual scene between Walter and a liquor store owner named Herman, Hansberry directs, "There is nothing 'racist' in Herman's attitude to Walter Lee. He is genuine, helpful, is simply voicing a typical shopkeeper's plaint" (59). The film script not only brings the Youngers into direct contact with cultures of urban segregation in Chicago, it also suggests that a full picture of that system requires dexterity enough to capture the menacingly benign surfaces of racial exclusion.

"HOWDY DO!" TO THE SHADOWS OF CLYBOURNE PARK

The screenplay's most important addition is that we see the Youngers first arrive at their new house in Clybourne Park. The screenplay highlights the danger that seemingly safe and definitely white suburbs held for the Youngers, such as the threats that greeted young Hansberry's own family outside their house in the summer of 1938. Thus Hansberry confronted head-on the strangely persistent tendency to wrest a happy ending from the Youngers' story, as if they had achieved an uncomplicated American dream of home-ownership. Hansberry makes plain what anyone intimately familiar with segregation already knows: the Youngers have a less-than-friendly reception awaiting them. Hansberry lays bare the fierce residential policing of color lines by juxtaposing the segregated streets of the South Side with a well-manicured suburban neighborhood. The "something sinister" infecting the neighborhood is quite plain, even more so than Lindner's semiveiled threats: "At some windows curtains drop back quickly into place, as though those who are watching do not want to be seen; at others, shadowy figures simply move back out of view when they felt that Walter and Ruth's gaze is upon them; at still others, those who are staring do so without apology. The faces—the eyes of women and children, in the main—look hard with a curiosity that, for the most part, is clearly hostile" (155). Hansberry underscores the shadowy presence of white supremacy lurking just behind window curtains, with an almost vampiric fear of daylight and the camera's eye. The white onlookers ogle but do not wish to be seen.[19] Their unapologetic and hostile curiosity belies potential sympathy for the white women and children in the domestic spaces of policed segregation. Such scenes of racial animosity in bright suburban light become iconic in the post–civil rights imagination.

Beneatha's initial response to Clybourne Park, which precedes Lindner's visit, is crucial. Hansberry directs, "*She feels a twentieth-century urge to ridicule absurdity and suddenly lifts one hand and stands alone, turning about, waving silently at watchers, shouting merrily*: . . . "Howdy do! Howdy do!" (156). Beneatha's cheerful, knowing, unabashedly defiant welcome is the signature moment in Hansberry's reframed story of desegregation. When legislative reforms, street preaching, antilynching campaigns, impassioned appeals to freedom and the nation's loftiest ideals, picket lines, and thoughtful letters to the *New York Times* stop short, what else to do but cross the color line with a greeting of "Howdy do!"? Standing in the bright external shot on the street, the Youngers provide a contrast with the white figures lurking in the shadows. Throughout her career, Hansberry remained very skeptical of the theater of the absurd following Bertolt Brecht and others in favor of her commitment to realism. But in this moment, the young, idealistic, and whip-smart young woman performs a realistic absurdity. With carnival-mirror reflection of Lindner's welcome, Beneatha greets the very folks who are most likely to firebomb the house that night. The film that eventually got made did show the Youngers exploring their new house in Clybourne Park. But Beneatha's "Howdy do!," like the ominous neighbors peering behind curtains, is remarkably absent.

When Beneatha returns to the apartment after the Clybourne Park scene and finds Walter dancing with Ruth, Hansberry once again casts civil rights in a playfully absurd register. Walter announces, "You know, when these *New Negroes* have their convention (*pointing to his sister*), that is going to be the chairman of the Committee on Unending Agitation. (*He goes on dancing, then stops.*) Race, race, race! . . . Girl, I do believe you are the first person in the history of the entire human race to successfully brainwash yourself" (157). He continues, "Damn, even the N double-A C P takes a holiday sometimes!" (158). This scene, appearing in all three versions (stage play, unfilmed screenplay, Hollywood motion picture) seemingly divests the Youngers of any sustained activist plan by way of knowing irony when decoupled from scenes of desegregation.

Not everyone agrees that the play's ending is unsatisfactory or politically backward. Michelle Gordon praises the ending because, she says, "[r]ather than altering the ending to promote assimilation or provide a reassuring sense of inevitable racial 'progress,' this change in fact proves crucial to maintaining the revolutionary potential of the drama: Ending the action prior to the Youngers' arrival in Clybourne Park supplies Hansberry with the only prospect of keeping it real, so to speak, while breaking the cycles of desegregation and ritualized white violence" (130). With the preceding shot on location in Clybourne Park, Gordon's revolutionary reading becomes more plausible.[20] J. Charles Washington has a positive analysis of Mama's desire for the house: "The only way a Black person could escape discrimination in the South of that time was to move to the North. . . . Hers is, in short not the true American Dream, but a second-class version of it reserved for Black Americans and other poor people."[21]

Nevertheless, most critics consider the original ending rather apolitical or depoliticized, largely agreeing with Walter's assurance to Lindner, "We don't want to make no trouble for nobody or fight no causes, and we will try to be good neighbors" (148). Notwithstanding the threat behind the conditional phrasing of "try," the play and ultimately the filmed version divest the story of direct engagement with civil rights protest or black nationalism. Jeanne-Marie Miller argues, "The Youngers will move into the white neighborhood, not with the goal of integrating it, but because the house is one they need, want, and can afford" (136). Miller distinguishes the play from protest literature due to its anemic portrait of segregation through allegory and simplification by Lindner as the sole figure of white supremacism. Can a single white character do that much narrative work? Moreover, can a single African character such as Joseph Asagai, or a lone symbolic plant in the apartment's only window, get at the complexity of antiracist struggles and the diversity of black experience? Probably not. The screenplay has more space and provides options to better frame the aesthetic and ideological struggles over how to wrest dignity from a white supremacist world in the coming post–Jim Crow world.

LENA GOES TO MARKET

The second most important change in the screenplay is that Lena leaves the apartment. Twice. Not only does Lena go to Clybourne Park in the original screenplay, but there are also early scenes of Lena on her last day as a domestic in a middle-class white family's household, scenes cut from the film version in which Lena has already quit. Lena is the character most bound to the domestic and familial arena, as well as to the southern Jim Crow past, by virtue of her embedded migration narrative. The screenplay explores how Lena's commitments to a suburban home arise from her experiences on the streets of Chicago and in the gender- and race-segregated economy. Hansberry emphasizes Lena's hands and her face through slow, extended, extreme close-ups, which amplify Lena's terse declaration: "I am sixty-five years old and I *am* tired" (38). The screenplay provides crucial background to Lena and Walter Sr.'s long work history, including their inability to get decent-paying jobs, which Lena might frame as northern Jim Crow. For instance, Lena knowingly offers her current employer an anecdote about asking for a small raise from a woman for whom she had worked for twenty-two years. She recounts, "'Why, we ain't never thought of you as nothing other than just another part of our family!' I just stood there and looked at that sister and thought to myself, 'I don't know what kind of member of no family you have down on their knees scrubbing all them floors and washing all them sheets all these years.' I quit right then and there" (40–41). Lena demonstrates a keen understanding of race relations and the white mind, even if her protest options are limited. In a counterreading, Lipari detects an "uncompromisingly loving attachment to her young white charge and her empathy for Mrs. Holiday's life with an oafish husband" (88). Either way, Lena's interactions with Mrs. Holiday point to a key way that Hansberry "illustrates the complexity of interracial and interclass relations" (88) in race-segregated Chicago. Lena's economic dreams are in no way an endorsement of white privilege, which counters iconic scenes of black domestics in white households in other key African American texts, most notoriously Pauline Breedlove's embrace of her white family in Morrison's *The Bluest Eye*.

Lena's face divulges no ill will toward her current employer, even though Hansberry provokes such reactions in her reader-viewers. Hansberry frames Lena primarily through the eyes of the white, well-meaning, but ultimately ignorant Mrs. Holiday in whose reactions we see the slow recognition of race segregation—its petty injustices and iron-clad economic barriers. As Mrs. Holiday listens to Lena's story, as typical as it is devastating, Hansberry provides the following direction: "She is still absorbing and having a response to the quite unprovoked stream of conversation. Her eyes suggest that, like everyone else, she receives and reacts to it in her own context: in perhaps some way that has to do with her own life or a member of her family; or abstractly, with pure and simple human rapport. It is, for her, a moment of sympathy in depth, perhaps for the first time in her association with the older woman" (40). In all her good intentions, Mrs. Holiday offers no help, so she is not as far removed from Lindner as she might like to think.

She meekly agrees with Lena's decision to quit her past employer, but she registers no real understanding of her analogous relationship. Though she learns that Lena had been a welder during the war, she shows no structural understanding of the economic limitations facing Lena when things return to business as usual. She even attempts a patronizing compliment by ventriloquizing her husband's disappointment: "'He was very upset.' (*She tries a little smile.*) 'You don't know how big a compliment that is. Jerry is the one who always fired everybody else'" (36–37). Lena passes on the opportunity to school her fellow citizen across the racial divide. Instead, we learn through a quick flash to Lena's face that "[h]er jaw is set the same" (37) as she ironically asks Mrs. Holiday to thank her husband. Though Lena does not confront Mrs. Holiday's ignorance and complicity, Hansberry cues her viewers to the pervasiveness and claustrophobia of race segregation.

In this scene we see Hansberry's prescient black feminism, so noted by later generations of readers and critics. In her study of black women's participation in the 1950s left, Mary Helen Washington suggests that Hansberry, with Alice Childress and Claudia Jones, "developed a model of feminism that put working-class women at its center."[22] To wit, in the screenplay Lena is referred to by name, rather than as "Mama" in the notes. Mrs. Holiday slowly realizes that her own household economy must change because, as Lena instructs, "[y]ou all can't afford no second person round here, and you ought to know it good as me" (38). Lena's subtle jab at her own pay notwithstanding, Mrs. Holiday announces with frustration that her husband and she "agreed that I would have to quit the agency for a while . . . I mean, you never feel right about going off and leaving your kid with—well—just anyone, the way some people do" (37). Hansberry shows how middle-class white women's relative independence and entrance into the public workforce depends on cheap black female labor in the domestic arena. Hansberry writes, "Mrs. Holiday closes her eyes and absorbs the truth with a slowly nodding movement of her head, and her expression finally changes to show that she has stopped resisting her own deep awareness of something she would rather, for personal interests, be able to argue against" (38). Far from Lindner's conscious use of race-restrictive covenants, this white (female) innocence cannot withstand full engagement with the geography of race segregation.

Hansberry's reader-viewers travel that racialized geography with Lena as she goes to market to procure apples on the way home from her last day as a domestic. First she goes to a local market where the white clerk shows little patience for Lena's discerning eye. Inspecting the apples' quality, Lena asks, "Who was chewin' on 'em before you decided to sell 'em to me?" (53). Lena refuses the second-rate goods available to folks living on the South Side, which the clerk meets with exasperation and an offer to shop elsewhere. Accepting the invitation, Lena attempts to establish cross-racial authority with her age: "Was you brought up to talk to older people like that, or you just turned wild here late?" (53). In this sole scene of Lena's outrage, we see a pedestrian struggle against the daily injustices of Jim Crow's urban cousin. Lena is a heroic figure of racial protest, contrary to her detractors who read her as compliant and committed to some naïve version of the American dream. Indeed, Lena's neighbor, Mrs. Johnson, contends, "Lord, Lena, you still out here trying to change the world" (54). Lena responds simply, "I ain't trying to change nothing. I'm tryin' to buy me some apples to make my family a decent pie and these here bandits want *thirty-five cents* for some fruit that was at the Last Supper!" (54).

In defiance of a system where the poorest residents pay the highest prices for the worst goods, Lena spends considerable time and energy to cross de facto lines of segregation and head to the famous "open markets" of Chicago. There she finds stall after stall of handsome fruits and vegetables as the camera jokingly lingers with an extreme close-up shot of "large, red, voluptuous apples" (56). Then, on her way home, we see "[a] young white woman, wrapped for the chill, is dragging a small boy into the house from the sidewalk and a cluster of toys and playmates. The house is small, neat, attractive, and too much like every single other one on the block. There is a tiny lawn with a few brand-new trees stuck in the ground—and all viewers are certain it is the kind that has a small, fenced-in backyard" (57). The culminating dream of a small home appears early in the unfilmed screenplay and as a direct response to a refusal to buy the substandard goods available in the black areas of the South Side. Carter detects a connection "between her rebellious visit to the distant market and her defiant purchase of the house in a white neighborhood, both aimed at seizing a better deal from life" (76). Further, Hansberry's description of the house is unsentimental, even a bit critical of its uniformity and diminutive comforts. Nevertheless, from Lena's point of view, the house appears as a rational response to the daily indignities and limits of life in segregated Chicago, both de facto and de jure.

In the stage play, Walter's self-determination stances come off as individual-
istic and not tethered to any larger movement, leading to integration as the
default response to counter Jim Crow's northern cousin for lack of any viable
alternative. The film script, however, includes Walter Lee's direct encounters
with black nationalism so that Hansberry addresses self-segregation's allure
by placing Walter Lee among a diverse background of black men beyond
Willy and Bobo, including Joseph Asagai. His frustrations and hopes begin
to have a history and explanation, more in line with Asagai's than not. In the
play, Walter Lee and Asagai share very little in terms of experience, point of
view, and even ideology. Walter Lee is a frustrated black American male who
can't provide for his family in a patriarchal order; Asagai is a mouthpiece
of postcolonial independence, Afrocentric intellectualism, and ethnic self-
confidence. The screenplay, however, frames black masculinity, masculinist
race politics, and Walter Lee's liquor store dreams within a coherent ideology
of economic self-determination. What Beneatha and Asagai find at college,
Walter finds on street corners. A speaker exhorts from a ladder on a street
corner, "And so, my black brothers, then what happens? Tell me, then what
happens! The black man gets off the train day after day from Mississippi and
Georgia—yes?" (130). The speaker then rattles off a master-narrative of the
Great Migration to Chicago, the Promised Land, and the black brother's
desire to become a male provider. The street preacher concludes with a
flourish: "He goes to the very man who has stolen his homeland, put him in
bondage, defamed his nation, robbed him of his heritage! The White Man!
. . . You go to him for a job and he hands you a broom!" (132).

The camera happens upon black nationalist rhetoric almost incidentally:
"Shot discovers Walter sitting on a curb. . . . Walter comes upon a street
meeting. He is still wandering in his dejection and indifferently finds a
place in a crowd where an orator on a ladder is exhorting his listeners" (129).
The crowd's varied reactions do not necessarily point to a critique of black
nationalism (its appeal, its rectitude, and so on); rather, Hansberry casts black
nationalism as an everyday presence on the streets of Chicago, as ubiquitous
and familiar as segregation. The speaker's challenge is to instill a feeling of
unity and like-mindedness based on shared experiences and frustrations. This
is a common spectacle for residents of the South Side, if not for Hansberry's
audience. She instructs, "The crowd has not yet begun the almost automatic

and rhythmical response which will eventually begin. They have heard many such speakers, and since what they talk about rarely changes, they linger mainly for the performance—waiting to see if this one or another can rouse them, if it will be a good performance" (130). The speaker is a good performer: he draws the crowd's participation in a polemical call-and-response around black nationalist logic regarding the way things are in white supremacist America.

Walter Lee and Asagai share positions as listeners and spectators. The speaker contrasts glorious Africa with "that small, cold continent" Europe (133). Hansberry notes, "Asagai stands impassively watching, as interested in the spectators as in the message of the speaker" (133). Bigsby faults Hansberry for creating an unreal African character, going so far as to describe Asagai as mere "oracle" (161) because, unlike each Younger, "Asagai's self-assurance remains untested" (160) and we never see him face daily frustrations and indignities. This street corner scene, however, endows both Walter Lee and Asagai with complexity. They represent the variety of black men's experiences and perspectives to which black nationalism might appeal. Wilkerson suggests that in the screenplay, "Hansberry subtly tilts the balance toward Walter Lee from Lena Younger by emphasizing Walter's role as a representative of African American men."[23] But Walter is only one possible manifestation of African American masculinity. In fact, Hansberry instructs, "[Asagai's] eyes scan the faces of the people around him. In the background, one among many, is the face of Walter Lee, listening. Asagai does not know him. Separated by many faces, they watch. The crowd cries out 'True!' at the last of the speaker's remarks" (133). Separated by experience, background, nationality, and even ideology, Walter Lee and Asagai convene as common spectators around black nationalism, while neither are its mouthpieces. The crowd includes a cross-section of the African American (male) community, with one key exception: George Murchison. Hansberry widens the camera's angle to see a "European sports car which pulls up, containing George Murchison; he calls out to Walter who recognizes him and goes over" (134). Perhaps inspired by the speaker, perhaps not, when George opens the door, "Walter squeezes himself up with an excessive display of distaste to fit into the tiny car" (135). Hansberry presents upward mobility as a cramped package.

With this external scene of Black Power and Nation of Islam street barkers, the screenplay connects Walter Lee's black nationalism and Asagai's anticolonialism to broader movements and also to each other. The ensuing film cut these external shots, thereby casting black nationalism and anticolonialism as strange and stylized encroachments into the apartment. The most notable manifestation of black self-determination inside the apartment is Walter Lee's scene of abjection when he decides to accept money from Lindner, who Walter positions as "*The Man*. Like the guys in the streets say—The Man. Captain Boss—Mistuh Charley . . . Old Cap'n Please Mr. Bossman" (141). Without having encountered those guys on the street, Walter Lee's revelation sounds like irrational race hatred. Self-determination doctrines also inform the purposefully comical scene of Beneatha's thoroughly colonialist performance of an African welcome song, which Walter Lee joins as an African hunter after a night of drinking. That famous scene dramatizes the fragile naïveté that undergirds Beneatha's idealism and Afrocentric rejection of assimilation. Walter Lee's participation is playful, but in the screenplay, when he jumps atop the dinner table to deliver a mock speech to his "black brothers" (a move Murchison soundly rejects when he enters), the scene directly mimics the street preachers of the earlier scene. Hansberry inserts a Malcolm X figure into the backdrop along with a coherent critique of Western whiteness and imperialism. Walter Lee is not irrational, only misguided in his translation of economic self-determination into his ill-fated liquor store scheme. In an interview with Studs Terkel, Hansberry reflected on some of the reactions to the play, especially the way Walter Lee is distorted in celebrations of the play as a universal rather than a Negro play (a position with which Hansberry had very little patience). She explains, "I think it's conceivable to create a character who decides that his whole life was wrong and that he ought to go out and do something else altogether different: a complete reversal of things that *we* think are acceptable. This to me is a kind of affirmation. It isn't just rebellion, because rebellion rarely knows what it wants to do after it's through rebelling" (*To Be Young* 283). With the street preacher and shared spectator position with Asagai, Walter Lee's dream seems a heroic attempt to embody self-determination ideals, if not an ill-conceived scheme by a desperate citizen of Jim Crow Jr.

Plucked from the South Side: *Raisin*'s Film Début

The film version of *Raisin* that eventually got made in 1961 remains loyal to the stage version. Lipari describes it as "a nearly isomorphic visual and verbal replication of the play,"[24] though the apartment is much brighter. The film is so loyal to the play that most reviews commented on the lack of filmic qualities. The *New York Times* called it "stagelike," Spike Lee later called it "stagey," and a reviewer in *Newsweek* cautioned, "Listen, Don't Look" because the dialogue remains superior while the confining apartment of the stage play isn't enough to fill a movie.[25] That is why most critics end up discussing the film and play as rather interchangeable.[26]

The film did add scenes outside the apartment: three scenes of Walter in a bar and some of Walter chauffeuring his white employer. But the film contains far fewer street scenes than Hansberry's original screenplay envisioned. The 1961 film opens directly with Walter Lee and Ruth in their bed, thereby cuing viewer expectations toward a domestic drama, whereas the original screenplay opens first with panning shots of the South Side before slowly moving into the apartment through the tiny window, which Hansberry parenthetically underscores, "(I repeat, T-I-N-Y)" (4). The original screenplay sought to place the Younger apartment in the South Side segregated geography from the film's very first image. On the contrary, the film largely hemmed them back into their apartment. According to Lipari, the trimming of one-third of the original screenplay is an example of the production of whiteness, "the maintenance, containment, and repair of rhetorical constructions of whiteness . . . associated with goodness, universality, and innocence," especially regarding the decision by Columbia studio executives to remove all white characters "other than the sole unambiguously racist character Karl Lindner."[27] In the end, Keppel explains, "[t]he script that Hansberry believed that she had written was not the one that the public would receive. . . . The critical establishment of 1959 read Hansberry's text as fundamentally a confirmation of, rather than a challenge to, the American ethos."[28]

Responses to the film are mixed, largely lamenting how the film reproduces or even exacerbates some of the problematic aspects of the play. Spike Lee concludes, "It seems to me all the cuts had to do with softening a too defiant black voice."[29] For Wilkerson, the cuts were "implicitly political" and "a measure of the cultural ignorance of the time."[30] Hansberry herself worried about the market pull of Hollywood and its potential corruption. She explains in the *Herald Tribune* in 1961, "I did not feel it was my right or duty to help the American public with yet another later-day minstrel show."[31] Nonetheless, film technology was enticing because, "[l]ike many Chicagoans who are born to the romance of the Sandburg image of the great city's landscape, I was excited by the opportunity to deal with it visually and send the formerly housebound characters hither and yon into the city."[32] For Keppel, Hansberry's film script is a deliberate effort to counteract misreadings of the play as overly invested in Negro stereotypes and unreflectively committed to the American dream.[33] Wilkerson argues that film technology could "widen the camera's view beyond the cramped Younger apartment to encompass the 'City of Big Shoulders' and its contradictions."[34] Still, as Carter notes, "Hollywood had a long history of presenting degrading and stereotyped images of blacks and often depicted them as exotic creatures with simple desires very different from those of the rest of humanity."[35] For Hansberry, this was simply bad art, art that was untruthful and did not live up to her oft-quoted brand of realism: "not only what is but what is possible."[36]

In the play, Hansberry already struggled with scenes cut for length then restored in later runs, scenes that offer direct meditations on segregated geographies even within the apartment. For example, the unexpurgated play features the neighbor Mrs. Johnson, who worries about the trouble Mama will find in Clybourne Park, citing stories of house bombings and how "these here Chicago peckerwoods is some baaaad peckerwoods" (102). She continues, "Ain't it something how bad these here white folks is getting here in Chicago. Lord, getting so you think you right down in Mississippi! . . . 'Course I think it's wonderful how our folks keep on pushing out. . . . Why if we left it up to these here crackers, the poor niggers wouldn't have nothing" (100–101). Mrs. Johnson maps how Jim Crow migrates and adapts. With Mrs. Johnson, revolutionary rhetoric is not confined to Walter Lee's economic plans or Beneatha's college idealism—the sweet lady down the street could be a street preacher. The screenplay promised to further map this new segregation geography. Though she ultimately deemed the film version "a thing of beauty," Hansberry noted that most footage of Chicago was cut.

There are varying explanations for why so much of the original screenplay was cut. Critics are rather unanimous, though, in condemning the cuts. Lipari detects the perpetuation of the myth of white innocence, while Reid faults the "forms of censorship" that accompany any Hollywood influence on black cultural productions. Reid explains, "The Columbia production team 'agreed that the addition of race issue material . . . should be avoided,' because 'the introduction of further race issues may lessen the sympathy of the audience, give the effect of propagandistic writing, and so weaken the story, not only as dramatic entertainment, but as propaganda, too.'"[37] Reid cites Beneatha's stifled pan-African revolutionary stances and a revised scene about Travis asking for money to pay for an African American schoolbook (a "special" book on "the poor-Negroes-in-history"), which was deleted by the production team (including a story editor who happened to be named James Crow!). Carter traces how the producers "wanted to hold as close to the original money-making magic as possible while reducing the risk even further. They therefore resisted any new material, but particularly those scenes that made the play's implicit social criticism more overt, striving, above all, to keep racial content and expression of racial protest to the minimum."[38] According to this line of thinking, social criticism was best confined to the legislative arena. Regarding her family's own desegregation struggles, Hansberry writes, "The fact that my father and the NAACP 'won' a Supreme Court decision, in a now famous case which bears his name in the lawbooks, is—ironically—the sort of 'progress' our satisfied friends allude to when they presume to deride the more radical means of struggle."[39] Hansberry wrote this in a letter to the editor at the *New York Times*, "with reference to civil disobedience and Congress of Racial Equality stall-in," but the lesson extends to her experience with Hollywood and its desire for safe narratives of progress.

Segregation Narratives in a Post–Jim Crow World

As the fig leaf of de jure legitimacy was removed from segregation's body during the civil rights movement, writers had to shift strategies. Some banished all remnants of Jim Crow in Black Arts projects that replaced his supine stance with Black Power postures of defiance or Afrocentric narratives of lost or regained nobility. Others, however, extended the segregation narrative tradition by returning to the nation's immediate past to figure out Jim Crow's enduring relevance. One possibility was to carefully connect past practices and experiences in the Jim Crow South with the forms of racial division found elsewhere, especially those that would prove most resilient in the face of civil rights victories. During the late 1950s and early 1960s, segregation narratives began to divide into two broad camps: those that painted experiences and practices of segregation as a thing of the past or soon-to-be past, and those that emphasized the endurance of old segregation practices and creation of new ones. The first camp tends toward linear narratives that place the Jim Crow South in the past and juxtapose it with experiences elsewhere and later, especially with back stories of the Great Migration, such as in Baldwin's *Go Tell It on the Mountain* (1953), which extends earlier narratives of migrations north, such as in Marita Bonner's "The Whipping" (1940). Farrah Jasmine Griffin suggests that midcentury migration narratives shifted their emphasis away from initial confrontations with the new terrain of the urban north and toward extended stories about navigating such cityscapes and the communities that developed.[40] In that shift, we see the other broad camp that emerged during the interregnum of the civil rights movement: a focus on segregation's persistence in the absence of stark Jim Crow legal codes. Prime examples include the early sections of Malcolm X's autobiography (1965) and LeRoi Jones's work before he became Amiri Baraka. This second camp in particular helped usher in the neo–segregation narrative, whether by painting race restrictive covenants as directly linked to Mama's Jim Crow experiences for Hansberry or by connecting domestic segregation to transnational phenomena, such as colonialism for Wright in his pan-Africanist work.

Hansberry's unfilmed screenplay stands as a particularly good example of a late segregation narrative because it shrewdly diagnoses problems of representing segregation once the cardboard specter of Jim Crow and readily identifiable white supremacists are no longer the stuff of realism but rather of melodrama. When Hansberry brings the Youngers out of their apartment and into the streets of Chicago, she accepts the challenges of representing segregation in its shape-shifting forms and in daily life. This continues the literary line that includes Chesnutt's folkloric examinations of life on the color line, Anna Julia Cooper's and Du Bois's essays on racial division, Wright's protest literature, Larsen's domestic scenes of racial passing, and Himes's experiments with genre to play with the color line, both political and literary. In her study of (male) lynching in drama by black women playwrights, Angelletta Gourdine considers how Hansberry extends the work of Angelina Weld Grimké's depiction of black female responses to an actual lynching in *Rachel* (1916). She argues, "While the direct circumstances of Walter's death seem a separate issue from murder by lynching, the play suggests that the death of his child from poverty leads Walter to an unconscious form of protracted suicide."[41] For Gourdine, lynching becomes a persistent trope in segregation narratives, even when the text doesn't directly address lynching at all.

Whether or not we agree that Walter Lee's death is a sort of lynching,

Gourdine's general point stands that Hansberry consciously addresses a long history of African American experience with Jim Crow segregation and other forms of racial division. This explains why the screenplay takes such pains to extend and fill in the image of Lena, long accused of confirming stereotypes of backwardness and not being revolutionary enough. A reviewer in *Time* went so far as to call Lena a "Mammy" within a "soap opera in black face."[42] Carter suggests that the alterations "enlarge the portrait of Lena and afford a clearer view of her relationship to her society,"[43] especially regarding her experience coming to the North and entering the workforce at age fifty. The screenplay, more so than the original play and ensuing film, places the Youngers in a long African American history dating back to earlier eras and regions of segregation, Jim Crow and otherwise. Regarding Hansberry's next play, *Les Blancs*, Joy L. Abell argues that "Hansberry uses an African setting as a means of providing her a comfortable distance from which to critique the strategies and philosophies of popular civil rights leaders Malcolm X and Martin Luther King."[44] She also suggests that "[a]nother possible reason for the play's African setting is Hansberry's desire to demonstrate the similarities between African and African-American struggles for equality."[45] While this may be the case, there is a missing step in the path from the cramped Younger apartment to the African continent, from Walter Lee and Beneatha to Asagai: the streets of Chicago.

In arguing that the unfilmed screenplay, more so than the wildly successful Broadway play or the mildly successful Hollywood film, is Hansberry's most realized picture of segregation, I realize that I tread a delicate, if somewhat well-worn, path in seeking the "real" Hansberry. White, lesbian, feminist writer Adrienne Rich attempted a similar posthumous project in the civil rights magazine *Freedomways* when she announced that "Lorraine Hansberry is a problem to me because she is black, female and dead."[46] She questioned Nemiroff's white male hand in posthumously and selectively presenting Hansberry's archive to the public. Rich also speculated that Hansberry herself was self-censorious, such as when characters initially conceived as female ended up male by the time the story hit the stage. Nevertheless, it is important to view the screenplay in the bright light of Hansberry's fame, rather than seeing success as inherently sullying. In the short time between the début of the play and her decision to write the screen adaptation, Hansberry faced pressures and distortions that come with mainstream success. Further, the swift pace of the civil rights movement toward national prominence means that Hansberry appreciated *Raisin*'s success in the context of a swelling liberation movement arguing for national amelioration of Jim Crow segregation, antiblack violence, and centuries of assaults on the dignity and humanity of African Americans.

Critics of *Raisin* must contend with the enormous mainstream success of the play and the resultant contradictions between canonization as a symbol of the civil rights movement, on the one hand, and the elusive goals of that movement to fully desegregate U.S. society on the other. The Youngers entered the mainstream, but the actual black people Hansberry sought to represent remain, to borrow Morrison's metaphor from *The Bluest Eye*, on the hem of society. Keppel suggests that *Raisin*'s canonization necessitated that its revolutionary and working-class politics were abandoned. He explains, "As gifted a cultural pugilist as she was, Hansberry ... was denied her due as a leading citizen of her times. In her lifetime, Hansberry's political unconventionality necessitated that it was her play, and not its author, that would become iconic."[47] But in this narrative we lose the screenplay. The film version that was eventually realized looks a lot like the original play: it focuses on the individual family and domestic themes more so than political engagement with segregation's structures in urban life at large.

In the twenty-first century, Hansberry is now claimed as a revolutionary thinker, key early black feminist, and gifted writer by people across the ideological spectrum, even most of her former detractors (including Amiri Baraka). In his "Sweet Lorraine" (1987), Baraka dubs Hansberry "our Bard." Baraka contends, "I have always thought that *Raisin*, and indeed Hansberry herself, with her working class audiences, was the real beginning of the revolutionary theater of the 50's, the catalyst for the cultural revolution of the Black Arts Movement. With *Raisin* and Jimmy's *Blues for Mister Charlie*."[48] Baraka's posthumous revisionism aside, it is telling that Baraka returned to this tumultuous moment when de jure gave way to de facto segregation to conclude, "The Younger family is part of the black majority, and the concerns I once dismissed as 'middle class'—of buying a house and moving into 'white folks' neighborhoods'—are actually reflective of the essence of black people's striving to defeat segregation, discrimination and national oppression. There is no such thing as a 'white folks' neighborhood' except to racists and to those submitting to racism!"[49] In a post–civil rights era, we can rethink Hansberry's place not only in African American literature and thought generally but also in the specific project of representing segregation.

In the unfilmed script it is nearly impossible to miss Hansberry's skepticism and her whip-smart analysis of the depth of white supremacism. She portrays the limits of the court system—and therefore some of the more celebrated gains of the civil rights movement that followed *Raisin*—to fully speak to the lives, hopes, and dignity of black people in segregated America. Keppel, quoting Hansberry, argues, "If Hansberry could not prevent the selective appropriation of *Raisin* . . . it is nonetheless clear that she followed her own advice . . . by creating a drama centered not on the comfortable middle class but instead on the working class, whose struggles and decisions are 'more pertinent, more relevant, more significant . . . more *decisive*—in our political history and our political future.'"[50] Like many others, Keppel seeks to salvage Hansberry from the political whitewashing that mainstream success brought her. Such rescue missions suggest that Hansberry's case is a good index of a civil rights–era dynamic in which symbolic successes are heralded but the full moral challenge of integration remains an unfulfilled promise. Gordon identifies a segregation aesthetic in *Raisin* and argues, "Hansberry's conception of genuine realism renders human beings as active agents in their own liberation as well as in the oppression of others. This mode opens a cultural space through which to imagine alternatives to a truthfully represented, oppressive social reality."[51] I aver that Hansberry's segregation aesthetic is best suited to the unfilmed screenplay and to Hansberry's careful, revealing descriptions of Chicago and her savvy sense of how visual technology could picture urban segregation through the eyes of black and white characters of varying ideological stripes. In this way, Hansberry begins to attend to unfulfilled integration promises that writers must address in a post–civil rights era just around the corner.

Post–Civil Rights Revisions: Morrison's Neo–Segregation and Neo–Slave Narratives

The post–civil rights era exacerbated the aesthetic and political challenges Hansberry faced. The nation's official narrative became one of achieved equality while the fact of inequality permeated much of black experience and history. Writers faced the choice of whether to emphasize slavery or Jim Crow as the signal experience that could help make sense of the persistence of racial division, despair, and internalized shame and self-hatred. Morrison is a particularly good example because she chose both options with her depiction of the 1940s in her acclaimed first novel, *The Bluest Eye* (1970), and her Pulitzer Prize–winning meditation on slavery in *Beloved* (1987). Like this pairing, the neo–segregation narrative in general has received less scholarly attention than its much more famous fraternal twin, the neo–slave narrative. I say "fraternal twin" because the two traditions are born in the same era and political sensibilities, but they emphasize different legacies of racial disenfranchisement to frame contemporary African American identity and U.S. race politics. Following key work by Ashraf Rushdy and others, scholars now recognize the importance of the neo–slave narrative, defined either narrowly or broadly, especially Margaret Walker's *Jubilee* (1966), William Styron's *The Confessions of Nat Turner* (1967), Gaines's *The Autobiography of Miss Jane Pittman* (1971), Gayl Jones's *Corregidora* (1975), Alex Haley's *Roots* (1976), Ishmael Reed's *Flight to Canada* (1976), Octavia Butler's *Kindred* (1979), Sherley Anne Williams's *Dessa Rose* (1986), Charles Johnson's *Middle Passage* (1990), Edward P. Jones's *The Known World* (2003), and James McBride's *Song Yet Sung* (2008), in addition to *Beloved*. This list is illustrative, not exhaustive, and the definition of what counts as a neo–slave narrative remains slippery. For instance, Walker claims to have based *Jubilee* on actual oral accounts of slavery, which may make it a proto-example.

Not only did the neo–segregation and neo–slave narratives develop in tandem, the two traditions also overlap significantly, including some of the key writers associated with each. Morrison's *The Bluest Eye* belongs at the head of the neo–segregation narrative tradition, while her later novel *Beloved* stands as one of the more famous neo–slave narratives after that tradition came of age. *The Bluest Eye* is known for its deceptively simple depiction of poverty and internalized race-hatred, which results in the violation and psychological dissolution of Pecola Breedlove, a young girl who carries all the ugliness, hurt, despair, and fury of the black community. Claudia MacTeer, the reflective adult narrator, famously explains, "All of us—all who knew her—felt so wholesome after we cleaned ourselves on her. We were so beautiful when we stood astride her ugliness."[52] Pecola is a racial pariah who requires the complicity of all involved, which is to say her entire community. Joining Sula, Beloved, the women in the convent in *Paradise* (1997), and Florens in *A Mercy* (2008), Pecola is the earliest figure in Morrison's oeuvre who illustrates the violence and terror at the heart of seemingly virtuous phenomena such as love, beauty, pride, community, and mercy. *The Bluest Eye* now appears in literature courses across the nation, and its early appearance on Oprah Winfrey's Book Club helped solidify its status as an American classic. It has been the subject of a great deal of literary criticism, so I will confine my discussion to a few brief points about how and why we might talk about Morrison's début novel as an exemplary and founding neo–segregation narrative. Written in 1970 not long after key civil rights successes, *The Bluest Eye* returns to Lorain, Ohio, in the early 1940s to deliver a conscious representation of de facto segregation during the era of Jim Crow. The main character, Claudia, breaks from her community's universal love of whiteness, which manifests as a parental insistence on "unimaginative cleanliness" (22).[53] The child narrator in turn embraces dirt and her own nakedness. Claudia questions her community's disregard of Pecola, who carries her father's child, and explains, "I felt a need for someone to want the black baby to live—just to counteract the universal love of white baby dolls, Shirley Temples and Maureen Peals" (190).

On the surface, the novel is about fashioning a coherent sense of self—both individual and collective—amid a community on both sides of the color line that denies the dignity and beauty of black culture and black people. Each key moment of internalization of racial hatred throughout the novel is attributed to an epiphanic encounter with dominant white culture, which then gets repeated by and disseminated through totems of whiteness internal to the black community, such as white baby dolls, milk, and Shirley Temple.[54] For instance, Cholly Breedlove's hatred for and violence against black women results from his own violation by two white boys who, with their peeping eyes and flashlight, penetrate the pastoral scene of his first sexual experience in the bushes (150). This backstory is replicated when Rosemary Villanucci encroaches with her own peeping eyes on another scene in the bushes, this one involving Pecola's first period, leading Rosemary to accuse the girls of "playing nasty" (30). In another example, Pauline Breedlove trades her sense of self for the shiny allure of whiteness during an encounter with Jean Harlow on the silver screen. Mrs. Breedlove loses a tooth, and therefore the fantasy of looking like Jean Harlow. "I let my hair go back," she recounts, "plaited up, and settled down to just being ugly" (123). This defining backstory moment is replicated each time Mr. Henry, the MacTeers' philandering houseguest, compliments Claudia and her sister by calling them Greta Garbo and Ginger Rogers (16, 75, 78). Such encounters across racial lines in this starkly segregated community provide the answer to Claudia's confusion over how the universal love of whiteness came to be. Beyond the back stories from an earlier Jim Crow era, Morrison traces such encounters back to slavery and the initial European invasion of the globe by introducing the character of Soaphead Church, or Elihue Micah Whitcomb, the biracial misanthropic anglophile who "regarded as his life's goal the hoarding of this white strain" (167). In setting up these encounters across racial lines, especially Claudia's famous vivisection of her white baby doll, Morrison's project is clear: analyze the internationalization of racial self-hatred and the universal love of whiteness "[t]o see of what it was made, to discover the dearness, to find the beauty, the desirability that had escaped me, but apparently only me" (21).

The novel's representation of segregation and cross-racial contact is about more than racial hierarchies during Jim Crow, which cues its status as a *neo*–segregation narrative. Morrison returns to a moment of stark segregation in the Jim Crow recent past in order to say something about the moment of 1970 when a seemingly orderly racial caste system was being upended. The setting returns readers to a pre–civil rights era of stark racial segregation in the 1940s, while the narrator speaks from the vantage of 1970, an era when ideologies of Black Power and cultural nationalism made headway in questioning core tenets of civil rights, especially the then-dominant belief in integration ideals and the ability of the government to ameliorate racial injustice. As Claudia rejects the internalized love of whiteness in the black community, Morrison keeps one eye on the 1970s by discussing the blackness characters reject as "funk," a word rife with connotations of authentic black culture and pride for her 1970s audience. Geraldine is the foil who embodies racial uplift ideology and cultivated whiteness, close kin to George Murchison. She espouses "[t]he careful development of thrift, patience, high morals, and good manners. In short, how to get rid of the funkiness. The dreadful funkiness of passion, the funkiness of nature, the funkiness of the wide range of human emotions" (83). As she rejects the "funk" within, Geraldine replicates and polices her own Jim Crow system within the black community by differentiating between "colored" and "niggers," especially since "the line between colored and nigger was not always clear" (87). Though the scene takes place in 1941 and Geraldine exhibits the racial uplift ideology of the early part of the century, Morrison uses a discourse of "funk" lifted straight from the 1970s Black Is Beautiful movement. More in line with 1970 than 1941, Morrison inverts racial hierarchies and embraces "funk" culture. To be flip: this is George Clinton, not Marcus Garvey.

Morrison presents a rather unflattering image of civil rights through the figure of Maureen Peal, a "high yellow dream child with long brown hair braided into two lynch ropes" (62). With such skin and hair, Maureen is the embodiment of the twin history of Jim Crow and its vigilante violence, on the one hand, and racial uplift and optimistic beliefs in the U.S. democratic system associated with civil rights on the other hand. Whose dream is she? Morrison goes so far as to suggest that Maureen is a cynical extrapolation of Martin Luther King, Jr.'s utopian vision of integration. Morrison inserts all sorts of knowing jabs about the legacy of civil rights and the "unearned haughtiness" (63) of the new black bourgeoisie. We learn that Maureen Peal can afford her well-pressed clothes and her half-eaten ice cream cones because her family became well off through civil rights litigation, which ends up seeming self-serving and not politically virtuous. As Maureen unfurls her dollar bill, Morrison writes,

> "My uncle sued Isaley's," Maureen said to the three of us. "He sued the Isaley's in Akron. They said he was disorderly and that that was why they wouldn't serve him, but a friend of his, a policeman, came in and beared the witness, so the suit went through."
> "What's a suit?"
> "It's when you can beat them up if you want to and won't anybody do nothing. Our family does it all the time. We believe in suits." (68)

The scene takes place in 1941, yet the concerns in this passage are more in line with a post–civil rights project of assessing the movement's successes and limits. Morrison exhibits a profound pessimism about a civil rights model of procedural liberalism and neutral equality. She presents the legal system not as a tool to ameliorate racial injustice but as a cynical, morally bankrupt playground for people who "believe in suits" more so than their own beauty. While this scene is not one of the more remarked upon in the scholarly dialogue, it performs important work of the neo–segregation narrative: return to the Jim Crow past to comment on race relations in the present. In a post–civil rights imagination, readers would think suits like the one against Isaley's would have little chance of success in the 1930s, but they would be central to the types of sit-ins and other activities in the groundswell of the later 1950s that led to the legislative and judicial gains of the civil rights movement. Maureen is out of touch with, or even hostile to, the lives of Claudia and Pecola. Instead, Maureen is symptomatic of the culture of segregation that leads to "exquisitely learned self-hatred" (65). Readers filter Maureen's litigious version of racial uplift and King's dream through the lens of a post–civil rights era, not through the lens of the 1941 setting. For Morrison, the ideal of integration and liberal equality so enshrined in dominant versions of civil rights may not fully redress internalized self-hatred and therefore does not fully speak to the members of the black community existing at the hem of society.

To conclude this brief discussion of Morrison's début novel, let me draw a very broad distinction between the neo–slave and neo–segregation narratives. Beyond the obvious distinction that there is not currently a fully recognized segregation narrative akin to the very specific genre of the slave narrative, the functions and political sensibilities of the two are complementary rather than commensurate. According to Rushdy, the neo–slave narrative comments on the failures of the New Left and reclaims black history and subjectivity in a self-determination pose akin to Black Power. He explains, "Black Power—especially the politics of property, identity, and violence—as a way of commenting on the failures of the New Left and articulating their hopes for whatever comes next."[55] The neo–segregation narrative also often adopts a self-determination stance, but it remains invested in civil rights—especially the politics of legislation, national identity, and interracial strife. Such narratives comment on the failures of Black Power as well as of the American nation to fully enfranchise African Americans (black women in particular). Further, their aim is often to reclaim the nation as belonging to African Americans, a stance also akin to integration sensibilities. This is not to say that neo–segregation narratives reject black nationalism and its self-determination stances in favor of civil rights ideals, only that they tend to position the allure of self-segregation as a logical response to Jim Crow, but not necessarily as an end solution.

In an essay on black history, neo–slave narrative pioneer Margaret Walker signals the presence of the neo–segregation narrative tradition: "When segregation was thus established, black people were thus set back to a more subtle but equally egregious slavery, we began to meet the challenge of our environment and circumstance with a creative response both positive and productive."[56] Walker opens up a literary project of finding meaning in the survival, creativity, and experiences of those living under Jim Crow in addition to and separate from stories of experiences of chattel slavery. We might, therefore, also ask how segregation informs neo–slave narratives. Because writers use neo–slave narratives to establish connections between the present moment and the era of slavery, the interval Jim Crow period and its attendant lessons and experiences necessarily infuse such stories. In other words, Jim Crow haunts key neo–slave narratives, including Morrison's *Beloved*.

As Morrison explores the re-memory of slavery, *Beloved* also points to the potentially redemptive—cleansing, even—effects of voluntary self-segregation or separatism, the pretty cousin of compulsory race segregation. On this side of civil rights, Morrison confronts us with a legacy of slavery that persists in the psychological terrain of Jim Crow: the dominant group's power to dirty. Over the course of the novel, Sethe must come to understand and accept her decision to slit the throat of her two-year-old daughter rather than let her be taken into slavery. Sethe finds that the ultimate violation of slavery is a psychological sullying, realizing "[t]hat anybody white could take your whole self for anything that came to mind. Not just work, kill, or maim you, but dirty you."[57] The lesson of how African Americans can be "dirtied" at the whim of white people is not confined to systems of chattel slavery; it continues through Reconstruction, Jim Crow, and de facto racial segregation. Sethe's notorious infanticide, the horrific act at the center of *Beloved*, stands as the most extreme act of separation from whites. Still, her action belongs on a spectrum of possibilities in the race-segregated community surrounding 124 Bluestone Road, as well as the tradition of self-segregation that regained prominence following disillusionment with civil rights ideals. In both her neo–slave and neo–segregation narratives, Morrison explores how the civil rights gains of the 1960s did not fully ameliorate the self-alienation that is the twin legacy of slavery and segregation and that constitutes the core of our contemporary racial identities. Furthermore, while *Beloved* is most often read as a neo–slave narrative, the novel is set during Jim Crow's earliest days; that is, Beloved returns in human form just as Jim Crow emerges in the wake of Reconstruction and its failures. *Beloved* is a neo–slave narrative that takes place in a neo–segregation setting.

If *Beloved* and neo–slave narratives in general counteract cultural amnesia and "the serious work of beating back the past,"[58] then we must account for the intervening period of de jure race segregation. That is, Jim Crow is the midwife between the *neo-* and the *slave narrative*. From this angle, we might look anew at the narrative problems posed by interracial connections in key neo–slave narratives, such as the interracial female friendship between Dessa and the white plantation owner Miss Rufel in *Dessa Rose* or the interracial marriage and lineage between Dana, her white husband Kevin, and her white slave-owner ancestor Rufus in *Kindred*. The interracial intimacies carry extra layers of meaning when viewed through the lens of Jim Crow segregation systems and integration struggles. In *Kindred*, Dana's survival hinges on her ability to play her role as slave without allowing the era to mark her, even when she finds, "I'm drawn all the way into eighteen nineteen, and I don't know what to do."[59] The problem and necessity of historical distance is compounded for Butler and her readers because we cannot jump from 1976 to 1818 without taking account of the intervening years. As Dana notices the ease with which her well-meaning white husband ends up "unwittingly echoing Rufus" (91), Butler's readers comprehend their relationship through the lens of civil rights struggles to end antimiscegenation laws. While Dana discovers "how easily people can be trained to accept slavery" (101), we note segregation's persistence across eras, even officially integrated ones.

Why would an author emphasize one era of racial division over another, compulsory segregation or chattel slavery, to comment on the present? Whereas neo–slave narratives fashion a contemporary racial identity by connecting African Americans to a horrific past and a steadfast community ethic, neo–segregation narratives focus on identifying racial division that persists after de jure racial segregation is no longer the law. In general, neo–slave narratives anchor the formation of contemporary black identity in the familial ties, lessons, and survival strategies associated with slavery. In a 1976 essay called "Southern Black Culture," Margaret Walker chronicles African American history and describes the rise of Jim Crow out of slavery: "And so, we came to the end of the nineteenth century shackled and oppressed by a system that was equally as demeaning and dehumanizing as slavery had been."[60] The effects of both slavery and racial segregation as social systems may look similar, but they emphasize different reference points in service of complementary projects. Neo–segregation narratives directly question mainstream assertions that racial division is a thing of the past, asserting in particular that the problem of the color line is not fully solved by key successes of the American civil rights movement, such as *Brown v. Board*, the 1964 Civil Rights Act, and the 1965 Voting Rights Act. In contrast, chattel slavery has a clear end, which means the neo–slave narrative has other cultural work to do, such as tracing slavery's legacy in ensuing social structures, celebrating the survival of black ancestors under such horrid conditions, or refashioning a genealogical line cut by slavery and the middle passage.

Neo–segregation narratives also identify and celebrate survival strategies employed by African Americans during Jim Crow, such as allegiance with other minority groups and conscious performance of racial stereotypes. In turn, these strategies offer readers ways to navigate and change race relations in the present. As tropes, Jim Crow and the escaped slave speak to different contemporary needs and sensibilities, especially debates internal to black communities, as we will see in the next chapter on masculinist Black Power and its black feminist critique.

CHAPTER 2

JIM CROW RETURNS, JIM CROW REMAINS

Gender and Segregation in David Bradley's *The Chaneysville Incident* and Alice Walker's *The Color Purple*

Lorraine Hansberry's late segregation narrative and Toni Morrison's early neo–segregation narrative concentrate on what happens when people cross the color line, whether physically or psychologically. The stark racial lines of Jim Crow can serve other purposes too. Many neo–segregation narratives do not primarily concern interactions across the color line, but rather those on one side of it, though segregation still looms large on their horizons. These narratives focus on issues internal to black communities, especially around class, sexuality, gender, and ideology, while framing them with the shadow of Jim Crow and a shared knowledge of racial injustice and the impact of white supremacy on black lives. In this manner, writers sort through intraracial tensions around gender and black kinship in a post–civil rights era. They are informed by the Black Arts movement and its critique of white-oriented aesthetics and also responsive to Black Power doctrines of self-determination, but they do not necessarily call such movements home. They also remain committed to the legacy of the civil rights movement, which took up universal language and appeals for integration and unity. Ensuing identitarian movements were skeptical about the prospects of inclusive visions of an integrated nation-state to foster cultural pride or to speak to inequalities within black communities. By setting up camp primarily on one side of the color line, neo–segregation narratives explore what kinds of alternative social spaces are possible when defined by, for, and about black people, whether such communities are externally imposed or self-segregated.

Armed with suspicion of universalist designs and open to considering the merits of self-segregation, post–civil rights writers turn to the era of compulsory race segregation to engage debates between black feminism and masculinist Black Power. For instance, Ishmael Reed taps Jim Crow to take a swipe at contemporary (white) feminism in *Reckless Eyeballing* (1986). In the novel, black writer Ian Ball attempts to get off the "sexlist" (feminism's version of a blacklist) by writing an all-female play that exhumes Emmett Till's corpse to testify in a posthumous rape trial. Reed finds the high stakes, stark racial lines, and perceived moral clarity of the Till case useful for a satire of feminism and what the book casts as not only its betrayal of black men but also its outright defilement of them. That is, he worries that Black Power has been neutered. On the other hand, Till also figures prominently in black feminist projects, such as Audre Lorde's feminist meditations on the racial and sexual lessons we all inherit from Till in her 1982 poem "Afterimages," which extends the work of Gwendolyn Brooks's famous retelling of the white female accuser's story through fairytale tropes in "A Bronzeville Mother Loiters in Mississippi. Meanwhile, a Mississippi Mother Burns Bacon" (1960). Lorde portrays her black female speaker's experiences in a post–civil rights era as an "afterimage" of that which led to the brutal murder of Till. "I inherited Jackson, Mississippi," the speaker declares. "His broken body is the afterimage of my 21st year."[1] Further, Lorde casts the female body itself as an afterimage of Till's corpse. She writes, "Emmett Till rides the crest of the Pearl, whistling / 24 years his ghost lay like the shade of a raped woman / and a white woman has grown older in costly honor."[2] These projects invert neo–segregation narratives by bringing the figure of Till into the present.[3] Their intertextual lobs are part of a struggle not only for how to narrate Jim Crow in a post–civil rights era but also to enlist him in contemporary black nationalist or feminist movements.

This chapter turns to David Bradley's *The Chaneysville Incident* (1981) and Alice Walker's *The Color Purple* (1982) as particularly good windows onto how neo–segregation narratives lend themselves to black feminist–Black Power debates, which crested in the late 1970s and 1980s. These two novels are lauded for their reclamations of U.S. history from the point of view of black people. In *The Chaneysville Incident*, historian John Washington reluctantly returns to his home in North County, Pennsylvania, to access his family's past. He finds that his family story crosses the border into South County and dates back to Jim Crow and a vigilante lynching, then slavery and a failed abolition scheme, and finally to the founding of the American nation itself. Along the way, Bradley explores the history and policing of black masculinity under slavery and Jim Crow, which colors John's interracial relationship in a post–civil rights era. In the end, the black male body carries collective memories of African American experience not captured in the written historical record. *The Color Purple* is a helpful counterpoint because Walker provides a female-centered meditation on gender in African American culture, especially the way black family dynamics replicate Jim Crow's black–white power relations, which the novel positions as an extension of slavery's master–property relationship. In his 1984 essay "Novelist Alice Walker: Telling the Black Woman's Story," Bradley characterizes Walker's novel as the "ground zero of a Hiroshima of controversy" for its portrayal of black men.[4] Walker's novel also profoundly influenced how post–civil rights generations think about African American life in the early twentieth century, especially with Steven Spielberg's major Hollywood film adaptation (1985) and the heated round of political debate that adaptation inspired.[5]

By turning inward to black communities in Jim Crow, both novels consider the separatist possibilities associated not only with compulsory race segregation but also with post–civil rights ambivalence toward integration ideals. Separatist tendencies infuse African American history, from Liberian repatriation schemes after the Civil War to Garveyism during Jim Crow. Following the Nation of Islam's increased prominence in the later 1950s and the subsequent rise of Malcolm X, the following decades witnessed a resurgence of self-segregation tendencies with Black Power and then womanism. In their influential 1977 statement, the Combahee River Collective outlined the scope, principles, and genesis of black feminism, especially from proximate women's and black liberation movements, and noted:

> The reaction of black men to feminism has been notoriously negative. They are, of course, even more threatened than black women by the possibility that black feminists might organize around our own needs. They realize that they might not only lose valuable and hard-working allies in their struggles but that they might also be forced to change their habitually sexist ways of interacting with and oppressing black women. Accusations that black feminism divides the black struggle are powerful deterrents to the growth of an autonomous black women's movement.[6]

For novelists such as Bradley and Walker, Jim Crow offers a useful, semi-removed terrain for working through tensions between black and women's liberation. Bradley and Walker both offer a recuperative project in their familial narratives: reclaim black history by us and for us, even if the black families on display contain some white members. They each use Jim Crow segregation to sieve post–civil rights questions about sexism and separatism internal to black communities, a dilemma that tends especially to fall on black women.[7] Whereas Ashraf Rushdy argues that the neo–slave narrative arose partly to rebuke William Styron's move to speak in the first person in *The Confessions of Nat Turner* (1967), neo–segregation narratives respond to internal divisions that racial self-determination stances might paper over, especially around gender inequality. In his study of remembering in contemporary African American fiction, Keith Byerman notes that fiction of recovery—historical, personal, familial—allows the oppressed to gain visibility and voice, which holds the power to heal a race or nation. "But because this is primarily postmodern literature," he cautions, "such healing possibilities themselves are often problematized. The writing itself often challenges the assumptions of womanist and Afrocentric readings of it as therapeutic."[8] In this vein, I highlight the gender dimension in the healing narratives undergirding Bradley's and Walker's projects, one a revisionist history in line with black nationalist ideals, the other a specifically womanist revision of that history.

Why turn to the historiographic terrain of Jim Crow for pressing contemporary debates about black feminism and Black Power? Bradley and Walker not only gauge slavery's legacy after Reconstruction but also engage specifically post–civil rights debates about the limits of integration and related gendered struggles around equality within black communities. Scholars focus on how Walker creates a specifically black and/or women's community, emphasizing how she turns away from the color line to carve out "alternative communities or enclaves,"[9] be they within the black community, in a juke joint, in Africa, in letters, or in the imagination of one poor, rural black woman. Bradley, too, turns away from a post–civil rights model of interracial national amelioration and toward a black-centered familial history. Ultimately, Bradley and Walker refract post–civil rights debates about sexism and racial empowerment through a stark, male-dominated Jim Crow world in order to imagine a black community attendant both to self-determination and to feminist desires to do more than just integrate a nation but also to revise that nation from a decidedly minoritarian perspective. The results may also locate such possibilities in surprising places, such as Sofia in *The Color Purple* and her utter disinterest in white folk in lieu of anger.

Jim Crow Remains in *The Chaneysville Incident*

In Bradley's novel, an abrupt late-night call summons John Washington to return home when Old Jack Crawley falls ill and is expected to soon cross over. Old Jack is a father figure to John and a hermit who seems to have taken no note of Jim Crow's passing in a post–civil rights era. For John, the call represents a rather unwelcome return of his history to his present life as a history professor in an interracial relationship. "But I did not hang up," John tells us. "Not right away. Instead I lay there, shivering, and listened to the wire."[10] In this image of an open phone line, Bradley dramatizes John's nonsynchronous relationship to history and also his desire (be it acknowledged or repressed) to connect with that history, to make it talk to him even when nothing but a crackling wire is on the other end. His white fiancée, Judith Powell, says of Old Jack, "I thought he was somebody you made up.... I would have thought he was indestructible. Or a lie" (3). Judith imagines John's history as a set of myths and is surprised that a remnant exists in their present-day reality, which echoes the book's general dynamic of casting the Jim Crow South as an anachronistic intrusion into the contemporary north. As John travels from Pittsburgh back to North and South County, Bradley figures home, history, and familial identity as a place that *was* but still *is*.

In the ensuing genealogical narrative of familial reconnection and rupture, John's trip spurs him to resurrect the mystery of the 1958 suicide of his father, Moses Washington, who left behind an attic full of clues, documents, and unfinished business in the house John's mother still occupies. The more John digs up and comes to learn what Old Jack knows, the further back in history he is drawn, through segregation, small-town secrets, lynching, and finally an 1858 failed slave escape that ended in thirteen suicides, including that of his grandfather C.K. Washington in the same spot as John's father a century later. John's scope also widens outside the archive and the domestic home to oral history and Old Jack's mountain shack as well as the local courthouse. While initially reluctant to return to his home on the Hill, John eventually reclaims his family history through both archival research and his own imagination when such records fail. At that revelatory moment, he uncovers the incident at the heart of the novel's title and hears the breath-song of the ill-fated escape attempt by slaves who would become his ancestors. In this way, John's family history maps neatly onto core eras of African American history: C.K. Washington in slavery, Moses Washington in Jim Crow, and

John Washington in a post–civil rights era of integration. In this patrilineal line, Old Jack is the key figure who disrupts the clean passage from one generation to the next (with each generation ending in suicide), while John's white fiancée and suffering mother serve as foils for cross-generational connection.

The novel is about John coming to terms not only with how the structures of Jim Crow and slavery haunt his post–civil rights era but also with Jim Crow's and slavery's evidentiary remains. In the course of tending to Old Jack and digging up records, both official and testimonial, John learns about the limits of official records and the historian's process to capture the story of his antecedents in Jim Crow and slavery as well as the relevance of such family histories in his present life. What emerges is an argument about historical change, or rather the lack thereof. For instance, ruminating on the founding fathers' racism alongside changes in lighting technology, John muses:

> And one wonders—if one is a wonderer—if somewhere along the line things would not have been different if the electric light had come along earlier, or not come along at all. Could Franklin have written his "Essay on Populations" if he had had the unerring glow of incandescence showing up his bigotry? Could Lincoln have proclaimed Emancipation with the same glow highlighting his hypocrisy? Was the only difference between *Plessy v. Fergusson* and *Brown v. the Board of Education of Topeka, Kansas* the fact that the former was written by lamplight and the latter under—probably —a fluorescent tube? . . . Could King have penned that hopelessly naïve letter from the Albany jail with a flickering candle forcing him to stop and think while words steadied before his eyes? (204–5)

In this meditation on chance and alternative histories, the object of John's wondrous quest is persistent bigotry and the fate of cross-racial knowledge, of which slavery and Jim Crow are two manifestations of the same phenomenon—or, "the changing same," to borrow from Deborah McDowell's influential framing of black feminism. The final jab at the icon of integration, Martin Luther King, Jr., reminds us that Bradley's concerns are at least as much on the present, specifically the limitations or unfinished business of the civil rights movement and Black Power critiques of it, as on debates about who owns history. Still, John does not opt for Malcolm X or other key figures of Black Power in lieu of King. Moreover, Bradley does not opt to focus exclusively on slavery or the master-slave paradigm to explain contemporary society, as is the case in many neo–slave narratives and related Black Arts experiments, such as Amiri Baraka's *Slave Ship* (1967), one of the more enduring ventures to come out of his Black Repertory Theater in Harlem, as well as the key slavery allusions in the portrayal of cross-racial sexuality in the Obie-winning *Dutchman* (1964), Baraka's last work written as LeRoi Jones.

Ultimately, my reading of *The Chaneysville Incident* is twofold: first, the novel is just as much, if not more, a neo–segregation narrative as neo–slave narrative; second, Bradley's novel is a prime example of a *masculinist* neo–slave narrative. According to Rushdy, "*The Chaneysville Incident* is literally structured around and suffused with scenes of and ideas about death and burial."[11] John resurrects long-buried history and channels the thirteen slave spirits haunting the graveyard in their unmarked burial sites, which are adjacent to the monuments of their white owners. However, Jim Crow segregation, more so than slavery, is the heart of the novel. Like a suspension bridge, the Jim Crow era connects the historical mooring points of slavery and the present day; it also connects John's life to the failed escape from slavery. Jim Crow forges self-segregationist tendencies—separatism—and the related superiority myths that connect each discrete era of his family history, which is to say U.S. history.

NEO–SEGREGATION AND NEO–SLAVE PALIMPSEST NARRATIVES

In the first chapter, I pointed to Morrison's *The Bluest Eye* and *Beloved* to position neo–slave and neo–segregation narratives as fraternal twins. But *The Chaneysville Incident* goes further in showing the interrelation of the two traditions. John's historical project is to reclaim his past, both familial and racial, all the way to slavery. Yet the majority of the history he turns up concerns segregation and the Jim Crow era, especially its racialization of space. Still, Bradley is not interested in drawing sharp distinctions between slavery and Jim Crow. The novel refracts segregation through the lens of slavery, especially by inhabiting the symbolic terrain of North and South Counties in rural Pennsylvania (that is, the North). Much of the novel's argument is about the *lack* of meaningful change between the slavery, Jim Crow, and post–civil rights eras. Old Jack admonishes, "You let him grow up thinkin' the whole world changes on account of somebody draws a mark on a map, or passes a law. You let him grow up thinkin' like a white man, an' a dumb white man at that" (67). Old Jack further suggests that when de facto segregation sets in, "we had been scarred by so many of the little assumptions and presumptions that go with dormant racism or well-meaning liberalism that a little overt segregation was almost a relief" (66). Compared to North County mired in "dormant racism," South County is a throwback foil that continues to exhibit practices and attitudes of Jim Crow in a northern location and post–civil rights era. Old Jack goes so far as to describe it as "a little piece of the South down there" (236). George Henderson explores the relation between space, history, and storytelling and suggests that the novel takes place, using Du Bois's phrase, "south of the North, yet north of the South." Henderson explains, "Within this landscape there is no line that can be crossed easily into safety, no ground that can be tread upon lightly, no past that can be demarcated irreducibly or returned to innocently."[12] Somewhat contrary to the northward direction of the slave narrative tradition, the segregation narrative is more concerned with intricate social lines within racialized territory, be it North or South. With this geographic approach, Henderson argues, "Spatial practice . . . is always double-edged. It indicates in this case that while Moses and all of the black characters in Chaneysville are exiled to the Hill, the Hill is nonetheless that worrisome site called home."[13] For John, home is history and history is home, no matter how painful and buried. If "home" is on the Hill, it is built on a segregated landscape best surveyed with a Jim Crow lens.

If we focus too much on the novel as a neo–slave narrative, we miss a key part: the middle. Unlike the time travel device in Octavia Butler's *Kindred*, which transports Dana and her white husband directly from 1976 to slavery, John's passage from Pittsburgh and the present to slave experiences in North and South County passes through Jim Crow. That era takes up the bulk of John's historical research and its lessons for the present, especially debates about the consequences of cross-racial coupling, the endurance of segregated living conditions, and the persistent distrust of miscegenation. As a result, Jim Crow haunts this neo–slave narrative, the inverse of the haunting presence of slavery in Toni Morrison's *Beloved*.[14] We can see this in the way Bradley discusses slavery through a post–civil rights ambivalence toward integration. John frames legal abolition through the parlance of segregation as he muses, "They suppressed and repressed, on their own account, everything African. . . . When Abolition came (as a by-product of a totally unrelated economic and political conflict), *de jure* slavery was replaced by *de facto* oppression (which later became a matter of law as well)" (212). In the post–civil rights imagination, the rhetoric of de jure and de facto is wedded to debates over segregation and the limits of the courts to adjudicate the color line. The novel does not pose segregation as just an extension of slavery, as is common in neo–slave narratives, but rather poses slavery as another form of the long-standing and intricate maintenance of the color line in the legal sphere. Jim Crow remains the pivotal point of reference for all eras.

Ultimately, the neo–segregation narrative is the overriding project because Jim Crow segregation, be it de jure or de facto, is the barometer with which John measures justice and inequity. For instance, in one of his early academic soliloquies, John discusses how the rich ride planes, the middle class take trains, and the poor are found on Greyhound buses. "The various degrees of civilization represented by the sanitary accommodations," he explains, "inevitably reflect class status that the society at large assigns to the passengers" (9). Bradley lends clarity and analytical precision to this disquisition by positioning contemporary transportation as a modern-day take on the Jim Crow car, not the slave quarters.

Still, the argument for reading Bradley's novel as a neo–slave narrative is strong.[15] Henderson suggests that the historian protagonist continues the antebellum battle begun by Frederick Douglass over who gets to narrate the experience of slavery, how, and what gets left in and out. He argues, "The contradiction (the missing detail in one kind of story is the sine qua non of another) suffuses Bradley's novel precisely because the history that binds both is not over (nor of course did it begin with Douglass)."[16] Rushdy suggests that neo–slave narratives are palimpsests that "address the social problems, political issues, and cultural concerns of their moment of production by generating a narrative in which an African American subject who lives in the 1970s is forced to adopt a bitemporal perspective that shows the continuity and discontinuities from the period of slavery."[17] Throwing segregation into the mix, we have another narrative layer. Neo–segregation and neo–slave narratives often coexist as palimpsests, though which narrative overwrites the other is not fixed. It might even be more useful to think of segregation as the palimpsest itself, and different eras (slavery, Jim Crow, post–civil rights, and so on) as the narratives scraped off and rewritten onto that palimpsest. The writer's job is then to trace the "transgenerational aftereffects" of key group experiences in later narratives.[18]

The suggestion that neo–slave narratives can be written over neo–segregation or post–civil rights narratives upsets ideas about historical progression one more turn because *before* and *after* can swap places in segregation's haunting echoes in narratives that take place in both slavery and post–civil rights eras. A good example is when John uses Jim Crow frameworks to make sense of the story of his slave ancestor. John logs C.K.'s travels and reminds himself, "C.K. didn't have a Greyhound and a Turnpike. There was a stage-coach, but Jim Crow was no stranger to Pennsylvania—as a matter of fact, the term originated in the Fifth Street Theater in Pittsburgh" (340–41). Another example is John's discussion of white reactions in 1842 Philadelphia to an African American celebration of the British Empire's abolition of slavery in 1833. He discovers, "[S]o they went tearing into the Negro section, beating up on people and killing a few, and burning property left and right. It was a regular Long Hot Summer act, and the militia had to be called out to quell the riot" (344). Whereas Rushdy suggests that palimpsest narratives concern "late-twentieth-century African American subjects who confront familial secrets attesting to the ongoing effects of slavery,"[19] Bradley's neo–segregation narrative understands the history of slavery through segregation and civil rights frames, such as the Jim Crow car or race riots during long hot summers, be they 1919 or 1967.

More than cataloging slavery's continued presence, the neo–segregation narrative explicitly rejects teleologies of racial progress after civil rights. John insists, "The stories had changed then, it seemed. And Moses Washington, a decade dead by that time, had changed. And I had changed. And none of the changes had been for the better" (45). Bradley poses a counternarrative of decline or regression in the post–civil rights era. Old Jack is the figure who most pushes John to view the contemporary era through the lens of Jim Crow. When Old Jack relays a Chaneysville incident, this one a lynching of his friend in retaliation for an interracial tryst, he notes the participation of white town leaders: "'Cause havin' Parker Adams there, dressed up in a sheet, was 'bout the same thing as havin' a speech by the mayor, an' the Presbyterian preacher handy to lead the prayer. Whatever they was gonna do to Josh, it wasn't gonna be no lynchin'. It was gonna be damn near as official as the Fourth of July" (98). For Old Jack, national platitudes about equality and Jim Crow experiences of exclusion and racially motivated violence remain his go-to signposts to understand slavery, segregation, and integration. He has no patience for a historical narrative based on discrete eras.

Old Jack lapses into a self-consciously Jim Crow mode at the suggestion of any racial uplift narrative, no matter the era. For instance, when John goes off to college, Old Jack responds:

> "You know somethin', Johnny—'scuse me, I mean Mistuh Washington, suh—these white folks, ones wouldn't give you the time a day last year? Now they think you're somethin'. Course, they ain't 'xactly sure *what*, an' I 'spect as how they're jest as pleased you ain't gonna be around here makin' 'em try an' figger out what, but they sure do think you're somethin'. Why, you know the major hisself set up here an' tole me you was a credit to your race. Yes indeedy, that's jest 'xactly what he said. Course, I didn't correct him, an' tell him that you wasn't colored no more, on accounta you read enough a them damn books to turn your head clear white." (135)

With Old Jack's adoption of a minstrel pose, Bradley locates his proto–Black Power self-determination stance in the Jim Crow era, yet informed by a post–civil rights skepticism toward the integration project.

Eventually, John the professional historian and the novel as a whole adopt Old Jack's version of history and nonprogress. Tropes of memory, history, and burial become central as John initially suppresses his history. He avers, "I knew nothing about the Hill any longer, I had made it my business not to know" (17). The novel then tracks John's move from reluctant bearer of history to active agent reconstructing a narrative better than that captured in the historical record. While John's family history is buried and discontinuous, the novel desires wholeness and life beyond the printed historical record. John explains to Judith, "That's the end of it; a period at the end of the sentence. That's the way history is sometimes. Sometimes you don't even get periods" (367). With the innocent white female as a foil, John comes to comprehend history as a series of palimpsests on which the stories of slavery, Jim Crow, civil rights, and the present are written, revised, and rewritten again. Racial division is the only constant.

The Chaneysville Incident has proved fecund for critics interested in engaging debates about who writes history, from what perspective, and using what methodology, usually placing Afrocentric oral history and European archival work in opposition, and sometimes debating regional authority too.[20] For Byerman, Bradley's novel is primarily about "family or communal history," versus media or dominant historical accounts, and John's efforts to recover that history in a therapeutic narrative of sorts.[21] Lawrence Hogue suggests that the novel "wants to problematize the past's values, contents, conventions, and aesthetic forms."[22] This is important because John's revisionist history is personal and "our reading and interpretations of the historical past are vitally dependent on our experience of the past."[23] John cannot simply find his family history in the archive, but rather the novel must somehow offer direct experience of the past. Hence, John incorporates imagination, what Klaus Ensslen calls "active collaboration," into his revisionist history, which offsets the limits of the traditional archive and dominant historical record with a new kind of oral history.[24] Byerman suggests that Bradley's novel "argue[s] for the importance, ultimately, of the personal in the quest for historical reality." Picking up on the novel's central tropes of burial and ghostly voices, Rushdy suggests such revisionist projects exhume the graves of the past, both in the archive and the family plot. He explains, "The courthouse is a domain of privileged official records and data, while the graveyard is a domain of unofficial and subterranean information. Both are places that contain varying qualities of knowledge from which to generate narrative accounts of the past." [25] I would add that John's body itself holds history, even from the beginning: "I felt the growing of old tensions, a sudden chill at the base of my belly" (24). John's body is pregnant with history. The novel then tracks its gestation so that John finally gives birth to a patrilineal family narrative of resistance and oppression.

It is important to flag *The Chaneysville Incident* as a neo–segregation narrative as well as a neo–slave narrative in order to capture more fully the contemporary debates Bradley engages not only about Black Power, self-determination, and black feminism but also about civil rights. At one point, Judith mocks John's racial pontifications: "Aren't we noble. *My* people. *My* brother. Next thing you'll be telling me how you have a dream. And of course you're going to shoulder the burden for all those poor dead darkies that got exploited to death, and for the ones that moved away and got good jobs too, the ones that don't even know how beat on they were. That's mighty big of you, Johnny boy. But I'm not sure you're big enough" (281). In his role as race spokesman, Judith finds John wanting, inadequate as a Martin Luther King or Malcolm X figure. She goes so far as to emasculate him as she questions whether John is "big enough." For Rushdy, "Bradley is contributing to an ongoing dialogue about race in the post–civil rights era; moreover, he largely articulates his position against a vision of race that found favor in the nationalist moment in the Black Power era." So too, Byerman suggests, "But the fact that these are haunting presences indicates a refusal of the black nationalist view that the figures of the past are necessarily nurturing and helpful." In the end, for Rushdy, John gives up racialist thinking, especially by claiming a cross-racial genealogy, including his white fiancée and a grandfather light enough to pass, so that "John must learn to reconsider his desire for an essentialist system of racial classification, where those who are black look, speak, and think in a particular way and those who are white in another."[26]

I join these interpretations but underscore the gendered dimension of John's reconciliation of self-determination stances and integrated histories. John's concern is specifically patrilineal descent and black male experience under white supremacism, all the way back to the original mother figure in the slave narrative whose name remains unrecoverable (323). While Rushdy and Byerman may be right that Bradley ultimately rejects black nationalist ideology, his neo–segregation narrative still adopts its masculinist postures. In his study of black culture and modernism, Ed Pavlić convincingly argues that John descends into history and emerges a diasporic modern citizen able to connect black to white, West Africa to African America, and past to present.[27] I would point out that John's version of that citizen is specifically male. John's cross-generational connection relies on an interracial romance and family structure that does little to bring to the revised historical narrative the experiences of women on either side of the color line, instead positioning female figures (both black and white) as helpmeets.

A MASCULINIST NEO–SEGREGATION NARRATIVE

In recovering his family history, John recovers his manhood, a key trope in the black nationalist imagination. John's project is decidedly patrilineal, and it is consistently thwarted by his white fiancée and black mother. When Old Jack wheedles out Judith's race from a reluctant John, he frames miscegenation as naïve racial treason. "'Johnny,' he said. 'You started trustin' white people, ain't you?'" (69). John retorts, "Hell, no" (69). Bradley also positions John's mother as another kind of race traitor: the obeisant Jim Crow citizen. In their first scene together, John recalls his mother's early lessons on how to navigate Jim Crow. "Maybe it isn't right, but that's just exactly the way it is," she says. "And as long as you're going to their school, so long as they're teaching you what you need to learn, you have to be quiet, and careful, and respectful. Because you've got your head in the lion's mouth" (119). While one could wrest a model of strategic resistance from this lesson, for the most part John's mother is a problematic figure of capitulation. Bradley's novel is best read as a masculinist entry in post–civil rights debates over which gendered experiences occupy the center of our memories of Jim Crow and slavery. I would go so far as to see the gendered struggle as another palimpsest over which the neo–segregation narrative is written. John's reconciled history remains patrilineal because the experiences he resurrects, through records or imagination, are nearly exclusively male, thereby confirming the description of black male responses to black feminism in the Combahee River Collective statement.

Judith jeopardizes John's quest for historical connection not necessarily because she is white and female, which in itself troubles masculinist stances of racial self-determination, but because she espouses liberal white innocence, which requires denying connection to one's past altogether. During their courtship, Judith says sarcastically, "I was thinking all this time there was something wrong with you. But it's me, isn't it. I've got this horrible skin disease. I'm white" (73). Bradley infuses the heterosexual romance plot with debates over whether or not white citizens must atone for their father's sins, to use popular post–civil rights parlance. John genders history male and innocence female. Rushdy argues, "John's symbolic suicide . . . aligns him with his paternal line, and, by implication, his racial community because of its implied attitude toward death . . . , while simultaneously communicating to his white fiancée, Judith Powell, that he has related her presence into his familial narrative" (*Remembering Generations* 71). Not only is John the knowing historian, he also holds—and withholds—knowledge about Judith's past: she is descended from slave owners. Whereas many critics address the way John uncovers family secrets, it is important to note that the male historian keeps some secrets too. This leads to a whiteness and femaleness that remain innocent, which is to say ignorant. Still, with Judith, the heterosexual romance plot provides a convenient narrative way to fully claim and reconcile an integrated history, both slave and slave owner, both Jim Crow and Klan member.

The cross-racial heterosexual romance plot engages high-stakes debates between black nationalism and black feminism, though the figure of the black female remains largely absent while the white woman remains underinformed. In the 1970s and 1980s, the tensions between black feminism and black nationalism often manifested in historiographic debates about slavery, gendered roles, and relative innocence or culpability. Bradley enters this fray when John recounts the story of his grandfather: "There had been no love lost between him and his son-in-law, who had more than once suggested that the lightness of his skin and the manumission papers that he proudly displayed were both the result of a series of miscegenetic liaisons in which his female forebears had been ready, willing, and possibly even eager partners. They stayed, though they could have left. The rest of us had no choice, we lived there" (22). While Judith is a figure of white innocence, especially around segregation, John unequivocally adopts a black masculinist position of innocence too and accuses female slaves of complicity. With this posture, John indicts both his white fiancée and his black mother, who occupies his family home on the Hill while Old Jack lives out back, quietly reminiscent of Black Power ideas about the moral inferiority of house slaves to field niggers.

Liberal anxieties about possible complicity also nag Judith in this cross-racial heterosexual romance. She ponders, "But you know, now I think, what if however-many-great-whatever John wasn't just a sea captain; what if he was a slaver? What if the *Seafoam* was a slave ship? They all had pretty names, didn't they?" (242). John knows her thought experiment to be true, but he spares her confirmation of those fears. Rushdy argues, "The problems of the relationship between Judith and John are social, in the specific ways interracial romantic relations are in this society, historical, in that John insists on telling stories about the difficulties and travails attendant on interracial romances in the American past, and familial, since there is a connecting set of family secrets in the Powell and Washington families that threaten to disrupt this relationship entirely."[28] I would go one step further: John *fosters* Judith's problematic white innocence, which gains him a masculinist, as well as racialist, historical authority.

Critics often position Judith as a stand-in for white reactions to African American revisionist histories, and that group's ability (or lack thereof) to understand and appreciate such histories.[29] For Pavlić, Judith is emblematic of whiteness in general. At first, Pavlić argues, John's "relationship to Judith merely provides him with opportunities to confirm his racial antagonisms," but eventually she is key to John's successful revision of his family history and emergence into "syndectic fluidity" as opposed to "the dichotomies of his dissociation" between experience and ancestors.[30] For George Henderson, John and Judith have opposing views of history's presence. Henderson explains, "whatever John finds out through his professional exertions is, for Old Jack, always already surplus and dangerous information; surplus because John needn't have left the 'Town' to begin with and dangerous because it disturbs the boundary between black and white (in both senses)."[31] On the other hand, Henderson argues, Judith insists that John "needn't rehearse the historical litany of racial hatred" lest it jeopardize their cross-racial relationship.[32] At stake in these critical appraisals of Judith is the success of the integration project, and what role histories of racial hatred, disenfranchisement, segregation, violence, and slavery should have in the post–civil rights present.

The miscegenation plot speaks to post–civil rights concerns but also engages long traditions in segregation and slavery literature. Miscegenation plots often measure the success, or lack thereof, of the integration project and the resilience of the color line, from Nella Larsen's *Passing* (1929) to Thomas Dixon's chronicles of the early Ku Klux Klan and D. W. Griffith's portrayal of the pathological mulatto in *The Birth of a Nation* (1915). The miscegenation trope in segregation narratives extends the reconstruction romance tradition, such as Lydia Maria Child's *A Romance of the Republic* (1867), rife with tragic mulattas and intricate heterosexual plots dramatizing links between northerners and southerners as well as blacks and whites. In this tradition, the availability of legal marriage between black and white citizens serves as evidence of progress in defeating Jim Crowism.

Old Jack rejects this miscegenation logic. To John's plea that "Jack, things have changed a little—," Old Jack responds, "Listen to him: 'Things have changed.' I spent the best part a my life tryin' to teach you up from down an' left from sideways, an' now you come tryin' to tell me that things have changed to the point where they give a good Goddamn about what happens to a colored man" (64). Despite victories in repealing antimiscegenation laws, Old Jack rejects civil rights integration in favor of the clear logic of Jim Crow. He contends that John and Judith's engagement signifies a *lack* of progress, which fits well with Black Power sensibilities as well as casting Old Jack as a throwback to Jim Crow. Still, the novel as a whole does not embrace Old Jack's stark postures of racial separatism, nor does it opt for simple integration stances that would portray interracial romance as an anodyne for the history of segregation. We see this in John's response to Judith's declaration that her whiteness should, in his logic, earn his hatred. John rebuts, "I suppose that's the basis of it all; hate, black people, white people, those simple things. But it's so much more complicated than that. It has to do with . . . atmosphere. . . . It's just a stench, like somebody buried something, only they didn't bury it quite deep enough, and it's somewhere stinking up the world" (275).[33] For Rushdy, John's engagement to Judith, and by extension the recuperative possibilities of interracial romance, "reconstitutes both biological and fictive kin relation."[34] Further, Byerman suggests, "Judith must give up the privilege of her white skin and her related assumptions of an American history defined by justice, fairness, and freedom, while John must surrender his notion that atrocity, even if it is the major pattern of history, is the only part of the story to be told."[35] The integrated, post–Jim Crow history that gets beyond amnesia-ridden progress narratives rests on this interracial romance, even as John himself largely turns inward to a specifically black familial history.

Bradley's cross-racial romance plot rests on an unquestioned white female fealty to the black male historian, which sometimes strains the narrative's internal logic. Judith's fealty becomes curious at moments when John adopts overt postures of black nationalism, even if Byerman is right that Bradley questions such an ideology in the narrative writ large. John's relationships to women run from problematic to repugnant, from disavowal to rape. In other words, it is not clear why Judith would *want* to marry John.[36] This question is perhaps most pressing when Bradley portrays John as an Eldridge Cleaver figure. As the minister of information for the Black Panther Party for Self Defense, Cleaver gained celebrity with his calls for black self-determination, even through violent means, especially in *Soul on Ice* (1968). In that collection, Cleaver launched his high-profile homophobic attack on James Baldwin, caricatured by some in the Black Power movement as an effete poster boy for integrationism, and he notoriously sanctioned rape of white women as "an insurrectionary act" (he discusses raping black women as practice). John mimics Cleaver's infamous position almost verbatim when he tells Judith what he did after the funeral of his brother, who was killed in Vietnam: "'You see'—I looked at her—'in my hometown, white people and black people aren't buried together. It isn't anything official like down South. It's just the way things are done.'" He then succinctly recounts that afterward, "I went to see the girl. And I raped her" (75). Though he expresses some remorse, John frames the rape as retribution for black male death—be it physical or social—under U.S. segregation and black (male) disenfranchisement. Judith responds: "And you think it makes sense to blame white people, just because they're white . . ." (75). In this heightened debate between white liberalism and Black Power, especially around violence to male and female bodies, Judith acquiesces. John reports, "I had waited for her to move, to get up and leave, or at least to say something, but she had not. She had just stayed like that, holding me" (76).

Going one step further than Cleaver's outlandish posturing, Bradley creates a white female character that sanctions the logic, if not the act, of the rape and provides palliative comfort for the psychic wounds of the black male citizen of Jim Crow and his descendants. John and Judith have another muffled exchange over the politics of rape when discussing antebellum prostitution. John cites the sexual exploitation of slave women by their masters and other white men. Correcting Judith, he objects, "You can't call it rape if the woman doesn't have a right to say yea or nay to begin with. Bestiality is more like it—they weren't people, remember" (359). While John's point may fit some feminist analyses, his patronizing historian stance toward Judith removes the possibility of a (black) feminist analysis that places (black) women's experience at the center. In the end, Bradley stretches the heterosexual romance plot so far that Judith becomes a cardboard cipher in a masculinist world.[37]

Criticism of *The Chaneysville Incident* has not fully accounted for how centrally gender informs John's masculinist concern with race, heritage, and how to narrate a history of segregation and slavery. Discussions of gender in the novel tend to position John's eventual connection with female figures, through genealogical descent and heterosexual coupling, as leading to a more complete historical record. Jeffrey Leak poses Bradley's novel as a masculinist response to Toni Morrison's call in *The Song of Solomon* (1977). Philip Egan looks at the novel as a narrative of "one man's tortuous journey out of misogyny."[38] He adds, "But the tempting view that misogyny finds its source in Old Jack and its redeemer in Judith is only a partial truth," the other part being that John's mother and ancestral female lovers constitute an Oedipal tale that helps him recover the humanity of his female antecedents as he "outgrows" or "unravel[s] his mother-based misogyny," especially by "harmoniz[ing] the warring tendencies" of Judith and Old Jack.[39] So too, Cathy Moses detects "the masculine subject in search of his manhood" by "creat[ing] woman-free zones."[40] Moses draws on feminist ideas of feminine écriture (á la Hélène Cixous) to track how Bradley moves "from a masculine to a feminine mode of imaginative writing" over the course of the novel.[41]

Like in the neo–slave narratives *Beloved* and *Kindred*, Bradley's neo–segregation narrative uses the trope of cross-racial heterosexual coupling, whether by force or by romance, to stage encounters with histories of oppression, both under slavery and Jim Crow. By highlighting the masculinist aspects of the novel, we can see that gender is central to the questions of history embedded in the *neo* of neo–slave and neo–segregation narratives. We can best see the extent to which post–civil rights debates between black feminism and Black Power infuse the novel by way of John's mother, even more so than Judith. John's initial resentment, even hostility, to his black mother is never adequately explained. Throughout the novel, there is a shuffling of lines of kinship as John eschews his mother for Old Jack. Reflecting on John's evolving understanding of his parents' relationship, Moses suggests that eventually "John actually begins to see through a woman's eyes, a shift in his attitude towards women, and a change in the novel's construction of gender. Women are no longer peripheral."[42] While this may be so, John's conception of home and family history is conspicuously and avowedly patrilineal as he forsakes his mother's domicile for Old Jack's shack on the "other side" of the Hill. In the end, John wrests black history from a feminized victimology narrative of slavery and Jim Crow. He replaces that feminized narrative with a masculinist self-determination stance and a patrilineal record quite in line with black nationalist sensibilities. While *The Chaneysville Incident* is not a black nationalist novel per se, Bradley's neo-segregation designs enlist Jim Crow in a masculinist reclamation of black history in which black men bear knowledge and power, and (black) women stand in their way.

Jim Crow Returns in *The Color Purple*

Alice Walker's *The Color Purple* serves as a thoughtful rejoinder to Bradley's patrilineal reclamation of racial heritage, what Tuzyline Jita Allan describes as a "womanist gospel." Whereas Bradley exhumes Jim Crow's remains in John Washington's integrated, post–civil rights life, Walker returns to Jim Crow to gauge how white supremacist, patriarchal structures are replicated in black communities. Or, in the words of the novel's characters, "You think Reagan's bad, you ought've seen some of the rednecks we come up under."[43] Many critics pair Bradley's novel with Morrison's *The Song of Solomon* and Walker's novel with Zora Neale Hurston. The Walker-Bradley pairing, though, better allows a discussion of gender and Jim Crow in the neo–segregation narrative tradition. More so than Bradley, Walker consciously turns away from the color line and tells a story about the richness of black communities living under segregation, especially to reclaim stories of daily survival from the vantage of one poor, illiterate, black woman living in rural Georgia. Walker draws attention to gender dynamics within segregation, going so far as to suggest—and herein lies much of the controversy around the novel—that Jim Crow's black men take up where the slave master left off. As a neo–segregation narrative, Walker reforms and reclaims black community via a womanism swaddled in equal parts Jim Crow history and racial self-determination, equal parts Zora Neale Hurston, William Faulkner, and Marcus Garvey. She offers a portrait of a post–Jim Crow subject who can reconcile racial self-determination stances and black feminist desires for gender equality.

From the moment of its publication, but especially when it became a movie, *The Color Purple* served as a touchstone for public debates about black men and black feminism. The unprecedented volume of political debates around *The Color Purple* is a high water mark of identity politics before intersectional analyses of oppression became the norm and it was no longer so easy to oppose black feminism and black masculinity.[44] Why did Walker's novel become a signal text for a whole generation of black feminist literary criticism? In a flashpoint 1986 essay in the *New York Times Book Review*, Mel Watkins analyzed the heated debates about feminism, race, and the Hollywood film version of Walker's novel. He catalogued "the proliferation of violent interaction between black males and females, and of increased portrayals of black males as oppressors and brutalizers of black women in recent fiction of black women."[45] Citing a general desire in African American literary traditions for positive portrayals of African American characters and demonization of slavery and postslavery institutions, Watkins laments that "[r]ecently, however, some black feminists have chosen to ignore those parameters altogether. Their fiction often presents brutal, barely human straw men who exist only to demonstrate the humanity of the protagonists or antagonists with whom they are contrasted. These writers have, in effect, shifted their priorities from the subtle evocation of art to the blunt demonstration of politics and propaganda."[46] In the salvo, Watkins accuses "some black feminists" of being bad artists, not unlike James Baldwin's famous 1948 denunciation of Richard Wright as being in line with Harriet Beecher Stowe. The black feminist response was quick, compelling, and assured. Gayle Pemberton pointed out that Watkins was discussing Spielberg's film, not

Walker's novel, and argued for attention to Walker's womanist designs. Then Deborah McDowell convincingly traced the hostility heaped on Walker for disrupting narratives of black kinship and community wholeness. In a review of the controversy in 2002, Candice Jenkins concludes, "Walker's work . . . *deconstructs* a black family romance and represents unequivocally the ways in which 'traditional'—and traditionally idealized—family structures can endanger black women both physically and psychically, largely because of the patriarchal power that such structures grant to black men."[47] I would add that Walker's portrayal of Mister _____, albeit harsh, is not without nuance and evolution over the course of the narrative, thereby freeing him from the ranks of pure melodrama—and offering the possibility that Jim Crow's return in post–civil rights gender relations is not inevitable.

Given the large volume of criticism around *The Color Purple*, my treatment may seem cursory as a brief discussion of the novel as a feminist rejoinder in the neo–segregation narrative tradition. Considering *The Color Purple's* high-profile reception, Thadious Davis argues, "Overlooked too often in the Walker criticism is her fictional examination of racial and regional identity along with gender identity, and her portrayal of a contemporary need to reinstate a black southern experience into cultural and historical contexts despite the pain that a truthful reinstatement necessarily bears."[48] If gender is not emphasized enough in criticism of Bradley's novel, its neon-lit glow in the criticism of Walker's novel sometimes threatens to obscure surrounding concerns, such as regionality for Davis and Jim Crow for me.

When Walker returns to the Jim Crow period, she consciously turns away from the color line so that the heart of her story and Celie's world does not depend on interactions with white people. In fact, for the first third of the novel, references to white culture or people are intrusive blips and bobbles that occasionally punctuate Celie's rather small but also black-directed world. Whiteness appears sporadically, almost like gnats buzzing around the narrative: as gun-toting interlopers out in a field,[49] a can't-be-bothered storekeeper (15), figures in silly motorcar advertisements in magazines (53), and background people who pay black women to wash their dirty clothes (57). There are also brief alienating references to God as an old white man and angels as albinos (96). It is also striking that there is no overt reference to Jim Crow until the end of the first third of the novel, just before the narrative opens out to the north, the Atlantic, England, and then Africa. The first such reference is from the white mayor's wife, who reminds Sofia that she cannot sit in the front seat when they leave their property, which they shared while Sofia taught Miss Millie how to drive (109). The reminder is strangely jarring. The mention of Jim Crow is intrusive as the narrative recalibrates its frame to encompass the larger structures beyond Celie's heretofore small world.

Jim Crow then becomes an open secret, always present, occasionally noted on the periphery, but never in need of overt discussion. When Jim Crow comes out of the shadows a third of the way into the novel, a disorienting temporal shift happens: the reader must think back through the narrative and reframe past scenes with the now-visible historical frame of Jim Crow segregation. Walker peppers the narrative with allusions to Jim Crow in increasing amounts, such as Nettie's remark that in England, "We all used the same cups and plates" (145). For the first third of the novel, Jim Crow barely warrants the dignity of attention; instead, Walker's neo–segregation narrative expends its love and energy on the black people that come in and out of Celie's world.

For many, the novel's strategy of treating Jim Crow as an open secret was a key source of its perceived failure, especially when translated to film. Gerald Early, for instance, averred, "The characters are totally untouched by history itself and so is the audience, much to its relief. The changes that occurred in America from the turn of the century through the 1930s (particularly changes in the American South) have no effect upon the characters."[50] Early condemns the novel as another sorry chapter in white America's love of bootstraps narratives, which leaves ahistorical innocence intact. I offer an alternative analysis: Walker's turn inward—psychologically into Celie's interiority, socially into the black community—means the novel is less about history than survival. If Bradley augments the historical record with black experience, Walker simply turns away from the archive when it falls short of womanism's designs. References to white culture and characters take up more and more narrative space as the novel progresses, but not before Celie and others develop a strong sense of self outside of white culture. That way, they are not decentered by the color line's increasing intrusion into the novel's world.

While Walker consciously decenters whiteness from Celie's world, the few moments of cross-racial interaction are shameful, brutalizing, and all the more important to the plot. The most key cross-racial interaction is Sofia's violent altercation with the white mayor and his wife, Miss Millie. In response to "sassing" Miss Millie and clubbing the mayor, Sofia is beaten severely, jailed, and ultimately installed as Miss Millie's maid, the very woman whose audacious request for such an arrangement led to the initial "sassing." These detrimental cross-racial encounters catalyze bold proto–Black Power self-determination stances—by women. While playing the model, obeisant inmate, Sofia confesses, "I dream of murder, she say, I dream of murder sleep or wake" (94). In response to being raped by the prison warden, her light-skinned uncle, Squeak adopts a posture of self-determination: "She stand up. My name Mary Agnes, she say" (102).

Walker places some of the most silenced and abject female figures into the Black Power trope of self-naming, such as the familiar narrative of Malcolm X in which Malcolm Little becomes Red becomes Malcolm X becomes El-Hajj Malik El-Shabazz. With Celie's encouragement, Sofia and Mary Agnes wrest some semblance of dignity from Jim Crow, within and across the color line. In Nettie's story too, cross-racial interaction prompts a Garveyesque black nationalism tucked inside a Du Boisian uplift program. She frames her blackness as an "advantage" over white European missionaries and concludes, "we and the Africans will be working for a common goal: the uplift of black people everywhere" (143). Finally, midway through the novel, the core secret of Celie's genealogy is revealed in Nettie's letters and she finds that her real father was lynched when white storeowners resented the success of his farm and dry goods store (181). Strangely, this iconic story of lynching frees Celie from her genealogy of male abuse under Pa and Mister _____ and instead connects her to a family history of survival and dignity under slavery and Jim Crow.

Like *The Chaneysville Incident*, Walker's novel has been discussed as a neo–slave narrative, although not as often.[51] The textual evidence for such a reading is solid, but ultimately less compelling and voluminous than in Bradley's novel. For instance, Mister _____ appraises Celie as if her father has placed her on an auction block (9, 11). Also, Celie plots her and Nettie's "escape" from Pa and Mister _____ via literacy (10), a common trope in the slave narrative. The slavery frame continues as a minor trope, such as when Sofia explicitly positions herself as a slave while in indentured servitude to the white mayor's wife. "Don't say slaving, Mama," one of her children reproves. Sofia retorts, "Why not? They got me in a little storeroom up under the house, hardly bigger than Odessa's porch, and just about as warm in the winter time. I'm at they beck and call all night and all day. They won't let me see my children. They won't let me see no mens. Well, after five years they let me see you once a year. I'm a slave" (108). The boy concedes that she is a "captive," but is troubled that Sofia doesn't mark a clear difference between slavery and Jim Crow. This reflects directly what bothered Black Power advocates as Walker doesn't draw a sharp distinction between black and white patriarchy, such as the provocative choice to call the husband "Mister _____."

The neo–slave narrative in *The Color Purple* is well scraped from the segregation palimpsest, leaving few remnants. This allows the novel to be much more concerned with its black characters than a cross-racial litany of historical abuses across the color line. *The Color Purple* then, especially in its womanist orientation, is a good example of a neo–segregation narrative overwriting a neo–slave narrative. In her influential black feminist reading, Barbara Christian describes Mister _____'s departure from the narrative model of Jim Crow's black male citizen, such as in Harriet Wilson's northern narrative *Our Nig* (1859). Mister _____, she notes, "is a Southern black of the Reconstruction period whose family is descended from slaves and slave owners and who has observed the means by which white men maintain power. Rather than marrying a white woman, as Jim [in *Our Nig*] did, an act that in the South would precipitate his death, he imitates the men who have oppressed him."[52] She continues, "Just as he must at all times call white men Mister, a symbol of his power relationship to them, he insists that those below him call him Mister."[53] As the power differential between Celie and Mister _____ evaporates, especially around Shug as their shared object of desire and heartbreak, Walker offers an alternative to merely replicating slavery's power structures within Jim Crow black communities. That is why Jenkins suggests that Walker is "queering black patriarchy."[54] By turning inward to the black community, and by writing a neo–segregation rather than neo–slave narrative, Walker sets in motion a story about internal race hierarchy, as well as her characters' slow, hard-fought, and touching evolution away from such hierarchies. We see this especially in the way that Celie and Mister _____ eventually develop a friendship while sewing and conversing on the porch as equals, not master-husband and slave-wife. They are "two old fools left over from love, keeping each other company under the stars" (278).

Walker's concern with intraracial gendered hierarchies ultimately has much more to do with contemporary debates between black feminism and Black Power than over the historical experience of life under Jim Crow. For Walker, womanism responds to the pulls and insights of women's and black liberation movements by placing the experiences and perspectives of women of color at the center, but not necessarily in an exclusivist way. In her playful definition of a womanist, Walker describes her as "[n]ot a separatist, except periodically, for health."[55] Her womanist vision prefers universalist tendencies and commitments to wholeness over separatism as an endpoint. The neo–segregation narrative upsets post–civil rights progress narratives, not necessarily through the surprising appearance of symbols of Jim Crow today but also through subtly anachronistic feminist tropes, from overdetermined quilts to Celie's pants business. The most overt example of women's liberation anachronism is the vaginal mirror.[56] When Shug first gives Celie a lesson in female sexual pleasure and her "button" (her clitoris), Shug nudges, "Here, take this mirror and go look at yourself down there, I bet you never seen it, have you?" (81). This scene directly recalls apocryphal images of 1970s feminist consciousness raising groups and the Boston Women's Health Collective's *Our Bodies, Ourselves* (1973), which located women's self-liberation in knowledge of their own bodies. The hand mirror is a heightened symbol of that cultural moment, shorthand for women's liberation as much as a noose signifies a whole history of lynching during Jim Crow. Sporting a hand mirror, Celie is a post–civil rights womanist who finds herself in the Jim Crow era poor, black, and rural. Initially voiceless and abjectly marginal, Celie finds herself in a classic women's liberation conversion narrative, becoming by the end a proud, defiant, no-longer-silenced woman.

With the discovery of the letters from Nettie on missionary work in Africa, which takes up the second third of the epistolary novel, the narrative becomes not only bitemporal with the Jim Crow era but also bilocal with a comparative lens between U.S. segregation, on the one hand, and imperial cultures and the traditions of the Olinka people on the other. Jim Crow's clarifying power allows Walker to make her black feminist vision global, which suits well her universalist model coming out of second wave feminism (à la *sisterhood is powerful*). Nettie describes the reaction of Olivia, Celie's lost daughter, to news that the Olinka do not believe in educating their girl children. Olivia retorts, "They're like white people at home who don't want colored people to learn" (162). These analogies and comparisons of oppression across cultures, often and rightly accused of oversimplification and ethnocentrism, are made possible by the bitemporal exploitation of Jim Crow's bright line of segregation, which is unquestionably indefensible in the post–civil rights imagination. Lest Walker paint the Olinka as backward antifeminists, she portrays the Olinka as very gender-conscious. At one point, a man of the village assures Nettie, "we are not simpletons" (167). This allows Walker to hold a comparative mirror to American feminism, a common trope in transnational-minded second wave feminism in the United States. Nettie discovers she is "an object of pity and contempt" (167) because she is not attached to a man. She surmises, "There is a way that the men speak to women that reminds me too much of Pa" (168). Contrary to, say, Alex Haley's *Roots* (1976), Afrocentric connections are not the pure, unadulterated stuff of empowerment but rather a chance to reflect upon what Gayle Rubin famously described in 1976 as the endless variety and relentless monotony of women's oppression.[57] The trope of memory, so often associated in the U.S. black imagination with Africa and the rupture of the middle passage experience, is reversed so that Nettie remembers Jim Crow as home—and memory and home are not necessarily comforting sites in Walker's novel.

In post–civil rights debates between black feminism and black nationalism, black women had long been prone to notorious accusations of racial treason when perceived as aligning themselves with white feminists. Tensions were especially heightened when a proponent of one ideology advocated the primacy of one form of oppression over another. Walker projects those debates onto her Jim Crow–era characters, such as when Mister _____'s sister admonishes Celie, "You got to fight them, Celie, she say. I can't do it for you. You got to fight them for yourself" (22). This trope of black sisterhood in battle against black men recurs throughout, including when Sofia's sisters cart her and her children away in response to Harpo's blundering efforts to make her mind through physical violence (72). These moments of solidarity against patriarchal black men contrast Celie's ultimate betrayal of sisterhood when she counsels Harpo to beat Sofia because "[t]he wife spose to mind" (66).[58] By the end, though, the novel's version of womanism is inclusive enough to welcome characters such as Mister _____, Harpo, and Celie—once they've learned to live with the idea that black women can and should have as much liberty and dignity as they themselves are able to wrest from Jim Crow.

By the end of the novel, Celie embraces an earth-based global spirituality, or vice versa, which had fueled her defiance of Mister _____ even before she consciously embraced it. After all, it is the dirt that the wind swirls into Celie's mouth, not Celie herself, that first tells off Mister _____ (214). But ultimately empowerment rests in a *revolutionary indifference* to the Jim Crow social structures in which the black characters find themselves, a stance well suited to the neo–segregation narrative's turn away from the color line. We see this revolutionary indifference in key moments near the end of the narrative. First, Celie crafts a self-determination stance by not wrapping her happiness in fate or in others. As her anger at Mister _____ gives way to understanding (but not exculpation), she extricates herself from Shug's shadow and decides that if Shug returns, great; if she doesn't, well that will be okay as well (290). She balances autonomy with reciprocity when she realizes, "Just cause I love her don't take away none of her rights" (276). Celie comes to a similar conclusion about Nettie: if Nettie returns, great; if Celie must wait until she is ninety, well that's fine too (287).

It is Sofia who most espouses revolutionary indifference. Sofia is the one who emerges in the neo–segregation narrative having completely detached her self-worth and ontology from white people. We see this when Miss Eleanor Jane, the white daughter from her time of indentured servitude to the mayor's wife, keeps visiting Sofia as an adult and presses Sofia to take an interest in her life. Miss Eleanor Jane baits Sofia to coo over her boy, "You don't like him because he look like daddy" (272). Celie retorts, "*You* don't like him cause he look like your daddy, say Sofia. I don't feel nothing about him at all. I don't love him, I don't hate him. I just wish he wouldn't run loose all time messing folks stuff" (272). By completely extricating herself from white culture, Sofia's revolutionary indifference is more than survival strategy—it is a precious ore mined from the neo–segregation narrative tradition. Black-oriented self-love is raw material that, when forged with womanism and black self-determination, may be strong enough to buttress both black feminism and masculinist Black Power. Sofia becomes a post–Jim Crow subject ushering the way to a post–Jim Crow world.

Gender and (Post–)Jim Crow

In her influential case study of gender and Jim Crow in North Carolina, especially among the black middle class, Glenda Elizabeth Gilmore finds that "Few of the black women in these pages ever became well known, yet they crafted a tradition of political activism that deserves celebration and emulation."[59] While chronicling white supremacy's deleterious effects on African American economic, political, and psychological health, Gilmore concludes, "But what is most important about white supremacy remains least documented: African American resistance."[60] Gilmore reconstructs a tattered, scattered historical archive; so too, imaginative writers such as Bradley and Walker turn to fiction for such a task. In doing so, they also respond to debates about black feminism and separatism that have just as much to do with their post–civil rights arena as the historical record of life under Jim Crow. Byerman concludes, "It is only through boundary-crossings, transgression of suppression, and openness to multiplicity and horror that a useful history can be constructed. . . . The point, then, is not to be haunted but to be nourished for the tasks of the present."[61] Neo–slave narratives tend to track slavery's legacy in the present, either for empowerment narratives such as in *Roots* or to recall suppressed pasts of pain and rupture as in *Beloved*. Bradley's and Walker's neo–segregation narratives, on the other hand, remove readers from the immediacy of present debates between black feminism and Black Power while at the same time drawing on the starkness and urgency of Jim Crow segregation to clarify some of those debates internal to black communities.

In his reflective essay on meeting Walker (both in person and in print), Bradley suggests the use of this perceived historical distance in the realm of fiction. Bradley recalls his initial resistance to even reading *The Color Purple*, citing the high-profile debates between white feminists and black male reviewers and therefore the tightrope he would walk as a black male writer if he were to express any criticism of Walker. The novel, though, ultimately met with Bradley's approval ("she made me cry," he admits) precisely because of the way Walker brings historical distance between her black characters and contemporary feminism, especially regarding her portrayal of lesbianism and its association with the practice of radical feminism in the 1970s. "That Celie—after being repeatedly raped and beaten by a man she thinks of as her father, having him take the children she bears him away," he justifies, "should find herself uninspired by the thought of sex with men, and be drawn to a woman who shows her love and introduces her to ecstasy seems less a 'message' of radical feminist politics and more an examination of human motivation."[62] Of course, Bradley still marks Walker's terrain as "The Black Woman's Story" in the title of his piece, and thereby he claims for the black man's story the general domain of black experience, and perhaps that of Jim Crow (after all, it's not Jane Crow). Still, Bradley's response to Walker's return to a Jim Crow period is important because in doing so, for him at least, Walker escapes the trap of sloganeering, of simply passing along a party-line "message" in fictional form. This move, for Bradley, saves Walker from being a mouthpiece of (white) radical feminism and returns her to her vaunted role of pathfinder for a generation of black writers, himself included, concerned most with their own humanity and cultural history.

Narratives of a singular, shared black experience are now a post–civil rights staple, due in part to the success and determination of a generation of scholars and writers who created Black Studies, integrated the canon, and demanded that black experiences and perspectives inform traditional disciplines and official accounts of American history. These grand narratives of black experience are always gendered, whether consciously or not. Writers and scholars then jockey over whose experiences are most central in Jim Crow's memory and their place in teleological narratives that track shifting manifestations of ever-present racism, from colonial encounters to slavery to Jim Crow to institutionalized racial disenfranchisement following civil rights. A good example is Patricia Hill Collins's *Black Sexual Politics* in which she argues for a new progressive black politics responsive to the "new racism" emerging out of older versions. Collins surmises, "Politically, Jim Crow segregation introduced mechanisms of social control that built upon those established during chattel slavery. Lynching and rape emerged as two interrelated, gender-specific forms of sexual violence. Perceptions of Black hypersexuality occupied an increasingly prominent place in American science, popular culture, religious traditions, and state policies."[63] Thus Collins smoothly narrates the creation of the myth of the black male rapist and the sexually available black woman across the color line. But in a post–civil rights era, Walker and Bradley consciously turn away from the color line to tell stories with a focus on gendered communities on one side, not always or primarily concerned with what folks are doing on the other side. Jim Crow provides a particularly good venue for these writers to enter the fray of unsettled tensions between black feminism and Black Power, a tension that could rip apart black communities if not corralled on one side of a bright line of segregation. The next chapter explores the possibility that integration ideals may find footing on one side of the color line and in concert with both notorious histories of compulsory segregation and ensuing self-segregation desires.

CHAPTER THREE

JIM TOO

Black Blackface Minstrelsy
in Wesley Brown's *Darktown Strutters*
and Spike Lee's *Bamboozled*

Alice Walker and David Bradley set up camp far from the color line to explore the limits and merits of segregated communities, both self-driven and externally imposed. Other neo–segregation narratives seek out the most highly contested fault lines to take on the subject of self-segregation and race mixing. A good example comes again from the tradition of retelling Emmett Till's story: James Baldwin's *Blues for Mister Charlie* (1964), a play based "very distantly indeed" on the notorious murder and acquittal.[1] Baldwin distills segregation down to its most polarized form by dividing the stage between Whitetown and Blacktown, with a ditch running down the middle.[2] That stark color line is crossed only by a few stock segregation characters: the white racist, the white liberal, the turn-the-other-cheek black preacher, and the gun-toting black son spoiled by his time up North. In the opening scene, the Till figure is shot and discarded in the ditch. The ensuing play features scenes on both sides of the color line and flashbacks to what led to the unjust murder. Baldwin bucks the trend of casting Till as an innocent boy or sacrificial lamb by making him older, jaded, sexually active, and prone to taunting the citizens of Whitetown.[3] While Baldwin was largely committed to integration ideals, his play takes seriously calls for armed resistance and militancy as legislation made headway but changes to the daily lives of black people lagged behind. In his elegy for Baldwin, Amiri Baraka went so far as to claim that *Blues for Mister Charlie* "announced the black arts movement."[4] As early as 1964, segregation's stark lines offered a canvas on which to consider the increasingly frequent calls for self-segregation in a newly de facto era.

Post–Jim Crow literature often returns to events and practices that epitomize segregation cultures to respond to lingering unease about the merits and motivations of racial crossing. Beyond Till's case, the best example is probably blackface minstrelsy. This chapter looks at a particularly loopy corner of that history: black blackface, or what Susan Gubar calls "black black impersonation," Louis Chude-Sokei calls "black-on-black minstrelsy," Grace Elizabeth Hale calls "blacked-up black minstrelsy," and what Eric Lott positions as the "genuine article" in the counterfeit economy of Jim Crow.[5] Blackface minstrelsy is one of the more notorious episodes in the nation's ongoing love/hate affair with race, spanning slavery, Reconstruction, and the Jim Crow era. In the post–civil rights imagination, blackface is the polar opposite of Black Power and emblematic of the most reviled stereotypes and backward race relations of Jim Crow. Anyone who dares enter into such a tradition is sure to cause a media and pundit firestorm, as white actor Ted Danson did when he donned blackface for a 1993 Friar's Club roast of black comedienne Whoopi Goldberg. Despite Goldberg's defense of the shtick, there was general agreement that blackface is out of bounds, that irreverent postmodern irony is insufficient to counteract the stain of Jim Crow's signature act. Today the idea of a black blackface performer seems particularly unthinkable, despite their appearance throughout the historical record from Bert Williams to Josephine Baker. In neo–segregation narratives, black blackface can raise questions of complicity in white supremacist cultures and what constitutes racial pride, questions that remain in the wake of the legislative gains of civil rights and cultural gains of black feminism and Black Power.

I pair the depiction of black blackface minstrels in Wesley Brown's under-recognized novel *Darktown Strutters* (1994) with Spike Lee's Hollywood film *Bamboozled* (2000), in which contemporary black actors cynically perform in the successful television variety series "Mantan's New Millennium Minstrel Show." Brown's novel traces the life of Jim Crow, a celebrated traveling minstrel, from slavery through just after Reconstruction. It is a complex meditation on the injustices as well as rewards of racial segregation and, most importantly, the remarkably inclusive community it creates. Consciously exploiting minstrelsy's notorious reputation, Brown projects contemporary debates between self-determination and integration through a carnivalesque plot featuring the trials, survival strategies, and artistic successes of first an all-white show (save for Jim Crow) and then a multiracial minstrel troupe run by two sexually adventurous black women. Jim Crow refuses to "black up" while the rest of the performers do. The trickster novel begins when Jim Crow is a slave and the white minstrel Tom Rice happens upon him while dancing away in a barn, thinking he is alone. Shortly after Brown's faux replication of that historical borrowing, Jim also teaches the moves to his adopted son, Jim Too, who was left behind when his parents went North to freedom (a slave narrative left cued but unwritten). W. T. Lhamon notes this "ensures that the steps will be transmitted to black as well as white performance."[6] The ensuing multiracial narrative is not only attendant to minstrelsy's history on both sides of the color line but also to shifting multicultural attitudes of Brown's own time. The narrative is less concerned with slavery's legal codes than Jim Crow's cultural practices. An eventually blacked-up Jim Crow emerges as a strange figure of radically inclusive separatism. Thus Brown reconciles seemingly opposed doctrines of racial separatism, integration, and inclusive attitudes toward sexual, gender, and ethnic diversity.

Brown is influenced by civil rights writers such as Baldwin; Black Power political writers from Huey Newton to Eldridge Cleaver; black feminists such as Audre Lorde; and the Black Arts tradition, leading to Amiri Baraka's endorsement for his first novel, *Tragic Magic* (1978). Brown also recognizes the power and importance of literary meditations on the legacies of black forebears, such as in his plays on Booker T. Washington, W. E. B. Du Bois, and Baldwin. With Jim Crow as a minstrel in *Darktown Strutters*, Brown is able to straddle eras of slavery and compulsory race segregation, recast assumptions about racial heritage, and take on one of black literature's biggest questions: the nature of freedom. Neo–slave and neo–segregation narratives are both concerned with freedom, but they differ over its arena. We see this when Jim Too first perceives himself as a cultural agent armed with his father's moves. Brown writes, "Jim Too wondered if all this had something to do with a word he'd heard blacks use when talking among themselves. And it came as a surprise to him when he started hearing the same word—FREE—used whenever he danced."[7] The meaning of "freedom" is contested in a post–civil rights era when legal emancipation and even affirmative action and desegregation have fallen short of engendering feelings of full equality. In the infamous terrain of the minstrel show, Brown retroactively locates multicultural freedom in an unexpected place: Jim Crow culture. Brown troubles the dominant imagination of segregation as an unequivocally despicable practice easily discarded by later generations that perceive themselves as more enlightened. Informed equally by self-determination doctrines and multiculturalist celebrations of inclusion and identitarian elasticity, Brown ultimately claims a ragtag bunch of historical outcasts as cultural ancestors, even those now deemed problematic, such as grinning black minstrels, race traitors on the plantation, lusty bisexuals, poor whites with black envy, and Jim Crow himself.

The Blackface Minstrel as Post–Jim Crow Pariah

Brown plays with the way blackface minstrelsy is reviled in the post–civil rights imagination. Popular in nineteenth-century American theater, especially in the urban north, as well as folkloric traditions, white male performers lent humor and caricature to black life under slavery. Minstrelsy's cartoonish depictions of blackness, first primarily by white performers then also by black performers, gained mass appeal from the antebellum through post-Reconstruction periods. It was tremendously influential in shaping popular conceptions of African American culture as it was popularized first on the minstrel stage and then on the Hollywood screen in the early twentieth century. By the later twentieth century, blackface was roundly despised and denounced across political and racial spectra. In his foundational study of blackface in American popular culture, Eric Lott argues that such performances, T. D. Rice's Jim Crow in particular, constitute the first major recognition of black culture by white Americans. This created anxiety about color lines long before *Plessy v. Ferguson* formalized the sundry practices, laws, and cultures that naturalized and enforced a bright line between races. Lott explains, "Underwritten by envy as well as repulsion, sympathetic identification as well as fear, the minstrel show continually transgressed the color line even as it made possible the formation of a self-consciously white working class" (8). Lott carefully demonstrates the contradictory impulses of love and theft in cross-racial desires to "try on the accents of 'blackness'" (6), mocking them on one hand and enforcing and naturalizing separation between races on the other. Lott concludes, "[T]he minstrel show worked for over a hundred years to facilitate safely an exchange of energies between two otherwise rigidly bounded and policed cultures."[8]

Blackface's pariah reputation is ripe for exploitation by post–Jim Crow writers. Blackface minstrelsy is a cultural relic of a bygone era, banished to a pre–civil rights sensibility whose backwardness undergirds a racial progress narrative. Brown finds that blackface minstrelsy and its function of simultaneously establishing and mocking an all-too-permeable color line are useful for thinking about the relation between doctrines of self-determination and ideals of integration. Historiographic representations of blackface minstrelsy also help to further disentangle the segregation and slave narrative traditions that we saw overlap in Bradley's and Walker's novels in the last chapter, especially since blackface minstrelsy arose during the latter days of slavery but primarily in the North. Blackface performance, then, is a northern and urban correlative to the slave narrative, though it persists and evolves well after the Civil War and Emancipation Proclamation. Those two routines, one on stage and one in print, emphasize different kinds of racial dramas and attend to somewhat distinct concerns: the construction of racial identity and social hierarchies in the case of blackface minstrelsy; and freedom, literacy, and national ideals of equality in the slave narrative.

Blackface minstrelsy hit the national scene with a famous 1843 performance in New York City, though scholars date the tradition to T. D. Rice's Jim Crow plays in the 1830s that drew on emergent folkloric minstrel types; to an 1815 performance in Albany, New York; or even as far back as a 1751 production of Shakespeare's *Othello*.[9] According to Eileen Southern, the first organized black blackface troupe dates to 1867, after which time black and white performers were equally common.[10] The black blackface minstrel arises as a trickster figure, as Lhamon describes him, who upends ideas about the politics of minstrelsy, not only its dubious cross-racial desires but also the rewards and hazards of participating in and taking control of the (black) culture industry.

In his 1958 essay, "Change the Joke, Slip the Yoke," Ralph Ellison writes, "It is not at all odd that this black-faced figure of white fun is for Negroes a symbol of everything they rejected in the white man's thinking about race, in themselves and in their own group. When he appears, for example, in the guise of Nigger Jim, the Negro is made uncomfortable."[11] Ellison positions *Huckleberry Finn*'s runaway slave Jim as a blackface minstrel, as pure symbol in a novel otherwise committed to realism. For Ellison, Jim merely reflects Twain's ideas of blackness and therefore belongs in the blackface tradition then in its final heyday on the minstrel stage. This makes sense given blackface minstrelsy's status as a signature cultural product associated with that era's brand of racism. But what if we think of Jim as a *black* character adopting blackface, not merely as a white projection screen but an interested agent? Twain's Jim may be one of the earliest black blackface performers captured in literature. When we see him that way, we may get beyond what Gubar calls "the psychopathologies of black envy" in the white mind. We might see, Brown suggests, new aesthetic and political possibilities when African American cultural producers and performers use Jim Crow and minstrelsy not as a rejection of or signification on white racial fantasies but as a deliberate claim on the tradition. Perhaps we might even—and this may seem strange to contemporary attitudes—position minstrelsy at the head of self-determination politics more often associated with Black Power. Gubar avers, "When white people portray African Americans they embody (and displace) them."[12] In turn, I ask: When African Americans portray blackness in blackface, who or what do they embody and displace? For Brown, a black blackface performer named Jim Crow may be best equipped to playfully switch the scripts of segregation and integration, separatism and assimilation, racism and antiracism, to simultaneously live up to the post–civil rights ideals of universal equality and multiculturalism.

Liberating Black Blackface

Brown's key historiographic intervention is to focus on African American bodies in minstrelsy both ante- and postbellum, whereas the dominant historical record poses minstrelsy as a predominantly white enterprise until after Reconstruction. Brown paints minstrelsy, especially the cockamamie (to contemporary sensibilities) figure of black blackface, as a necessary complement to abolitionism—a pairing that for a post–civil rights sensibility maps roughly onto self-determination and integration. After Jim Crow gains considerable fame in both the North and South, he finds himself at a lecture by Frederick Douglass. A fellow audience member says, "With Douglass settin our minds on fire when he gets his jaws to goin and your feet putting the rabbit in our blood every time we get too set in our ways, there ain't no way we can lose!" (60–61). Brown poses minstrelsy as culturally liberating, a necessary co-constituent to legal struggles for abolition. The Black Power movement worried that integration projects required cultural assimilation. But with Jim Crow and Frederick Douglass working in cahoots, Brown challenges contemporary readers to consider the dream team of cultural and legal emancipation, even if team players appear as problematic as a black minstrel. If Lott is right that blackface minstrelsy was a safe site of cultural play and an effective form of cultural control, when African American subjects don blackface, new possibilities emerge to "put the rabbit in the blood" of established (or, rather, establishing) social orders. There were some high-profile black minstrels in the antebellum period, especially William Henry Lane (known as Master Juba) and sometimes Ira Aldridge, but the minstrel tradition is generally white in its beginnings.[13] Not so in Brown's novel. Jim Crow *precedes* Tim Rice—then outlasts him when Jim Too accepts his father's name. By placing black blackface at the center of minstrelsy *from the beginning*, Brown reclaims for antiracist contemporary readers a sense of ownership over what Lott constructs as the birth of American popular culture itself. Otherwise, black people are historical latecomers to their own tradition.

With Jim's bequest to Rice—as if he has a choice—Brown raises questions of cultural ownership. Slaves debate the relevance of Rice adopting Jim's moves:

> "He turned out to be another kind a white man."
> "What kind is that?"
> "Well, there's the kind like Crow that name you. And then there's the kind like Rice that claim you. I heard today he been travelin all over the country doin the dance you showed him and calling himself Tom 'Jim Crow' Rice." (4)

Naming and claiming are different modes of ownership. Rice is a rather complex and sympathetic figure, including holding antislavery sentiments, being gay (which Lhamon positions as Brown's response to William Styron's portrayal of white-woman-loving Nat Turner),[14] and despising his own whiteness before being shot on stage in blackface during the Civil War. Nevertheless, Rice is culturally wanting; he has a "hunger for things belonging to other people" (20), which manifests as a need to claim, if not name, others. This form of ownership trespasses where the law cannot: the psychological sphere of identity. Gubar explains that "burnt cork articulates two jostling propositions made by whites about blacks, a syntax which contributes to supremacist ideology: 'We can be (like) them' versus 'They need not exist.'"[15] Jim assures Rice that he can claim the Jim Crow dance once he makes it his own, a sort of inverse signifying. He says, "It belongs to you. And that's different from just copyin somebody" (3). This has implications for debates about cultural ownership and authenticity as well as legal debates about whether property (a slave) can own property (culture). Jim's theory of ownership also challenges contemporary ideas about freedom. In a heated discussion with Whisper, his slave wife, Jim says, "I guess next you gonna tell me you ain't no slave" (11).

She responds, "Only by law. And that's something I learnt from you, Jim. When you dance ain't nobody got a claim on you. Ain't that what you told that white man, Rice? That there was things in you he couldn't have, even if you wanted to give em to him" (11). Cultural practices may cross the color line, but for Whisper something ineffable can never be transported across segregated economies. In part, Whisper's statement is a shrewd assessment of the limits of legal codes to separate citizen from noncitizen, human from property, even in the extreme case of chattel slavery. More than that, Brown positions Jim Crow's moves, whether performed by white Rice or black Jim Too, as a space of extralegal freedom on very public display.

When Jim Crow teaches his moves to Jim Too, Brown engages ideas about national culture, historical time, and even a post–civil rights need to come to terms with one's roots in Jim Crow culture and minstrelsy. Brown writes, "Jim was pleased no end to see how easily he took to it. Jim Too's body had the get-up of a fly, and he had to be told that the nation didn't move at the same speed as his body" (6). Jim Too is out of step with his time and the national narrative, an uncanny recitation of how America has always perceived Jim Crow. Only this time he is not a throwback but rather an agent of change, the pulse in abolition's heart, with a foot-stomping inability to stay in place. In Brown's novel, Jim Crow is not just a projection of white desires to contain, mock, or perform blackness. Gubar considers the propensity of white people across social strata to imitate black culture, or "cross-racial impersonation," and notes, "whites have said what it meant to be black and have represented African Americans throughout the nineteenth and twentieth centuries. . . . [T]he humanity and subjectivity of African Americans have often been staged by white people performing blackness."[16] Of course, African Americans also construct, negotiate, and perform black identity. But Brown's central challenge is to reclaim Jim Crow and the figure of the minstrel as a site of possibility. For instance, when Rice makes a deal with Jim Too's owner and installs him in the minstrel show, Jim Too says, "I didn't know white folks was interested in seeing anybody colored in a minstrel show unless they was white folks actin like they colored" (37). Already his father's moves have become a part of white culture and divorced from their origins. Rice, however, responds, "Once they see you dance, that won't be true no more," (37). Rice cues Jim Too to the possibilities available to him on the minstrel stage, both to improve his own lot (minstrel shows beat plantation life any day) and that of black people in the public imagination.

Eventually Jim Too becomes Jim Crow, adopting his father's namesake upon learning of the lynching that followed their master's murder by his own cane. This fatal act befits Jim Crow Sr.'s knack for determining his own path, even within the confines of slavery. When he arranges the sale of a fellow slave, Jim Crow Sr. explains, "But that's what I wanted to do! Slavery helped but slavery didn't do it. I did! And like it or not, that's a kind of freedom we gonna have long after this slavery is over" (27). Foreseeing the end of slavery, Jim positions self-determination as true liberation, not unlike Black Power's impatience with the legislative designs of civil rights. So too, Jim Too cum Jim Crow strategically finds liberation in minstrel performance. For William Mahar, minstrelsy's signature object, burnt cork makeup, is an aesthetic technology of racial critique. It "served as a *racial marker* announcing that a single actor or an ensemble offered what were selected aspects of (arguably) African American culture to audiences interested in how racial differences and enslavement reinforced distinctions between black and white Americans."[17] And the flip side: "The makeup was also a *disguise* for white performers who chose parody and burlesque as techniques to satirize majority values while still reinforcing widely held and fairly conservative beliefs" (1). Lott also notes that "the early minstrel show was a Janus-faced figure for the cultural relationship of white to black in America, a relationship that even in its dominative character was far from self-explanatory."[18] While the white theft and mockery of black culture is insulting, even heinous, the minstrel performance itself provocatively stages dramas among different kinds of freedoms and portrays strategies for achieving them.

Black blackface minstrelsy has a rocket-fuel power to stir up social orders. Early in the novel, a slave takes Rice for a fellow slave and cries, "Fix me Lord,'fore I start mistakin slavery for free!" (2). Even before it is fully fledged, minstrelsy turns the most sedimented oppositions on their heads. We see this power in audience reactions, a recurring trope throughout the novel that gauges shifting social orders across the novel's progression through slavery, Civil War, Reconstruction, and finally the birth of the Jim Crow era. The first show happens on a plantation as a dance contest between Jim Too and Rice's Diamond, which riffs on the historical 1844 match between Master Juba and Diamond John in which the black blackface performer famously defeated the white one. The intricate social order around the plantation becomes off-balance. "But as the excitement leading up to the contest started to build," Brown writes, "it was hard for people to stay where they belonged"

(16). A riot breaks out among all manners of attendees: slaves punch other slaves, women disrobe, white women stab their men, and black people take revenge on whites with whatever tools are available, from picks to knitting needles. A few slaves simply walk North. Afterward, the plantation owners attempt to erase all evidence from the historical and folkloric records. Brown writes, "They were all shaken up by what had happened and seemed to be waiting for Churchill to tell them that the bottom of the world had not fallen through the top" (33). After emancipation, minstrelsy retains its power to induce a topsy-turvy world, which creates considerable anxiety among whites. As the black-run minstrel troupe travels the nation, "nothing was more upsetting than black people laughing out loud" (184), which explains the creation of the notorious "laughing barrels" that Ellison features in his essay "An Extravagance of Laughter." This prompts the creation of sundry Jim Crow laws after Reconstruction: "Many whites, who only knew about blacks from minstrel shows, found it strange living around the blacks who didn't act the same as the ones on stage" (184).

Outside the novel, the subject of black blackface also stirs up historical and scholarly narratives. In his book-length study of Bert Williams, *The Last "Darky,"* Chude-Sokei explains quite simply that by the early twentieth century "the notion of minstrelsy and its discourses of authenticity were so formalized and institutionalized that the very notion that a black performer could *outperform* a white performer in a white form such as minstrelsy was unimaginable."[19] As a West Indian immigrant, Williams's ascendance as one of the period's most famous black minstrels illustrates a conscious adoption of African American identity as a public—and profitable—performance. The very subject of black minstrels remains underexplored, almost un-touchable. "In fact," Chude-Sokei contends, "black minstrelsy is most often dismissed as either pathological or an unfortunate and pitiable sideline in the transition from a more passive era into a much more self-assertive and militant one."[20] Esther Godfrey takes a poststructuralist approach and avers, "[U]nlike drag culture, blackface operates with no interest in appearing 'real.' The exaggerated makeup and costumes of drag seem blasé in comparison with the parodic tropes of the minstrel show that denaturalizes race from the physical body."[21] Doubling this effect, black blackface especially doesn't fit into easy narratives across the political spectrum, whether during the heyday of minstrelsy or in the contemporary moment. Given this, Brown turns to black minstrels and black blackface to stir up and upend ideas about where we are likely to find proponents of cultural empowerment and liberation.

To Black Up or Not to Black Up

The central dilemma in Brown's novel concerns Jim's refusal to black up. His refusal inspires heated reactions as Jim's non-blacked-up performances are interpreted as "uppity" moves, by both his fellow performers and, more dangerously, his audiences. After refusing his troupe's advice, a postshow mob takes it upon itself to inscribe the minstrel face directly onto Jim's body: they carve a smile upon his left cheek. The white mob, all in blackface, explains, "We wanna see darkies when we go to a show, not some uppity nigger who think he too good to act the coon like he supposed to!" (63). Jim's scar is an inscription of white ideas about acceptable blackness. It becomes a worm, itching at him for the remainder of the novel. The partial grin performs Jim's subjection to white will even when he refuses to black up, underscoring how his performances and the cultural meanings they inspire are out of his control. So too, when Jim learns to read at the behest of an underground railroad worker, his reputation inspires would-be runaways even though he had no such intent. Jim continues his refusal to black up during Reconstruction when he joins the black-run troupe. The pressures to do so shift and also remain the same: blackface protects the performers at the same time that their performances stir up social orders. Postbellum audience expectations, Lynn Abbott and Doug Seroff explain, were also fraught: "White southern audiences demanded unreconstructed minstrelsy from black entertainers, while white northern audiences resisted black musical comedy that did not prominently feature coon songs. It is surprising how much was accomplished, given the limitations."[22]

Jim's refusal to black up is Brown's take on the historical figure of Master Juba/William Henry Lane and his 1844 outperformance of white John Diamond. Jim's non-blacked-up face in the novel opens possibilities in the historical record: a self-determination stance in the unlikely space of the minstrel stage. In the novel, Diamond, a white minstrel and Irish immigrant, explains, "You got an advantage not many blacks get. You're a dancer on the top shelf. And there ain't no way whites can hate that out a you. And if you put this on, you can even beat them at their own game. Cause while they tryin like the devil to hate you for what you are, your face makin em laugh at what you ain't" (41). Lott explains, "[B]lackface was simply less objectionable than the appearance of black people onstage, particularly given the caricatures that resulted."[23] He also notes, "[I]t was possible for a black man in blackface, without a great deal of effort, to offer credible imitations of white men imitating him," which engenders a "simulacral dilemma" when whites attempt to control the production of something perceived as authentic black culture. The white face under the black mask could have a reassuring power. Lott explains, "Early audiences so often suspected that they were being entertained by actual Negroes that minstrel sheet music began the proto-Brechtian practice of picturing blackface performers out of costume as well as in . . . and there are several existing accounts of white theatergoers mistaking blackface performers for blacks."[24] If the purpose of white blackface is to become and displace black bodies on stage (to love and steal them, in Lott's terms), the purpose and politics of black blackface is less clear and therefore provocatively disorienting.

Black blackface proves to be an effective social critique during both slavery and Reconstruction. Brown writes, "The Featherstone Traveling Theatre kept up its two-faced show, imitating a country that also had two faces when it came to making good on the promises Lincoln made to bind up the nation's wounds after the Civil War" (184). Black blackface stands as the only honest home for the nation's inclusive promises. Lhamon argues, "Brown estimates minstrelsy as a national tag-team wrestling match, intermittently fatal and often violent, over 'who's who,' with everyone except Jim Crow donning blackface for different reasons." He continues, "Brown is silently laughing at the absurdities of racist tides that first disallowed blacks into racial representation, now disallow whites."[25] Yet Brown also brings white performers into the black-run minstrel troupe. The project becomes integrating white people into a black nation, not the inverse, or what James Baldwin famously described as the ill-fated effort to integrate a burning house. Even a luck-starved white man with a spectacular broken body act becomes a beloved, if illicit, part of the traveling show as a rogue balcony jumper. (He didn't make the audition cut.) Black blackface's two-faced critique is influential, especially since it appears on official national scenes, both in the novel and historical record. A good historical example is Nancy Green, an ex-slave working as a domestic, who Hale describes as a "representation of a representation of a representation" when she performs as the four-year-old trademark Aunt Jemima at the 1893 Chicago World's Fair.[26]

While Jim's refusal to black up may suit contemporary post–Black Power sensibilities, the character who most espouses doctrines of self-determination and "any means necessary" is Jubilee, who tries never to stop smiling lest he descend into uncontrollable rage and violence. Jubilee explains his decision to black up: "So I played the fool, did the darky, acted the coon, put on the mask, did whatever it took to get me to the good side of the white folks. . . . Well, freedom didn't come. I went out and got it!" (113–14). Jubilee critiques legal emancipation as insufficient, an abolitionist palimpsest for Black Power critiques of civil rights integration. If Jim Crow is a Master Juba figure, Jubilee is more akin to the infamous Billy Kersands who, in the 1870s, filled his mouth with billiard balls to play on exaggerations of blackness long before the crest of black black minstrels in the later Jim Crow era. Brown also offers a figure of white liberalism in Rice, who increasingly refuses to black down. "Rice needs to be on a stage in black face," Diamond explains. "'Cause if he ain't, he don't have no idea who he is or what he's doin. Which puts him several cuts above most men I've known who do a lotta damage tryin too hard to be white" (77). For Rice, a gay white minstrel with abolitionist views, blackface is a comforting public performance more tolerable than other spaces afforded to whites of conscience. Rice semiconfirms Michael Rogin's insight that blackface minstrelsy allowed ethnic white immigrants, primarily Jewish in his study, to transition to an ethnicless white identity. Rice, however, is not a recent immigrant and has no overt ethnicity to shed. Instead he prefers to remain in that transitional stage of blackfaced whiteness. Antebellum Rice and postbellum Jubilee end up agreeing on blackface's honesty. "'You tryin to tell me there's less shame for a colored man putting on burnt cork than join the Union Army?' Jim asked" (77). Jubilee responds by describing the Union Army outfit as "white face" (106) for those free blacks who enlist.

To black up or not to black up ultimately serves as a proxy for post–civil rights debate over whether to engage legal or cultural arenas for black liberation. Brown writes, "'When I black-up,' Jubilee said, 'I ain't gotta follow in behind what no white man did who put it on before me. Which ain't gon be the case for all these colored men rushin to put on that Yankee blue!'" (89). Jubilee's true liberation lies in self-consciousness behind the mask:

"You think you too good for blackin up. . . . I ain't the dancer you is, Jim. But nobody gave me a way out a slavery and set me up in my own private car. I had to find my own way out and leg it the best way I could. I know blackin up is US DOIN WHITE FOLKS DOIN US! But minstrelsy ain't the only place where that goes on. Like most of our people, I know I gotta stretch the truth in order to live. But long as We know what we doin, it don't matter what white folks think!" (134)

Brown rescues Billy Kersands from the dustbin of racist history. Jubilee is a figure of Du Boisian double consciousness and Malcolm X–style self-determination. He harbors a threat of violence lurking behind his grin.

The night of the culminating minstrel show, Jubilee is caught on the street by restless white audience members, including the rogue white balcony jumper. After killing two, leaving one for dead, and another perched atop a confederate statue, "Jubilee stuffed their bodies into the laughing barrels marked FOR COLORED" (193). Jubilee's violence and his ultimate death by mob violence "change the joke," to draw on Ellison's famous formula, and critique not only segregation but also its place in the historical record. After the massacre, Brown reports, the newspaper's official account placed all blame on the troupe itself, presenting the mob as an orderly search party seeking Jubilee. The fires and deaths were explained as a failed escape on the part of the troupe members themselves, complete with the imprimatur of the town minister testifying that "the people who had followed the traveling show had only gone to do the Lord's work" (207). Not only do we distrust the historical record, Brown executes the second half of Ellison's formula, to "slip the yoke." He poses Jubilee, a proto–Black Power figure, as the most recognizable civil rights martyr: Emmett Till. "Jubilee's body was found rotting in the Missouri River," Brown writes. "The newspaper said the cause of death was drowning. But some blacks who saw Jubilee's body didn't believe he'd drowned trying to escape. It turned Jim's guts when he heard a man say Jubilee's cheeks were puffed up and his head was beaten in so bad it looked like ground beef. When his mouth was pried open, they pulled out his tongue, ears, balls, and penis" (208). The description signals Till's corpse, whose lynching is five decades in the future for the novel and four decades in the past for readers.

By substituting Reconstruction's smiling fool Billy Kersands for segregation's ultimate martyr Emmett Till, Brown echoes the circulation of the original Till story and photographic evidence. Dora Apel explains, "The photos of Emmett Till and his funeral, because the victim's family controlled their production and circulation, remained outside the network of lynching photos that circulated among white supremacists. The image of the black subject *as a subject* violated the code of lynching photographs by which black bodies were always objects to be acted on by white subjects."[27] However, Brown disallows anything akin to Mamie Till's strategic use of spectacle lynching economies and their power to shame. Upon the troupe's arrival in St. Louis, "[t]hey were met at the outskirts of the city by the sheriff, the mayor, and other city officials who told them that in the interests of public health and safety the burials would have to take place immediately" (208). Jubilee's body is buried outside public view while Jim Crow lives on. Jim may be the main character, but Jubilee is the moral center because, more so than Rice, the Featherstone sisters, Diamond, or anyone else, he contests Jim's refusal to black up.

Just as Jubilee exits the narrative, Jim blacks up as a unifying gesture as troupe members begin to fight among themselves over fears that Jubilee's lynching party may go after them too. Starletta eulogizes, "It's been coming since the white folks started hunting down our dreams and dragging them back into slavery" (196). Brown fiddles with historical progress narratives and cues pervasive worries of returning to earlier eras, be it slavery in this novel or segregation in Brown's time. Jim's decision to black up arises as a strange corrective to keep the troupe moving forward. Lhamon argues, "Brown shows a thoughtful black dancer, in Jim Too, coming to understand the risk and menace and charisma in blacking up—no matter what color is beneath the mask. . . . According to Brown, however, Jim's refusal to mask is a mistake. His earnest projection of an authentic self simplifies who he is."[28] While I generally concur, I note that Jim's reasons are never explicit. Instead, other characters project their explanations, be it "uppity" for white supremacists, foolish or dangerous for fellow minstrels, dishonest for Jubilee, or accusatory for Jim's lover, Starletta. Jim's politics, like the black minstrel behind the blackface mask, remain elusive. In this unexplained self-determination stance, Brown retains a sense of possibility—political, cultural, identitarian—in the historical figure of Jim Crow, no matter his current perception in the cultural imagination.

The Jim Crow Car, Hotbed of (Antiracist) Separatism and (Segregationist) Inclusion

In part two of the novel, which marks the passage from slavery to Reconstruction, Jim Crow becomes an adjective (137) and a verb (133). The Jim Crow car becomes a general designation, not a particular description of Jim's transportation between minstrel shows. As Jim Crow passes from the particular to the general, and sediments in the nation's legal and cultural arenas, black characters lament, "There was a time when the Jim Crow car was something special to colored folks" (133). As Reconstruction fails, Jim courts blame for racial disenfranchisement, rather than credit for inspiring liberation desires. Before Jim Crow the performer becomes Jim Crow the national institution, the Jim Crow car operates as a space of relative privilege due to the Janus-faced relation of segregation and separatism. Brown has fun with the genesis of the Jim Crow car: "Rice told the cast that the success of the show was riding on making Jim bigger-than-life. So it was better for the show if he was left alone and had the Jim Crow car all to himself" (54). In slavery, the Jim Crow car provides a nonmonitored space, even allowing Jim to attain literacy. Eventually, all Rice's troupe members travel in the Jim Crow car, previewing the integrated black-run troupe in the Reconstruction era.

If Brown is right to reclaim the possibilities of segregation-as-separatism in Jim Crow culture, "Why, then," Lhamon asks, "has Jim Crow acquired its bad rap?" He explains, "The main reason Jim Crow became a disdained entity was that his modus operandi was to keep coming back, to keep causing trouble, picking scabs, jumping and turning and sneaking like a little hoptoad right in your face, polite people. Beyond that, he represented cross-racial affiliation which was repellent to many people in the nineteenth century and seems hopelessly romantic to many people of all hues and persuasions at the end of the twentieth."[29] Lhamon adds, "Another reason for Crow's bad rap is that the early Jim Crow is not the late Jim Crow. Jim Crow went from fond alliance to hateful segregation as the Civil War approached and then as the Nadir replaced Reconstruction."[30] Brown's novel wrests early Jim Crow from late Jim Crow, and his attendant lessons for post–civil rights sensibilities. As Jim makes his way back to New York City from St. Louis following the massacre, the train is overfull and whites ride in the front of the Jim Crow car. One black woman protests, "This here's the Jim Crow car.

We even got the real Jim Crow back here with us. So if you don't like sittin still for what you hearin, you can go on and stand up in the white class car!" (215). Brown imagines the Jim Crow car as a space of strategic separatism and even privilege, while still protesting segregation's injustices. Like Brown, Lhamon is not so quick to jump on the band wagon of dismissing Jim Crow as an ineluctably racist icon that belongs with the offal of history. Lhamon also notes a prebellum archive beyond middle-class journalism that tends to put Jim Crow in a fighting rather than an obeisant pose.

Jim Crow thinking, with oscillations between segregation and separatism, infuses the social orders of minstrel audiences. Brown writes, "When folks came to see the show, the actors Jim Crowed the theater by settin up an all-white section in the balcony. The white folks pitched a fit, 'specially when none a the colored gave up their seats down below on the first floor. Damn near had a riot till folks in the show cooled things down by tellin the white folks they was seated in the balcony so they could look down on the colored like they was used to doin" (137). The black-run troupe embeds separatist politics and Jim Crow privilege on open display in a format easily mistaken as supplicant to doctrines of white supremacism. A hairsbreadth from being a deconstructionist, Brown playfully notes that whether from balcony or floor, Jim Crow car or whites-only space, it is difficult to tell which group occupies the superior position. Of course, white characters can cross segregation's lines into the Jim Crow car with impunity, but not vice versa. So the ability to wrest separatism and Jim Crow privilege from white supremacist segregation is highly contingent. Those in the Jim Crow car must first cede the inevitability or even rightfulness of segregation in order to carve out a space of separatist privilege.

What does Brown gain and risk by positioning Jim Crow as a figure of separatism and privilege, a proto–Black Power ancestor for a post–civil rights era? This move is disorienting because, for contemporary sensibilities, the minstrel and the separatist are polar opposites. That is, Master Juba is no Malcolm X. Brown riles the historical imagination as much as the minstrel show does the social order. "Freedom had gone to the heads of these Negro wenches—which was the last place on their bodies it should've gone to," Brown writes about the Featherstone sisters. "They'd forgotten their place; and if they were allowed to carry on like this for too much longer, there was no telling how many other folks would start forgetting their places too" (165). Jim Crow laws arose as a corrective to keep the boundary-crossing antics of minstrelsy in check, so that the minstrel stage remained apart from the national stage. The massacre of the Featherstone Traveling Show arises when the white search party spies the troupe achieving solidarity around a campfire by exchanging clothes and roles. "They not only carried on their race-mixing and sex-switching among themselves," the white lynch party discovers, "but the one called Jim Crow sang a song that told how this blasphemy started in a place called Paducah and how they were going to mongrelize the whole country with their foul and filthy ways!" (198). The true horror for the lynch mob, that icon of white supremacy, is the possibility that Jim Crow thinking will infuse the nation. Brown's trick is to substitute one Jim Crow mentality for another. Which one wins is a matter of historical record and Brown counts on his contemporary audience to come to the novel despising Jim Crow so that they leave wishing to rescue another possible Jim Crow: the one of privilege and pride.

And inclusion. The Jim Crow car becomes a space of not only black empowerment but also radical inclusion. Let me explain: Jim Crow is hardly the most outrageous member of the Featherstone Traveling Theater. Run by two libertine black sisters who achieve solidarity by only sleeping with partners (of any sex) during menstruation, the troupe features black women dressing as men, a man named Two-Faced with whiteface in back and blackface in front, a poor white woman named Sweet Knees passing for black passing for white, an American Indian woman with no voice whose body acts out sentences better than any mouth, a woman named Sorrow who only sings, and a white man named Trash who doesn't like "white" too close to his name, not to mention the over-the-top antics of Jubilee. Brown goes out of his way to position minstrelsy—both the ante- and postbellum troupes—as protofeminist and proto–queer positive, which is surprising in both the historical record and in dominant Black Power sensibilities. Even before we meet the rambunctious and confident Featherstone sisters, we meet Zulema, a black woman in Reconstruction-era New York City. Jubilee and Zulema argue,

> "White men in black face the only ones think they can be two people at once."
> "And what you think you doin when you decked out like a man?"
> "But I ain't a man."
> "White men ain't black neither."
> "Ain't the same thing." (100)

When Jim first sees Zulema on stage, he assumes she is a man in blackface, mixing Gubar's racechange and sexchange. Lott explains, "White men's fear of female power was dramatized with a suspiciously draconian punitiveness in early minstrelsy, usually in the grotesque transmutations of its female figures."[31] While minstrelsy was notorious for gender crossings among male performers, double figures of female minstrels, like black blackface, pose new possibilities via illicit crossings, even within the relative free-for-all of minstrelsy. Mahar also addresses the curious place of gender in minstrelsy "because male conceptions of the differences between men and women figured so prominently in blackface repertory" (5), especially as it reinforced male dominance and female marginalization in the public sphere.

Brown's depiction of the minstrel troupe as a queer positive space is equally important. Jim is rather uncomfortable with gay sexuality, though he is in favor of heterosexual libertine sensibilities. When discussing Rice's homosexuality, Jim reports to Diamond:

"He wasn't alone!"
"So?"
"It was a man!"
"That bother you?" Diamond asked.
"It don't bother you?"
"You know, I'll never forget the day those two bounty hunters brung you into Louisville tied across that horse like a sack a flour . . . THAT bothered me!" (55)

Brown distinguishes between systems of subjection so that slavery and homosexuality are morally distinct: one is despicable and the other is permissible, a desirable portion of the spectrum of human interaction. This is a key intervention into not only the historical record but also Black Power homophobic postures. While painting the Jim Crow car and other segregationist spaces as sites of antiracist separatism and privilege, Brown infuses them with multiculturalist sensibilities of radical inclusion in line with feminism and gay liberation.

Brown positions the Jim Crow car as a site of cultural emancipation that draws on the most inclusive and empowering aspects of multiculturalist, feminist, Black Power, and gay liberation sensibilities. Key thinkers of the Harlem Renaissance argued for the necessity and inevitability of a second emancipation, this time psychological. This second emancipation would happen in the cultural arena, as Alain Locke famously explained in the introduction to *The New Negro* (1925). In the blockbuster civil rights essay *The Fire Next Time* (1963), James Baldwin reprises the theme, but this time on both sides of the color line. Whereas the slave narrative engages the legal arena and the passage of slaves toward subjecthood, usually in the North and via literacy, the segregation narrative is especially interested in questions of freedom as they work themselves out in the cultural arena.

Brown reclaims a notorious cultural site from the past to achieve contemporary desires for future liberation. With the Jim Crow car and other segregated spaces as locations of antiracist separatism and radical inclusion, newly emancipated characters can create a progress narrative out of the nation's two-faced promises of Reconstruction. A black man says to Jubilee and the rest of the troupe, "I still get paid more in orders than I do in money by the same people who used to hold me a slave. That don't sound so new to me. . . . You all put on a good show. But all that cuttin the fool in the street and actin free and easy with the white folks ain't gonna do nothing but get some of us hung from one a them poplar trees like the two colored fellas lynched right here in Mercer County last year" (162). The black-run troupe becomes aware that their privilege—their ability to cross-social lines and lampoon national scripts on stage—is increasingly divorced from the hemmed-in daily lives of black citizens and their allies. The historical substitution of Jim Crow laws for Jim Crow minstrelsy forecloses the possibilities Brown resurrects in his novel. Jim Crow's disorienting dual origins in blackface minstrelsy and southern segregation codes reflect Brown's designs to upend expectations and social orders, both in the historical imagination and for his contemporary readers. Lhamon explains, "When Americans were winding up to the Civil War, 'Jim Crow' meant the opposite of what it indicates today. 'Jim Crow' referred to free and runaway African Americans moiling together with volatile European Americans. Tracing back this allure delivered a deep paradox: before the concept of 'Jim Crow' stood for America's justly despised segregation laws, it first referred to a very real cross-racial energy and recalcitrant alliance between blacks and lower-class whites."[32] Jim Crow is a trickster figure for "working-class integration," which positions him well to sort through the internecine battles between integration and self-determination for Brown's post–civil rights, post–Black Power readership.

Black Complicity, *Bamboozled*, and Brown's Historiographic Mode

Brown's historical backflips remind us that when Jim Crow frames contemporary issues he can upset dominant narratives of racial progress. This is especially true for blackface minstrelsy. There is an expectation of historical distance, then Brown undercuts it. This strategy infuses other discourse too. Accusing an actor, politician, or any political figure of being a latter-day minstrel is a powerful weapon in the culture war arsenal. For instance, in reelection year 2004, *New York Times* columnist Bob Herbert questioned the honesty of "compassionate conservatism" and its professed inclusiveness by framing the 2000 G.O.P. convention as an instance of Jim Crow *today*. Herbert described the event: "[A] parade of blacks was hauled before the television cameras (and the nearly all-white audience in the convention hall) to sing, to dance, to preach and to praise a party that has been relentlessly hostile to the interests of blacks for half a century." He noted, "I wrote at the time that 'you couldn't tell whether you were at the Republican National Convention or the Motown Review.' That exercise in modern-day minstrelsy was supposed to show that Mr. Bush was a new kind of Republican, a big-tent guy who would welcome a more diverse crowd into the G.O.P. That was fiction."[33] The power of Herbert's accusation of "modern-day minstrelsy" relies on a dominant historical imagination that locates Jim Crow *then* and is ever-vigilant to make sure he stays there. This historical narrative drives the discourse accompanying appearances of overt blackface or accusations of covert minstrelsy. Examples include Ted Danson's blackface roast appearance; a gay white drag performer's notorious character, Shirley Q. Liquor; contemporary race comedy, including such touchstones as the 1990s sketch show *In Living Color*; Eddie Murphy's fat-suit films; and the Wayans brothers' *White Chicks*. Sometimes the desire for historical distance can provide clarity for self-analysis, such as when Dave Chappelle discussed on the *Oprah Winfrey Show* his high-profile 2006 decision to walk away from a lucrative deal with Comedy Central for his blockbuster comedy show. Winfrey pointed to a particularly regressive sketch in which Chappelle appeared as a blackface minstrel with pixies encouraging him to perpetuate racial stereotypes. Chappelle explained, "It was the first time I felt that someone was not laughing with me but laughing at me."

But what happens when black blackface minstrelsy appears outside the historiographic mode, not in a neo–segregation narrative but set in the present day? Spike Lee's 2000 film *Bamboozled* is the most obvious, if not slippery, instance of a contemporary narrative that exploits the perceived moral clarity of blackface. In the satirical film, black television executive Pierre Delacroix, a George Murchison–esque caricature of upward mobility and Europeanization, is frustrated that he can't get positive images of black people on television. He attempts to escape his contract by pitching the most obviously racist and backward—and therefore doomed to fail—project he can imagine: an all-black blackface variety show called "Mantan's New Millennium Minstrel Show." The show plays on every offensive stereotype imaginable: a hip-hop band called "Alabama Porch Monkeys," sketches involving watermelon eating, and old white ladies declaring themselves "niggers." Delacroix is surprised by the smashing success of the show, much to the delight of his white boss, Thomas Dunwitty, who fancies himself more black than Delacroix.

The exact inverse of Jim Crow's blacking-up moment in Brown's novel occurs in the climactic scene of *Bamboozled* when Manray, the show's star, refuses to don blackface anymore and performs sans mask, for which Dunwitty swiftly fires him. In the dénouement, a group of black activists, horrified at the racism of the entire project, kidnap Manray and publicly execute him. All are then killed abruptly in the ensuing police drama, with the exception of "One-Sixteenth Black," a white group member who is only arrested despite his desire to die with his black cohorts. Lest Lee's over-the-top satiric message get lost like Delacroix's, the film ends moralistically with historical footage of black images from Hollywood film that contemporary audiences will deem horribly offensive and racist, from the white supremacist film *Birth of a Nation* (1915), featuring white men in blackface, to *Our Gang* (1922–44). The footage is a tape, which Delacroix watches as he bleeds to death after being shot by Sloan, his adept and morally anchored assistant who compiled the tape. John Strausbaugh deems the film "masterfully squirm-inducing" (270) and Lee himself conceives it as an update on a project from his film school days in which a "young African-American screenwriter is asked to write and direct a $50 million remake of *Birth of a Nation*."[34]

Lee's film brings old-fashioned minstrelsy into the twenty-first century to illuminate the complex, institutionalized, covert, and pervasive racism of contemporary mainstream media. In a demonstration outside the studio, the Reverend Al Sharpton shouts into a bullhorn that there can be no minstrel shows in the twenty-first century. Without the historical imagination attached to minstrelsy as the ultimate in backward racism, the contemporary entertainment industry might be a messy thicket for Lee, especially when African Americans are now part of the culture machine. Linda Tucker contends that "*Bamboozled* assesses the clarity with which each character sees his position relative to the white supremacist capitalist patriarchal system within which each functions and/or from which each tries to escape."[35] Blackface minstrelsy is not necessarily wrong per se, but wrong because it should no longer be acceptable *now*. By appearing in the post–civil rights era, blackface can flush out its twin, white supremacism, which also went underground. Like Brown, Lee's film plays with historical narratives of when and where blackface should be located, if never celebrated, and when and where it should not appear at all. Regarding the *New York Times'* decision not to run an advertisement for the film, which Lee imagined as an over-the-top Barnum & Bailey–style poster, Art Sims, Lee's longtime publicist, notes the dual desire and repulsion around such history: "We had a pickaninny with a watermelon, and people were freaking out. To this day, I think that is our most requested poster; people just love that."[36]

Most attempts to pin down *Bamboozled*'s overt-but-slippery message rely on collective agreement about minstrelsy's backward politics. This contrasts the work of scholars from Lott to Lhamon who question such historical assumptions and remind us of blackface's more playful or radical ends. For Godfrey, *Bamboozled*'s politics are slippery because exaggerated performance in any minstrelsy destabilizes and reifies given categories. Not only is there "the liberating potentiality of unearthing the worst of racial stereotypes that prove enticing," but the very same performances can also be put to other, less celebratory uses, such as "offer[ing] whites a chance to alleviate white anxiety and guilt concerning America's racist history under a new black sanctioning" of such madcap embraces of exaggerated stereotypes.[37] The minstrel show, and perhaps Lee's fooling around with it, fits well within a "commitment to the subversion of essentialized identities" and the underlying contemporary disdain for postures of authenticity—racial, gendered, or otherwise. But those sensibilities don't fit well within self-determination projects that seek to acknowledge and foster distinctly black culture and black cultural production, a project associated with Black Arts and Black Power. Tucker looks at *Bamboozled* in conjunction with Aaron Blandon's independent film *The Last*

Blackface (2000) and Ice Cube's Hollywood film *Barbershop* (2002) and finds that in playful or knowing narratives of black (male) minstrelsy "the empty space of representation ... can offset the containment wrought by reductive and stereotypical representational practices." Tucker deems *Bamboozled* a progressive attempt to wrestle with pressures to present positive images of black men, which fits comfortably with bourgeois politics of respectability. Nonetheless, she worries that, within the film, "[a] gap exists between each character's awareness of his containment and his ability to mobilize that awareness with an eye toward functioning more freely within or to escape altogether from the sector(s) of the prison writ large that contain him."[38]

Bamboozled's risky dance with blackface minstrelsy ultimately relies on the perceived *then*-ness of the practice.[39] As post–civil rights viewers, we are on the lookout for latter-day minstrels and quick to boot them back to the nineteenth century where we think they belong. That sensibility informs Tucker's critique, Mel Watkins's discussion of comedian Chris Rock, and Strausbaugh's and Lhamon's less-than-glowing portraits of hip-hop. Gubar wonders why racechange is so prominent in the twentieth century, in both racist and antiracist projects, by both black and white performers. She identifies two constants: "first, the ways in which a culture that systematically devalues blackness and established whiteness as the norm effectively endorses, even enforces, black-to-white racechange; second, that historically such racial metamorphoses nevertheless (and paradoxically) constituted a crucial tactic used by civil libertarian activists and artists as a means of disentangling the category of race from skin color."[40] Brown's historiographic novel of black blackface attempts to get outside this Gordian knot. He "slips the yoke" by claiming the most backward, untouchable, and racist figure imaginable—Jim Crow in blackface—as a figure of self-determination, perhaps even Black Power.

Even as blackface minstrelsy fades from popular practice in an increasingly multiracial society, Gubar suggests that "the pressures to separate black from white remain extensive" and lead to the titillating world of cross-racial impersonation.[41] These pressures also come in the wake of the Black Power movement and its rejection of integration goals, such as in the consumerist For Us By Us (FUBU) movement or culturalist Afrocentric movements. Therefore, Jim Crow may be found even in—perhaps particularly in—those places that would most deny him. In his study of black men and masculinity during the Jim Crow era, Marlon Ross goes so far as to suggest that the portraiture common in the Harlem Renaissance is easily read as an instance of minstrelsy, considering especially the propensity of European visual artists, such as Winold Reiss, to patronize black male subjects.[42] Jim Crow pervades the blues and jazz traditions too. "As late as the mid-1910s," Abbot and Seroff note, "the term 'up-to-date coon shouter' was routinely applied to the likes of Clara Smith, Ma Rainey, and Bessie Smith; but around 1916 they were redefined as 'blues singers.'"[43] In fact, many such performers got started in minstrel shows because it was the era's most accessible stage. Like segregation's transition from de jure to de facto, we are vigilant about minstrelsy's evolution into covert forms and predisposed to disavow anything that smacks of minstrelsy today, from Flavor Flav to Midwestern white suburban kids embracing hip-hop.

What cultural work is done by Brown's historiographic narrative of black blackface versus a film about a contemporary minstrel show? Tucker provides a provisional answer in suggesting that *Bamboozled* draws a historical continuum between contemporary media depictions of black masculinity and nineteenth-century minstrelsy. Since the white boss Dunwitty considers himself authentically black, she concludes, "Witty's appropriation and performance of a counterfeit black identity makes Lee's point that the literal blackening of one's face is not necessary in modern manifestations of the minstrel principle."[44] Tucker deems Delacroix's show a failure because the audience removes the satire as the show gains massive success. Moreover, she deems Lee's film a failure because, while he reinserts irony, there remains a "failure to represent alternative space within which black masculine agency can thrive beyond the confines of the white supremacist, capitalist, patriarchal realm."[45] In other words, Lee's film fails because it is not speculative fiction. Can importing nineteenth-century blackface minstrelsy into contemporary spaces ever get beyond the racism and white supremacism that are inextricable from Jim Crow?

Neo–segregation narratives that return us to the Jim Crow era—the opposite of Lee's time travel—can better achieve the progressive cultural work Tucker and others seek. By working in the historiographic mode to address post–civil rights concerns, Brown lives up to the disorienting nature of Jim Too's and black blackface's political possibilities. Brown consciously tweaks the historical imagination, as we see in an early passage that meditates on the relation of story and historical events. Brown sets in motion competing claims around the true story of Churchill selling Kentucky into slavery and

Kentucky's subsequent escape (or not). One storytelling slave says, "You tell what you heard and I'll keep spreadin what I just told you. And we'll see in a year from now which story folks'll remember, yours or mine. None of us probably ever gonna see Kentucky again. So I figure my story's as good or better than anything we gonna hear" (20). For Brown, the story that best embodies the desire of its audience will survive and thrive, not necessarily that which is most historically accurate. This historiographic principle also means that we must continually retell the story of our origins, even those to which contemporary sensibilities are most allergic, such as Jim Crow and black blackface. Thus we can wrest cultural survival and pride from the most dire situations and historical figures.

Can a historiographic novel about Jim Crow succeed where purposefully anachronistic depictions of Jim Crow in the contemporary moment cannot? While Delacroix attempts to divest and distance himself from blackface in his cynical satire of modern-day minstrelsy, Brown's black characters ultimately embrace blackface in the post-Reconstruction era. Lhamon concludes, "Wesley Brown shows that the most powerful aspect of minstrel performance was neither its inevitable quotient of demeaning attributes nor its opposing urge to authenticity, both trying to approach an exclusive essence, but instead its radical portion of contamination, literal overlap, and identification with its muddier process."[46] Lee and Brown muddy our ideas about a seemingly clear racist history, while at the same time the seeming clarity of Jim Crow and blackface minstrelsy in the contemporary imagination provides a narrative tool. Gubar explains the "double bind" that black-face minstrelsy poses to African American artists: "To adopt minstrelsy is to collude in one's own fetishization; but to relinquish efforts to adapt it is to lose completely a cultural past appropriated by whites."[47] Writing from a post–civil rights era, Brown finds black blackface a useful narrative tool that can transform Black Power's self-determination desires into a multicultural and inclusive space that also embodies civil rights integration projects. In her influential study of postmodern literature, Linda Hutcheon positions historiographic metafiction as a particularly rich and self-aware example of the co-constitutive nature of literature and history. She explains, "There is no pretense of simplistic mimesis. Instead, fiction is offered as another of the discourses by which we construct our versions of reality, and both the construction and the need for it are what are foregrounded in the postmodernist novel."[48] Though Brown's novel is not full-blown metafiction, he does riff on historical figures and playfully incorporates faux historical documents, such as Jim Crow's parting daguerreotype as "THE CONNIVING UNCLE TOM" who, unbeknownst to the photographer for the national "Rogues Gallery," moves just as he is captured on film for posterity (218–20). In the historiographic mode, Brown can manipulate the nation's history—continually rewritten and rewritable—so that contemporary desires for inclusion are housed in a past era and practice normally seen as hostile to post–civil rights ideals.

CHAPTER FOUR

JIM CROW IN IDAHO
Clarifying Blackness in Multiethnic Fiction

So far I have concentrated on neo–segregation narratives by African American writers. But what about white or ethnic minority writers who turn to Jim Crow and his black subjects? And in the process, what happens when we find Jim Crow's citizens far from their expected location in the segregated South? A good example is American Indian writer Sherman Alexie's bestselling novel *Reservation Blues* (1995) in which Alexie drops the blues guitarist Robert Johnson into a present-day Spokane Indian reservation. What is this fabled African American artist from the Jim Crow South doing in the middle of an American Indian reservation in the contemporary American West? Alexie's story concerns a group of young American Indians trying to reconcile traditional ways of knowing, signified in the character of Big Mom, with contemporary American culture, which incites their desire to rock and roll. The novel culminates in a failed New York City record deal and the group's return to "the rez"; meanwhile, Robert Johnson remains on the reservation in conversation with Big Mom, who is rumored to have taught iconic music legends such as Janis Joplin and Jimi Hendrix.

Robert Johnson is a playful, conspicuous choice to help connect contemporary American Indians with their cultural heritage. Alexie's work is well versed in, and resonates with, the Native American literary renaissance and the American Indian Movement (AIM), yet Alexie famously takes an equal opportunity approach to all American history and popular culture as he employs a range of references, from Coyote and Custer to *The Brady Bunch*, often in the same passage. In *Reservation Blues*, African American culture under Jim Crow carries particular significance. Still, the arrival of "a strange black man and his guitar" does not evoke immediate recognition by reservation inhabitants.[1] Alexie writes, "The whole event required the construction of another historical monument" (5) so that black history becomes a tribal council–sanctioned part of American Indian history. As Thomas Builds-the-Fire, the storyteller protagonist, inherits Johnson's guitar—and, by extension, his legendary deal with the devil—Alexie develops a reservation blues novel, a song of American Indian economic deprivation, ethnic colonization, and cultural renewal.[2] Alexie's inventive multicultural project is buttressed by an imported master narrative of Jim Crow segregation and the perceived authenticity of its associated black cultural traditions. "'This isn't my guitar,' Thomas said. 'But I'm going to change the world with it'" (13). The significance of Johnson's instrument becomes clear to Thomas and his band because "Y'all need to play songs for your people. They need you" (23). More than a cross-ethnic borrowing, Alexie uses Johnson's blues model and its emergence from Jim Crow segregation to navigate the American Indian reservation system and the attendant desire to sing a beautiful song from that location.

Jim Crow tropes and figures pop up curiously and persistently in key white and ethnic American literary projects. So too, specific segregation narratives inform contemporary multiethnic American fiction well beyond Alexie's novel, most notably with Chang-Rae Lee's novel *Native Speaker* (1995), an Asian American adaptation of Ralph Ellison's *Invisible Man* and Richard Wright's *Native Son*. But Lee's direct revision of African American segregation narratives is more exception than rule when it comes to multiethnic neo–segregation narratives. Instead, like Alexie's use of Robert Johnson, the historiographic mode yields to a more speculative mode as writers attempt to forge genealogical bonds and partnerships that may have been rather unimaginable in the historical context of compulsory race segregation. So Wesley Brown's surprising move to locate multiethnic inclusion in the separatist space of the Jim Crow car is more in line with the multiethnic use of Jim Crow than the themes of constructing or reconstructing racial genealogies that we find in *The Bluest Eye*, *The Chaneysville Incident*, and *The Color Purple*. The multiethnic neo–segregation narrative deliberately flouts the bright line of race segregation while still using that backdrop to bring order to how race and ethnicity are lived in post–civil rights America.

Alexie and Lee bring Jim Crow figures and designs into the present, so their works are not neo–segregation narratives per se. Still, such techniques of cross-racial comparison, borrowing, and reinvention do result in full-fledged neo–segregation narratives. A good opening example is Tony Kushner's play *Caroline, or Change* (2004), which is set in 1963 Louisiana and features a complex, hardworking, and deeply angry black woman working as a maid for the Gellmans, an upward-looking middle-class Jewish family transplanted to the American South. We see the titular character through the eyes of young Noah, a thinly veiled autobiographical counterpart to Kushner, who is fascinated and frightened by his family's maid. To teach Noah to be more careful about money, his mother declares that Caroline can keep whatever change he forgets in his pocket. In a part-experimental, part-paternalistic gesture, Noah leaves more and more change in his pocket, until he accidentally leaves his Bar Mitzvah gift, a twenty dollar bill. Caroline feels shame, frustration, and anger that she comes to depend on the pocket-trifles she ferrets out of the laundry. Caroline is a cipher who serves as a lightning rod for Kushner's blues-charged moral deliberation about what it means to grow up during the American civil rights movement. Change can be as paltry as a few coins in a young boy's pocket, which can purchase clothes for Caroline's children, or as grand as an inspirational speech by Martin Luther King, Jr., or the assassination of John F. Kennedy. Like Mama Younger, the new generation perceives Caroline as a Jim Crow subject: cautious, obeisant, cheap, and soon to be irrelevant. But like Lena Younger in Hansberry's original screenplay, Kushner doesn't consign Caroline to the dustbin of Jim Crow history, instead seeking moral lessons from her. Caroline, though, may not be interested in offering wisdom and insight to the gawking son of her employers.

In approaching neo–segregation narratives by nonblack writers, I am mindful of the challenges and pitfalls of comparative ethnic approaches in American literary studies, especially when literary texts incite anxieties about cross-ethnic borrowing and set in motion matters of racial authenticity, propriety, and solidarity.[3] I am also mindful of the particular debates about nonblack depictions of black Jim Crow subjects. Ground zero of this tradition is John Howard Griffin's sociological experiment in *Black Like Me* (1961) in which he passes from white to black in the deep South with the aid of tanning beds and skin-darkening medication. Griffin then "traces the changes that occur to heart and body and intelligence when a so-called first-class citizen is cast on the junkheap of second-class citizenship."[4] Griffin's whiteness is both central and strangely safe from his own inspection. His stated project is to uncover white Americans' racist complicity, but in the narrative it is impor- tant to always remember—and therein reinforce—the privilege he gives up, to remember with "secret awareness" the whiteness at the heart of his black experiment (17). Griffin's experience, many note, is not really that of a black man, with attendant background experiences, history, and community, but rather that of a white man passing into unfamiliar territory while retaining his privilege, complete with a duffel full of two hundred dollars in traveler's checks and twenty dollars in cash (22). *Black Like Me* was widely popular, especially among white audiences, though it earned an equally large volume of criticism for how it displaced black people while seeking to give voice to black experiences of Jim Crow.

This tradition of racial crossing persists through the post–civil rights era, such as in Philip Roth's contemporary passing narrative *The Human Stain* (2000). The Hollywood film version of that novel stars Anthony Hopkins, thereby lending further uncanny credibility to the whiteness underneath these fictive black characters. Numerous scholars have raised questions regarding credibility, appropriation, and problematic constructions of whiteness in *Black Like Me* and its literary descendants.[5] Lest I rehash these debates, I turn to more self-consciously multiethnic literature, not just white literary depictions of blackness, because it harbors more interesting and complex uses of Jim Crow. In *ReWriting White* (2004), Todd Vogel provides a good avenue into such a tripartite racial reference system by examining how writers responded to nineteenth-century ideas about whiteness and the cultural capital it afforded. Vogel pairs African American writers with writers from another minority group because, he explains, "African Americans served as the foundation of the economy and because they played a crucial role in shaping Americans' understandings of whiteness and race in general, their history acts as a touchstone for comparison."[6] In the post–civil rights imagination, Jim Crow provides a similar reference point, even though whiteness and the privilege it entails remain as powerful as ever, if not more visible. Writers of all backgrounds turn to Jim Crow—African American experiences in particular—to understand race and ethnicity in a multicultural era.

What does it mean when race-specific experiences of segregation, which the figure of Johnson imports to the reservation, frame multiethnic novels not primarily concerned with African American history and experience? While such stories are imaginative, even speculative, fiction, the cross-racial frame has a firm basis in the historical record since Jim Crow laws policed the lives of other nonwhite ethnic minorities. This took place, for instance, through legal decisions over how new immigrant groups map onto existing black-and-white Jim Crow laws. It is also present in cultural and economic systems that pitted minority groups against each other, as in the notorious model minority idea that portrayed dutiful Asian American citizenship against the stereotypical foil of black delinquency.[7] A secondary question arises: With black Jim Crow characters, how do nonblack writers, whether white or of an ethnic minority, address long-standing concerns about cultural appropriation, or what Susan Gubar calls "black envy"?

This chapter examines Tom Spanbauer's *The Man Who Fell in Love with the Moon* (1991) as particularly illustrative of the promises and pitfalls of how multiethnic-minded neo–segregation narratives approach the above questions. *The Man Who Fell in Love with the Moon* is a quixotic novel set in the American West at the turn of the twentieth century. The novel is therefore also well paired with Alexie's novel because it brings Jim Crow subjects into the same region far removed from the segregated South, but a century prior. In neo–segregation narratives not primarily concerned with African American identity or history, Jim Crow buttresses contemporary ideas about whiteness and ethnic identity. The perceived moral clarity of signal black experiences harbors the power to orient other groups around pressing matters of national identity, ethnic belonging, and multiethnic inclusion. This is particularly true for the white literary imagination. Spanbauer's novel is a rich example of how contemporary writers far removed from African American literary traditions use Jim Crow practices, especially lynching and minstrelsy, as a racial barometer to sort out intricate identitarian lines in multiethnic milieus. Spanbauer delivers a part-historiographic and part-fantastic depiction of the settlement of Idaho, a contested terrain populated by various Anglo, Indian, Mormon, Chinese, and nomadic characters, often of ambiguous or hybrid racial background, all of whom jockey for ownership over the land—and their own stories. Late in the narrative, an all-black minstrel show suddenly appears, almost a deus ex machina. This development helps sort out the cross-racial mess that Spanbauer has deliberately set in play. Like Robert Johnson in Alexie's novel, the unexpected arrival of the African American minstrels imports the perceived clarity of Jim Crow race relations into Idaho, which provides Spanbauer's characters a grid upon which to map their own budding cross-ethnic alliances. But this also poses the danger of cross-ethnic masquerade, or even cross-ethnic pilfering, a concern to which I will return at the chapter's end.

Spanbauer's Ethnosexual Confusion in the American West

The Man Who Fell in Love with the Moon is by a gay white writer interested in matters of identity and belonging. The novel won a 1992 Pacific Northwest Booksellers Association Prize and Spanbauer went on to become something of a local legend among writers in his adopted hometown of Portland, Oregon, as well as in gay literary circles. The novel is set in southeast Idaho and its locations and characters are quite familiar to locals, especially those in Spanbauer's hometown of Pocatello, Idaho, an old blue-collar railroad community known around the state for its Democratic majority in a Republican stronghold state and its de facto social segregation among American Indians, Anglos, Mormons, Hispanics, and the newer crop of university and high-tech energy professionals.[8] The novel is far from well known but it sometimes finds its way into studies and syllabi on a wide range of subjects including race and sexuality, health sciences, and American culture, as well as sometimes even a literature course or two. The novel's failure so far to garner widespread recognition may be due in part to Spanbauer's refusal to stay within market niches (gay literature, western literature, coming-of-age narratives, American Indian literature, and so on) in the identitarian late twentieth century and, more specifically, his overt sexualization of cross-ethnic contact. Since this neo–segregation narrative is likely the least known in my study, I will first sketch its key characters, dilemmas, and plot events, especially with an eye toward underscoring its purposeful multiethnic confusion preceding the minstrels' arrival.

The irreverent story centers around a young man named Out-In-The-Shed who, as his faux Indian-sounding name implies, lives in a shed. The shed sits behind Ida's Place, a classic Old West whorehouse, where Shed earns his keep as a prostitute for the male patrons who may not go for the three women inside. The narrative is a fairly conventional coming-of-age tale in that Shed is searching for a cultural identity and a sense of belonging. There are some serious unknowns surrounding the protagonist's identity: Shed is of ambiguous American Indian and/or Anglo heritage; he is bisexual; he was raised by a prostitute, Ida Richilieu, who may or may not be his birth mother; and he finds spiritual communion with the Anglo pioneer Dellwood Barker, who talks to the moon and becomes Shed's lover despite the fact that he may or may not be Shed's father. Shed's presumed birth mother is Buffalo Sweets, or the one everyone calls "Princess" in a tongue-in-cheek nod to whites who claim an authentic Indian princess in their heritage. Princess worked as one of Ida's whores until she froze to death while hunting Billy Blizzard, the devil in the shape of a white man who raped Shed when he was a young boy. Beyond the ethnosexual confusion of the question of Shed's identity, Spanbauer uses elements of local color, bodice-ripper romance, bawdy dialogue, and western adventure tales to add plot twists and turns that make this story of a small western town settlement a carnivalesque romp.

Shed's real name is Duivichi-un-Dua, a Shoshone- or Bannock-sounding name, but Shed has little memory or facility with Native words. We learn about Shed, his cultural identity, and his sexuality through his entrance into Anglo written language via Dellwood's tutelage. Shed explains, "I don't know if *Berdache* is a Bannock word or a Shoshone word or just Indian. Heard tell it was a French word, but I don't know French, so I'm not the one to say. What's important is that's the word: *Berdache*. 'B..E..R..D..A..C..H..E,' Dellwood Barker spelled, 'means holy man who fucks men.'"[9] These cheeky spelling games underscore Shed's contemplative, slightly dumbfounded approach to questions of identity, cultural belonging, and geography. Words themselves are strange tools that tell Shed about his place in the world, while at the same time allowing Spanbauer to orient his contemporary readers well versed in identity politics about who accepts whom. For Shed, language and the stories it permits are problematic things. We first get a sense of the geographic time and location when Shed explains, "The name for Excellent was an Indian name I forget, which meant Good-Hot-Water-Out-Of-The-Ground" (6). In this impious approach to both Anglo and Native cultures, Spanbauer sets in motion a problem of how to talk about belonging when the stories, language, and ethnic groups simply don't fit. Shed explains, "That's just how people are—tybo or Indian. The only difference between *tybo* stories and the stories *we* tell is what those stories are about. We being Indians, which I was only half of. The half I liked to call the me part of not me" (7). In this meditation on race and story, Shed recites a simple racial taxonomy—*tybo* (white) or Indian—but even he doesn't fit his categories.

Spanbauer privileges an erotic attachment to land, identity, and family. In this vein, sexual desire drives Spanbauer's celebration of cross-ethnic coupling. To wit, Shed's sexuality is what makes him the hero. "Once I heard said I was as good as any woman in pleasing a man out in the shed," Shed explains, "and I'll tell you right now that's a damn lie. Ain't no woman could do what I could do out there and anybody who tells you different's a Mormon" (9). This leads to "'C..H..A..S..T..I..S..E..M..E..N..T,' Dell-wood spelled, 'Means getting spanked for liking to fuck'" (113). In search of freedom, movement, and cross-ethnic solidarity long before the arrival of the minstrels, Spanbauer pits Shed and his multiethnic band of libertines in direct opposition to rigid morality and its institutionalization through a government installed by later immigrant settlers, especially his hostile view of Mormon pioneers. Spanbauer thus transports contemporary ideas about identity and sexual inclusion to a mythical Old West, thereby drawing on the long-standing role of the frontier in the American (literary) imagination as a canvas on which to paint dreams of freedom and fulfillment.

Shed is uniquely able to tell a story about cross-ethnic contact, intimacy, and family because of his questionable origins. As a multiracial (maybe) and ambisexual (certainly) character, Shed is able to navigate Spanbauer's disorienting world, even if tybos declare him crazy. The arc of the story is not just Shed's search for his original identity and a sense of belonging but, more importantly, his search for healing and family. In this way, Shed is a classic foundling child, a narrative device well tested in its ability to mix up social orders and reformulate ideas about family, ethnic belonging, and nation, such as the heroine in Helen Hunt Jackson's *Ramona* (1884), Dianthe Lusk in Pauline Hopkins's *Of One Blood* (1903), and Joe Christmas in William Faulkner's *Light in August* (1932). The figure of the foundling child sets in motion questions not only of ethnic and national identity but also sexual identity.[10] The question of self-determination, so prevalent in ethnic communities, becomes this foundling's quest to locate home, family, and the special way of knowing called "moon language": "*What's moon language?* folks would ask. '*Language from the heart*,' I would answer. 'But it's not the truth, moon language is not the language from the heart. Moon language is mind language'" (315). Moon language appears in direct opposition to tybo ways of knowing, and it defies a social order that discourages cross-ethnic contact and intimacy. In order to achieve clarity in this identitarian confusion, and perhaps to escape the thicket of whiteness, Spanbauer leaves the community—going all the way into outer space. Shed draws on half-remembered Native ways of knowing and telling, but he also learns a great deal from his wayward Anglo father figure because "Dellwood Barker's human-being story, and the words he used to tell his story, were pretty much the same as with other tybo folks. How Dellwood Barker put his words and his story together, though, was another story" (113).

In this multiethnic world with Shed at the center, Spanbauer looks at white culture through the language and experiences of the indigenous people of the region. That is, he portrays whites, including himself, as tybo. Shed adds more layers to the mix and sees himself through the vantage of *tutybo*, or black white people. For Shed, after all members of his family are dead, have been murdered, or have fled, it is his story itself that will satiate his quest for identity because, in the final pages, "Telling this story is what I'm doing—learning to tell the story. Me, the one who has lived—the brave hero" (351). However, while Shed may be the hero of this narrative, African Americans in a traveling minstrel show from the Jim Crow South ultimately provide a viable model to achieve integrity in a life of performance and identitarian desires for belonging.

Jim Crow as Magnet for the Iron Filings of Multiethnicity

In a common grammar school science exercise, students learn the organizing power of a magnet. They approach a messy pile of iron filings with magnet in hand. When used with care, the magnet brings beautiful order by aligning all the filings according to positive and negative ends. Blackness—especially when invested with the history of Jim Crow and attendant racial terrorism—holds a similar power to bring order to the seeming disarray of multiethnic relations for Spanbauer, and for multiethnic-minded neo-segregation narratives more generally.

Out of nowhere and two thirds into the story, four "authentic negroes" arrive in a wagon: "*The Wisdom Brothers—Ulysses, Virgil, Homer, and Blind Jude. Authentic Freed Negro Slaves!*" (241). Their wagon advertises their performance: "*Singing Songs of Jubilee, Pure Plantation Melodies, and Songs of the Sunny South.* . . . A Union Jack flag was sewn on the back flap. The word *Freedom* was scratched onto the canvas under the flag with an ink pen" (241). The Wisdom Brothers are an all-black minstrel show from the South. They carry the history of slavery and Reconstruction written on their wagon and they fit well in a story about identity ambiguity and play. For Spanbauer's contemporary readers over one hundred years later, the Wisdom Brothers carry the history of the failure of Reconstruction, ensuing Jim Crow laws, and the racial terrorism of lynch mobs, especially given their arrival at the doorstep of two white women prostitutes eager to extend their services. The history of minstrelsy in the United States is well documented and it lends itself to ideas about race-as-performance prevalent in current critical race studies. In the novel, though, the black minstrel performers do more than tell us about how whiteness and blackness perform for each other: the perceived clarity and settled status of Jim Crow segregation helps bring some sort of cross-racial order to the multiethnic West.

When the all-black minstrel show happens through the saloon town—as unexpected as Robert Johnson's arrival on the Spokane Indian Reservation in Alexie's novel—the narrative is finally able to comment with certitude on injustice and contemporary matters of ethnic divisions and their histories. Spanbauer aligns the mixed-blood Indians, loose women proprietors of the local saloon, and ethnic immigrants *with* the African American performers and *against* the newer, religiously intolerant settlers. The cross-identitarian alliance of the various marginalized figures is made possible by the starkness of minstrelsy's racial lines and the clear politics of lynching. When the Wisdom Brothers ride into town, Ida jumps at the business opportunity with an extemporaneous speech shrouded in purposefully hackneyed declarations of patriotism and a progress narrative of rising up from slavery: "Our country fought a bloody civil war, brother against brother, for the cause of freedom. Abraham Lincoln, our greatest president, was murdered because of his stand against slavery. We fought a bloody war, brother against brother, and we won. The Emancipation Proclamation had ended slavery in this country. Negroes are free people, just like us white folks are free. Free to pursue life, liberty, and happiness" (245). The Wisdom Brothers import to the multiethnic West a familiar national history of broken promises, a recognizable lens through which readers can now view the rest of the novel.

The four black men are freed slaves making a way for themselves in the newly forming terrain of Jim Crow segregation. Those familiar historical lessons about black experiences and broken American promises impart order onto the not-so-clear lines of liberty and freedom in the newly settled West. Though much of the novel has at least some resemblance to actual historical events and figures, the Wisdom Brothers descend onto the semifictional terrain of Excellent, Idaho, out of nowhere. The recorded history of African Americans in the West at the time of the story is quite thin. Only one known autobiography of a black cowboy exists, despite their not insignificant numbers: *The Life and Adventures of Nat Love, Better Known in the Cattle Country as "Deadwood Dick"* (1907). Further compounding this sparse literary trail, Love's depiction of the West is questionable from the point of view of both historical accuracy and Spanbauer's interest in acknowledging the racism of the location. Blake Allmendinger notes that Love rarely breaks out of the us-versus-them, cowboys-and-Indians mentality. "Perhaps because he was writing for a mainly white readership," Allmendinger argues, "Love denied having been the victim of prejudice. Instead he described his kind treatment at the hands of white bosses, his acceptance within a color-blind cowboy fraternity, and his subsequent rise to fame in a nonracist frontier environment."[11]

The arrival of the Wisdom Brothers is directly preceded by the equally abrupt arrival of a new group of immigrant settlers: Mormon pioneers. Rather than adding yet another identity to the rich cross-ethnic tangle, Spanbauer casts the Mormon pioneers as not only uninterested in cross-ethnic contact but also hostile to it. Shed reports, "The Mormon women started herding their children out of [Ida's Place] as quickly as possible, the children all staring up at us as if they'd never set eyes on human beings that weren't Mormon before" (184). Spanbauer attempts a comedic depiction of intolerance, but in depicting the Mormon families as a herd of domestic animals, he risks dehumanizing an entire group. He does not display the cross-ethnic understanding that has been privileged throughout the rest of the novel and that is generally prized in a multicultural age. The Wisdom Brothers, then, must invest cross-ethnic contact and identity play with a moral and political capital that contemporary readers are prone to ascribe to the familiar history of Jim Crow segregation and lynching.

Throughout the novel, Shed is perplexed by his own origins and ethnic lineage, while Spanbauer persistently undercuts ideas about ethnic authenticity and revels in fluid, hybrid, or unknown identity. But it is not until the arrival of the Wisdom Brothers that the narrative insists on racial variety and ethnic crossings as an ethical mandate and demographic reality. Spanbauer exploits expectations of stark racial division in the segregation tradition that the Wisdom Brothers import. To Shed's surprise, not only can the Wisdom Brothers consort with white prostitutes the same as anybody else but also he finds "[s]omething else, too. They weren't black. Those Negroes weren't black. They were brown, different shades of brown—it's the same with tybos; for example, Ida Richilieu and Alma Hatch—both of them were tybo, but Ida was white white with dark nipples and black hair, while Alma was mostly pink with pink nipples and brown hair that went blond. Same as with the Wisdom Brothers—parts of them were black, but mostly they were the color of wet pine bark, or loamy soil. Smelled as good, too, especially Homer" (252). This is a revelatory scene for Shed because pigmentation variety leads to a whole new outlook on identity, bodies, and destiny. The effect is to humanize all involved and permit cross-racial union—sexual or otherwise—especially given Shed's sexual interest in Homer.

The Wisdom Brothers foster gender play too. Shed reports, "Blind Jude wrapped the feathered boa around his neck. I put Ida's hat on him, the one Alma Hatch had given her, with the peacock feathers. He stood himself exactly as Ida stood herself" (254). The identity play and familial intimacy fits well—indeed, is prerequisite—in a minstrel show. The Wisdom Brothers incite all sorts of movement and performances across lines of gender. Shed, Dellwood Barker, and the Wisdom Brothers become happy, empowered female prostitutes in disguise. At the same time, "Ida Richilieu had turned into a black man. 'The Emancipation Proclamation has ended slavery in this country. Negroes are free people, just like white folks are free. Free to pursue life, liberty, and happiness'" (254). Ida's repeat performance is part cynical take on American promises and part emancipatory play across social lines. Either way, the all-black minstrel troupe invests Spanbauer's identity play with grand political overtones typically associated with African American histories of slavery, Reconstruction, Jim Crow, and civil rights.

When scholars study the history of African Americans in the West, they question settled ideas about well-known movements, such as the Great Migration and New Negro Renaissance, and also ideas about the West. Allmendinger studies how African American writers, especially those with roots in the region, look at more familiar sites of the urban north and rural South through the lens of western experience. He finds that some Harlem Renaissance writers with western roots, such as Taylor Gordon, held up their hometowns as beacons of "unrestricted freedom of movement and social equality" (63) in contrast to the alienating and racist urban north. On the other hand, some writers such as Wallace Thurman looked back at their western roots (Salt Lake City and Boise in Thurman's case) with scorn and mockery. "But when he complained about racial segregation, lack of equal access to education, and the absence of an African American professional class," Allmendinger reports, "he sounded openly bitter."[12] Allmendinger concludes that when African American writers employ the frontier or a frontier mentality in their works, such as Ralph Ellison (of Oklahoma roots) in *Invisible Man* (1952) and Langston Hughes (of Kansas roots) in *Not without Laughter* (1930), the West plays a significant role in African American literary traditions. The West remains a fecund site in the African American literary imagination, from Pauline Hopkins's *Winona* (1902) to Toni Morrison's *Paradise* (1997) and Suzan-Lori Parks's *Getting Mother's Body* (2003), which I discuss in the following chapter. Black writers turn to the

West "to imagine a better world that includes women and racial minorities,"[13] though many writers eventually find that the West is not able to house these liberatory aspirations.

If the West serves as the not-East in the African American literary imagination, signature African American experiences of segregation also carry very different histories and connotations in the West. What happens when the threat of lynching appears in a story about the West but is associated with Jim Crow segregation in the South? Scholar-photographer Ken Gonzales-Day chronicles his search for the notorious "hang trees" of his native Southern California and finds that the story of lynching in the West differs markedly from the more familiar political and social terrain of the spectacle lynchings and racial terrorism in the South. The era of spectacle lynchings is a notorious, shameful chapter in U.S. history. "No one tries to defend the lynching of African Americans in the South as a popular form of capital punishment (as many Anglo-Americans once did)," Gonzales-Day explains, "but the lynching of blacks, Asians, Indians, and Latinos continues to be defended in many historical texts and popular representations as an unavoidable part of taming the West."[14] Gonzales-Day's work demonstrates that the racial history of lynching in the West has yet to be fully told, while scholars of lynching in the South must work to reopen seemingly closed avenues of inquiry.

In *Legacies of Lynching*, historian Jonathan Markovitz argues that lynching remains a metaphor that tells us about racialization and contemporary racial politics because "[l]ynching was always intended as a metaphor for, or a way to understand, race relations." Markovitz explores how "the very process of remembering lynching and of using those memories to help shape our understanding of the present are highly complex matters that are intimately linked to ongoing processes of national racial formation and 'common sense' [Gramsci] understandings of race." Markovitz concludes, "Lynchings have provided a 'lens,' or way of seeing and understanding race relations and race spectacles."[15] If Markovitz is correct that spectacle lynching is now a "malleable" metaphor for contemporary race relations, it follows that contemporary depictions of Jim Crow segregation and spectacle lynchings are powerful tools in novels primarily concerned with groups outside core African American experiences.

The threat of lynching in Spanbauer's novel, when beamed through the prism of seemingly settled politics of white supremacism and racial terrorism, allows a cross-ethnic solidarity that brings some semblance of clarity to the confusing social and political terrain of Spanbauer's multiethnic West. Shed reports, "There were about a dozen men on horses riding in circles around the shed and the Wisdom Brothers' wagon. You could hardly see because of the dust. They were shooting off their guns into the air and whooping and hollering the way men do herding cows. Two of the men held signs. *Nigger, Read and Run*" (256). Coming from a narrator whose use of language and spelling typically catapult him into existential reveries about identity and origin, the clarity and simplicity of this sign is noteworthy. The arrival of the Wisdom Brothers catalyzes a stark separation—segregation, really—among the residents of Excellent. After the Wisdom Brothers' show at Ida's saloon, "Everybody started cheering and clapping—even some Mormons were clapping—Mormon women and children, that is" (247). This collective town gaze directed at the minstrel show quickly fractures because "'The Book of Mormon tells us all about these people,' the Reverend Helm said. 'Now, kindly, I ask all Latter-day Saints who are faithful to leave this saloon'" (246). In this scene of unity, Spanbauer paints the newer Mormon settlers as intrusive, patriarchal, and divisive. As a side note, there is an irony because Spanbauer evidences a very partial understanding of Mormon culture by referring to a church leader as "Reverend" and he potentially misreads what the *Book of Mormon* does or doesn't say about African Americans. In any case, because the Mormons' intolerance is directed at the Wisdom Brothers, Spanbauer draws on the settled political history of southern segregation, rather than the openly confusing terrain of the West, to draw a clear line between inclusion and intolerance. Strangely, Spanbauer uses these figures of exclusion and victims of Jim Crow segregation to set up a new kind of segregation in the West. Only this segregation is ethical—certainly a surprise in a story that plays to contemporary multicultural attitudes of inclusiveness.

The lynching threat recasts the main characters' anti-Mormon sentiment as an antiracist stance. Throughout the novel, the figures at the moral center—Shed, Dellwood, Alma, and especially Ida—carry anti-Mormon bias with such fervor that Spanbauer risks putting off his readers. To some extent, their anti-Mormonism is understandable through a multicultural sensibility because the nonnormative lives of Shed and Ida fail to live up to rigid community standards, which are aligned explicitly with the Mormon characters. That is why Shed contrasts his intimate relations with Dellwood, Ida, Alma, and the rest of his extended family with the new moralism imported by the newer Mormon settlers. This leads Ida to aver that their "glorious" foursome is "[b]etter than any Mormon family" (225) because "the glorious days, according to Ida, were the days the four of us spent together, before the trouble came in between" (225). Thus Spanbauer sets the new Mormon immigrants as trouble-bringing interlopers disruptive to the interethnic family created by two loose women, a mixed-blood protagonist, and a contemplative Anglo wanderer. Nevertheless, without the Wisdom Brothers and the threat of lynching brought by their immersion in the glorious family, the main characters' anti-Mormon sentiment risks seeming unwarranted and vituperative. The Wisdom Brothers quickly adapt to the anti-Mormon sentiments of their newfound family. Spanbauer writes, "'Pernicious!' Owlfeather said into the mirror. 'P..E..R..N..I..C..I..O..U..S,' he said. 'Ain't it delicious, being so pernicious. Fuck those Mormon sons o'bishes'" (255). This bald statement of hatred becomes an ethical commitment to inclusion when Spanbauer aligns it with the right side of the history of Jim Crow segregation and its concomitant practices of racial terror.

In his review in the *Washington Post Book World*, Richard Lipez praises the work as "[a] novel that combines winningly rebellious characters who are brimming with life, along with a wise and powerful sense of the heartbreak of nineteenth-century American history."[16] Spanbauer also draws on a long history of Anglos "going native." In her study of that tradition, Shari Huhndorf finds, "As the nineteenth century progressed, however, the conquering culture began to reimagine the objects of its conquest. Popular images of Native peoples, though never monolithic, grew increasingly ambivalent. Indians continued to serve as civilized society's inferior 'other,' but more and more often European Americans looked to Native America to define themselves and their nation."[17] Spanbauer enters this tradition with a cross-ethnic twist because the characters move among seemingly distinct and divergent identities and histories beyond an Anglo/Native divide. The clarifying power of blackness in this raucous multiethnic story set in the Old West allows Spanbauer to invest with ethical certitude the "winningly rebellious" attitude toward identity that is prized in contemporary multiculturalism but is also dangerous and potentially fatal in the hyperpoliced worlds of Jim Crow segregation and frontier towns. Against a tybo social order that excludes or denigrates the Sheds, Idas, and Dellwoods of the world, Spanbauer retrieves a redemptive moment in the West. Before government-sanctioned white settlement and Native displacement, the multiethnic confusion of the West achieves clarity through the magnetic power of Jim Crow in the contemporary imagination.

Non-White Like Me: Moral Clarity or Cross-Ethnic Pilfering?

I have traced how a gay white writer throws in Jim Crow characters to sort out the ethnic confusion he puts into play, and even—somewhat counter-intuitively—to invest his characters' postures of intolerance with moral clarity. But what difference, if any, is there between this moral clarity and oversimplification? Ojibwa author David Treuer joins many scholars in pointing out, "There is a long history of fake Indian texts, just as there is a long legacy of fake Indian artifacts. There is even a long history of fake Indians."[18] Though Spanbauer does not consciously pose as an impostor Indian,[19] we must still ask whether he seeks cross-ethnic solidarity without sufficient attention to the specificity of geographic and ethnic experiences. Instead, perhaps Spanbauer flattens out intricate social hierarchies in yet another example of appropriation of ethnic otherness by white writers. What are the implications for whiteness and its place in the dominant social order when this story continually defers to American Indian and African American characters and histories to sort out (white) identity? To consider the ramifications of Spanbauer's strategy, I return to the work discussed at the outset of this chapter: Alexie's *Reservation Blues*. These two instructive uses of black figures in western spaces more populated by Anglo and Native people signal the breadth and diversity of Jim Crow in the multiethnic imagination. Contrary to Spanbauer, Alexie spends considerable time exploring the convergences of African American and American Indian cultural heritages without conflating or flattening them, such as in the long conversations up on the mountain between Big Mom and Robert Johnson. His cross-ethnic borrowing, therefore, is a more politically and aesthetically successful.

Placing African American experiences at the center of other ethnic American literary narratives is potentially disorienting, but ultimately it proves steadying. One of the women in the rock and roll band in *Reservation Blues* resents seeing herself through a black/white lens. Chess explains, "It's just that everywhere I look these days, I see white women. We caught Junior and Victor having sex with some white women. They're always having sex with white women. It makes me hate them" (138). She clarifies, "White women. Indian men. Both, I guess" (138). Faced with the overwhelming, self-erasing presence of white women, Chess easily falls into dominant racial dichotomies. "Anyway, all those little white girls would be so perfect, so pretty, so white," she explains. "White skin and white dresses. I'd be all brown-skinned in my muddy brown dress. I used to get so dark that white people thought I was a black girl" (140). Chess faces erasure in a black-and-white worldview. Likewise, placing African American experience at the center of a novel about the search for Native cultural pride risks once again effacing the very people with whom Alexie is most concerned. When the band returns to the reservation community, the community is not ready to welcome the blues, still seeing it as the influence of outsiders upon their wayward children. Alexie writes, "Those blues created memories for the Spokanes, but they refused to claim them. Those blues lit up a new road, but the Spokanes pulled out their old maps. Those blues churned up generations of anger and pain: car wrecks, suicides, murders. Those blues were ancient, aboriginal, indigenous" (275). While Alexie claims the blues as a Native form, the Spokanes may not accept his offer.

With or without tribal council and community approval, Alexie places Johnson atop the mountain with Big Mom and enshrines him as an elder who offers cultural redemption. On Big Mom's questioning, we find that Johnson imagines his blues as a song of freedom, freedom from a history of slavery and Jim Crow in which "Johnson felt the whip that split open the skin on his grandfathers' backs. He heard the creak of floorboard as the white masters crept into his grandmothers' bedrooms" (264). Thomas taps into a collective history, in which "Johnson's grandmother was not alone in that cabin. Other black men, women, and children sang with her. The smell of sweat, blood, and cotton filled the room. Cotton, cotton. Those black people sang for their God; they sang with joy and sorrow. The white men in their big houses heard those songs and smiled. *Those niggers singin' and dancin' again*, those white men thought. *Music don't make sense*" (275). Ultimately, Thomas shows his people that the blues offer a model to tap into their own collective history of pain, shame, oppression—and survival. The cross-racial sharing is a two-way street: after his long run from the devil, Johnson concludes, "On the reservation. I think I might just belong here. I think there's been a place waitin' at this tribe for me" (303). Johnson also offers cultural redemption to the Spokanes, as seen when "Big Mom walked out of the bedroom carrying a guitar made of a 1965 Malibu and the blood of a child killed at Wounded Knee in 1890" (206). If in the historical record

Johnson's disappearance from the earth opened up speculations about the veracity of his fabled deal with the devil, why couldn't he have ended up all the way on the other side of the country on the Spokane Indian Reservation, not unlike the Wisdom Brothers' unexpected arrival in Excellent?

Spanbauer is savvy about the fraught terrain of white writers depicting American Indian characters. If I am right that Spanbauer's ability to foster cross-ethnic solidarity and form a cross-racial family requires anti-Mormon sentiment, then the prospect of lynching African Americans from the South provides a palliative to Spanbauer's contemporary reader. Spanbauer layers on histories of slavery, freedom, Reconstruction, and Jim Crow so that the Wisdom Brothers' experience in turn-of-the-century southeast Idaho is inseparable from black experience generally, which carries an ethical aura for Spanbauer. Further, the Wisdom Brothers are inseparable from all of Western civilization given their names: Ulysses, Homer, Virgil, and Blind Jude. The arrival of the Wisdom Brothers allows Shed to think about his local family in national and global terms: "*Emancipation Proclamation*, I thought, *free*" (256). In this version of freedom, the Wisdom Brothers instigate scenes of cross-racial harmony, gender play, inclusivity, and sexual intimacy. Shed says, "Owlfeather sat down by me and took my head in his hands. Pretty soon, Damn Dave was laying next to me, holding me, and so was Blind Jude laying next to me. Four men laying on the floor dressed up like women. They didn't try to stop me crying. They put their arms around me" (256). Spanbauer paints this image of comfort and cross-ethnic harmony immediately before the much-anticipated lynching.

Spanbauer attempts to reconcile the pleasures and dangers of cross-ethnic identification by swapping the lynching script regarding who does the lynching—whites, yes, but Mormons in particular. The newly ordered multiethnic society (with Mormons on one side and Anglos, Natives, Chinese, African Americans, and all those in between on the other) comes to a climactic head when a follower of Reverend Helm sets fire to Ida's saloon. Many die or are horribly injured in the ensuing fire, including Shed (now in a sort of coma), Ida (near dead and legless), Alma (soon to be dead), Dellwood (soon to be gone), and the Wisdom Brothers (some dead, some to be hunted down). The victims of the actual lynching in the narrative, however, turn out to be Reverend Helm and Sheriff Blumenfeld. The town doctor reports, "Found 'em myself, just two days ago, hanging from a tree next to Merrillee's mill down there. Both of them brains pierced through ear to ear with a bayonet" (304).

Spanbauer sets in motion familiar lynching tropes, though the components are out of order: a search posse forms *after* the lynching to go after Dellwood Barker and other survivors of the fire, leaving the injured Shed and Ida behind, assuming (incorrectly) that they are left for dead. In this reversal of the familiar lynching story, the lines between victims and aggressors are potentially blurred. But Shed's visit to the segregated cemetery helps sort things out: "I looked around. At the Reverend Helm's funeral, Blumenfeld's funeral, in the main part of the cemetery, in the Christian part, Mormon folks stood in the sun, so clean, faithful, sure they were right. White people singing to God, burying their preacher and the assistant mayor" (307). Spanbauer portrays this posture of moral certainty as hollow, then he replaces this false sense of moral superiority with an ethical alliance with his Jim Crow characters, who perish in the skirmish.

After the fire, the lynching, and proprietary skirmishes, the social order looks very different. Alma and the Wisdom Brothers are dead, Ida ends up as "Peg-Leg Ida," Shed ends up blind (literally taking the place of Blind Jude), and the rest end up either dead or Mormon. Finally Shed hops on his horse named "Metaphor" to track where Dellwood has gone to die with his own horse called "Abraham Lincoln." In this new social order, there is almost no place left for a family like that of Shed, Ida, Alma, and Dellwood. The final blow comes when Ida learns that her free-and-clear title burned in the fire. Reverend William B. Merrillee traveled to Boise to purchase the land, in a story not unlike the long history of Anglos taking Native territory through legal maneuvering around "unassigned land." All Ida owns is the land around the shed. Spanbauer invests this new social order with a cynical vision of national identity. He writes, "The day William B. Merrillee finally came to town was the same day that Ida Richilieu got to be Peg-Leg Ida. It was Saturday, July fourth, one year to the day that the Wisdom Brothers were killed and Ida's Place had burned to the ground" (333). Even Out-In-The-Shed / Duivichi-un-Dua loses his name in the new tybo social order. Shed reports, "Sheriff spit in my face. Called me one of those tybo words for men loving men" (322).

As a gay white man writing about—and identifying with—American Indians, African Americans, female prostitutes, and other marginalized groups, Spanbauer provides a strange sort of reverse passing narrative. Rather than passing in order to access white privilege, *The Man Who Fell in Love with the Moon* passes as ethnic in order to access the moral weight assigned in a post–civil rights era to histories of subjugated peoples. In his study of ethnic white passing, Steven Belluscio finds, "The passing narrative . . . involves an extreme example of crossing the boundary that separates dominant and marginal cultural, racial, and/or ethnic groups—usually with the purpose of 'shed[ding] the identity of an oppressed group to gain access to social and economic opportunities.'"[20] In Spanbauer's case, when the passing narrative reverses from privileged to marginalized in an identitarian age, he risks confirming the deep suspicion around the long history of Anglos "going Native" for less than honorable reasons. In her study of white fictions of Native Americans at the turn of the twentieth century, Sherry Smith finds, "To acknowledge that they often failed to grasp the complexities of Indian peoples; that they often failed to transcend their own ethnocentric and even racist assumptions; and that early twenty-first century Indian and white readers might find their works sentimental, romantic, and simpleminded does nothing to negate their cultural power."[21] At the turn of the twenty-first century, there are more and diverse American Indian voices in print culture so the cultural power of Anglo fictions of Native peoples has diminished. Still, when placed alongside other stories of American Indian crossings with African American culture, such as *Reservation Blues*, it seems that Spanbauer's novel siphons the moral weight of Jim Crow/civil rights to provide a palliative fantasy of an ultimately innocent whiteness that requires no concessions, reparations, or even social justice. Spanbauer may simply be, in the words of Philip Deloria, entering that long-standing and notorious American cultural history of "playing Indian."

The Man Who Fell in Love with the Moon is very concerned with minority disenfranchisement in the West. Yet when it comes to white subjectivity, the novel is strangely exculpatory—even prone to amnesia. This is not surprising based on historians' accounts of white memories of Jim Crow, especially regarding culpability for the racial terrorism and intimidation that accompanied Jim Crow. Sherrilynn Ifill measures the resonance of histories of lynching in various communities today and finds significant impact on black Americans but less on the part of whites, even those who witnessed lynchings firsthand. "I found this silence by whites and their detachment from lynchings quite extraordinary," Ifill reports, "when contrasted with the rich and detailed 'memory' of blacks." She continues, "Whites also remain strangely caught up in a continued bond of complicity—pleading ignorance or faded memories to avoid at all cost talking about a shameful part of their history." Ifill compares this situation to postapartheid South Africa and suggests something akin to South Africa's Truth and Reconciliation Commission, which "ma[de] the job of forgetting difficult for whites."[22]

Spanbauer's novel is a good example of a rich, raucous engagement with lynching's history that simultaneously has removed any semblance of white complicity. The absence of this moral engagement with whiteness is striking because stories of Jim Crow segregation are almost inherently primed to evoke ethical reactions. Mara Scanlon suggests that lynching narratives, in her case Robert Hayden's 1962 poem "Night, Death, Mississippi," carry an assumed ethical or moral response. "And so," she explains, "the necessary answerability of the reader to a poem that voices prejudice and violence seems self-evident, whatever emotional, pedagogic, or sociopolitical form that answer takes."[23] With the subject of white complicity unaddressed, or even removed from the stage, when white writers don ethnic masks for neo–segregation narratives, the ethical dimensions of their novels become warped. The moral response cannot account for whiteness's stark absence from the courtroom of literature.

Despite the moralistic designs of bringing Jim Crow to bear on contemporary multiethnic fiction, Spanbauer's use of his black characters, and all his ethnic minority characters, may fall back into the problematic mold of what George Frederickson described long ago as "romantic racialism" in his foundational 1971 study *The Black Image in the White Mind*. Frederickson found that while white liberals came to largely reject racist ideals of an all-white America in the early twentieth century, they still acquiesced to beliefs about racial difference (and therefore hierarchies), which led them to proffer stories mired in black stereotypes borne of a shallow interaction with black people and experiences. "What was new about the image of blacks conveyed in the novels of white writers like DuBose Heyward, Julia Peterkin, and Carl Van Vechten," Frederickson argued, "was not the stereotype itself but the lack of moralism in the treatment of what would previously have been defined as black immorality or even animality; for these novelists incorporated sexuality into the romantic stereotype without appearing to condemn it."[24] Frederickson's description of white modernist uses of black primitivism uncannily echoes Spanbauer's white image of black blackface minstrelsy and the cultural play it affords, which is now valued in a self-consciously multicultural postmodern era. It is only two short steps from Van Vechten and John Howard Griffin to Tom Spanbauer's black image in the white imagination. Since Frederickson's study, the fields of African American literary studies and critical race studies have explored conventional understandings of how blackness and race are constructed, and African American imaginative responses to such systems as Jim Crow segregation. The field of whiteness studies arose later so that we are only now fully asking questions about texts such as Spanbauer's novel and their image of black characters. While Jim Crow's black subjects may help Spanbauer to orient multiethnic alliances, the clarity may be ill-gotten when the gravitational pull of whiteness itself is left unaccounted.

Jim Crow Experience at the Center of Ethnic America

Neo–segregation narratives by writers who share no blood kinship or direct cultural kinship with black people in the United States almost implicitly confirm widespread suspicions about white writers' uses of marginalized groups. In her 1997 presidential address to the American Studies Association, Mary Helen Washington provocatively asked, "What happens to American studies if you put African American studies at the center?" As the association's first elected black president and black studies pioneer, Washington narrated her long path to seeing the ASA as an intellectual home, which was not inevitable.[25] Washington pushed the field to recognize the full impact of this delayed shift beyond token inclusion. She cited the shared project of many black intellectuals over the century to show how they "identified white supremacy as a systemic and central feature of the American experience. Indeed, this is one of the most important aspects of what it means to put African American studies at the center of American studies and to use this paradigm as a starting point for reading the contemporary scene."[26] Placing African American studies at the center of American studies promised to facilitate more, and more innovative, "border crossings" among different groups housed—however uncomfortably—in national identity. Six years later, Washington participated in a bellwether panel that asked if the ASA could be an intellectual home for American Indian studies and scholars. She underscored that ethnic studies scholars might not perceive the ASA as home, though it might look like it from one ethnic group to another. She also revisited her earlier embrace of inclusion, now detecting a rather pernicious air of imperialism in that model. She concluded, "It's not so much that Native American studies needs ASA but that ASA needs Native studies."[27]

The American Indian studies scholars on the panel—Philip Deloria, Robert Warrior, and Jean O'Brien—were sympathetic to Washington's call, but also leery. The prospect opens up new avenues of research, such as uncovering rich histories of shared experiences between African American and American Indian cultures.[28] But it also fuels long-standing suspicions about cross-ethnic pilfering, leading some to advocate a counterproject of what Warrior, Jace Weaver, and Craig Womack call "American Indian literary nationalism." Now that ethnic and American studies are intertwined, especially in comparative ethnic studies, Washington's earlier call is a useful test case. In a way, Spanbauer's novel does precisely what Washington asked in 1997: place African American experiences and insights about American identity at the center of examinations of racial division in a multicultural setting. That cross-racial project is especially provocative when it ventures into the terrain that has so occupied American studies: the frontier.

This chapter focuses on the clarifying power of blackness in Anglo-Native fictions. Still, much the same can be said about seemingly peripheral African American characters and references to black experience that appear persistently throughout ethnic American literature. A good parting example is Maxine Hong Kingston's *The Woman Warrior: Memoirs of a Girlhood among Ghosts* (1975). At the end of her second chapter, when we finally meet the adult narrator, one of the first things we learn is that she came of age as a student at Berkeley in the sixties. In this memoir of silence and cut tongues, we learn that one of her first entrances into adult voice and American ethnic belonging is a repudiation of Jim Crow–style racism. The narrator recounts, "I once worked at an art supply house that sold paints to artists. 'Order more of that nigger yellow, willya?' the boss told me. . . . 'I don't like that word,' I had to say in my bad, small person's voice that makes no impact. The boss never deigned to answer."[29] The narrator's ad hoc boycott resonates with those by integration-oriented civil rights groups NAACP and CORE in the historical record. These moments are rather peripheral to the memoir and they have gone unremarked in the literary criticism, but they buttress this influential narrative of the formation of American ethnic consciousness.

Experiences of Jim Crow and civil rights often serve as beacons for ethnic minorities to chart their own place in the American social and political imaginary. In a conversation with African American novelist Charles Johnson, Kingston comments on the strangeness and necessity of a Jim Crow–centric model of ethnic identity. Kingston muses, "I think that we people who are non-black, non-white, we have a very special sight because the whole discussion during the 60s was about black and white. And from our point of view with 'Where am I in this?' and the answer was just like so complicated because you have to make your place in it."[30] Throughout *The Woman Warrior*, Kingston's famous ghost trope demarcates lines of belonging, separating home from alien, family from foreigner. Amid the twin pulls of ethnic belonging and cultural assimilation, African Americans are closer in kind to Chinese immigrants than white people because, while black Americans are still ghosts, they are "more distinct than White ghosts" (97). With *The Woman Warrior* and her companion novel of immigrant male experience, *Tripmaster Monkey*, Kingston joins a handful of seminal post–civil rights writers documenting Asian American experiences of segregation, including especially John Okada's depiction of Japanese American internment in *No-No Boy* (1957). Like Lee's *Native Speaker*, Kingston deliberately and consistently uses African American experiences to orient that literary tradition.

Not unlike the central role of Africanist presences that Morrison notices in white modernism, African Americans are pivotal to the development of ethnic consciousness across various minority literatures in America. Scholars now call for literary studies that look at how one minority group approaches another,[31] even while many American Indian studies scholars remain hesitant, if not outright skeptical. Comparative ethnic American literary studies formalized common practices in reading and politics when that field emerged out of long-standing conversations between ethnic studies and American studies, on the one hand, and American literature and postcolonial theory on the other. In her discussion of teaching African American literature to Korean students, Myung Ja Kim reports, "My own experience suggests that Korean students can learn to redefine and reposition themselves and their culture through learning about other cultures represented in American ethnic literature."[32] Such comparisons between groups are quite common, especially when articulating one immigrant group's experiences through the lens of African American experience because, as Ronald Takaki explains, "African Americans have been the central minority throughout our country's history."[33] Such cross-racial comparisons open up new avenues in literary studies, be it by tropes such as in Yung-Hsing Wu's study of the trope of invisibility in Lee's *Native Speaker* in comparison to Ellison's *Invisible Man* and Wright's *Native Son* that "makes it possible to imagine an ethnic intertextuality,"[34] or the magnet-and-iron-filings function that Jim Crow segregation holds in the multiethnic American imagination in the Spanbauer example.

Neo–segregation narratives by nonblack authors can resist or court, to varying degrees of success, the pull to fetishize ethnic difference by attending to distinct ethnic and racial histories that nevertheless inform one another. One successful option is to underscore the nature of the borrowing itself so that the segregation tradition is available to multiethnic America, even if it remains inextricably linked to black experience. "That guitar pulled at him, like gravity," Alexie writes. "Even though Victor had it for months now, Johnson could still feel the pull. Johnson wondered if he'd ever really be free again" (266). Alexie underscores that Thomas Builds-the-Fire can only borrow the guitar to play the reservation blues before it inevitably re-turns to Robert Johnson; the guitar cannot be bequeathed permanently. So when Jim Crow comes to Idaho, Spanbauer's purposeful ethnic confusion need not collapse into a bland soup of ethnic otherness—what Wu calls "a transcendent ethnic commonality" that is a pox in multiculturalist reading practices.[35] Instead, Jim Crow might come to Idaho to lend some sort of clarity, however manufactured, strained, or politically problematic it may be, to the multiethnic American West of the past—and present.

CHAPTER FIVE

JIM CROW FAULKNER
Suzan-Lori Parks Digs Up the Past, Again

So far I have concentrated on how literary writers return to the Jim Crow South to track what remains of him in the contemporary moment, in other locations, and in post–civil rights political and philosophical debates. What about interventions into literary history itself? The neo–slave narrative is a good orienting point because it is very concerned with literary history. We can see this in direct intertextual revisions, such as Ishmael Reed's sendup of *Uncle Tom's Cabin* (1853) in *Flight to Canada* (1976) or Alice Randall's similar take on *Gone with the Wind* (1939) in *The Wind Done Gone* (2002). This approach is also evident in the neo–slave narrative's origins as a literary rebuke of white writer William Styron's right to tell a story in the first person about Nat Turner and his slave rebellion. Neo–segregation narratives tend to be less inclined toward overt intertextuality, though they still also engage literary history and rebuke texts that harbor Jim Crow sensibilities. For instance, in George Wolfe's play *The Colored Museum* (1985) viewers board a plane to ride back in time to visit exhibits filled with iconic props and stereotypes from various eras of black history. One such exhibit, "The Last-Mama-on-the-Couch Play," is a takeoff on the pervasive mammy trope up through Lorraine Hansberry's *A Raisin in the Sun* (1959) and Ntozake Shange's *For Colored Girls Who Have Considered Suicide / When the Rainbow Is Enuf* (1975). Another good example, this time from popular culture, is the delightful and enduring industry of signifying on *Black Like Me*, that earnest 1961 experiment in crossing the color line. Examples include Eddie Murphy's white-faced sketches for *Saturday Night Live* in the early 1980s, scholar-activist Tim Wise's *White Like Me: Reflections on Race from a Privileged Son* (2004), and David Ehrenstein's 2008 lampoon of Barack Obama's presidential campaign in his *LA Weekly* article "Off-White Like Me."

The best example of a neo–segregation narrative consciously engaging literary history, especially its upper echelons, is *Getting Mother's Body* (2003), the Pulitzer Prize–winning first novel by experimental playwright Suzan-Lori Parks.[1] For a raucous, irreverent story of Jim Crow segregation and small town dreams, Parks reinvents *As I Lay Dying* (1930), William Faulkner's modernist story about the Bundrens, a poor white family in the rural South on a long, hot journey to bury their matriarch. For her reinvention, Parks offers instead the Beedes, a poor black family in 1960s rural Texas on a long, hot journey to *un*bury their matriarch. The Beedes head west to LaJunta, Arizona, in search of treasure: a diamond ring and pearl necklace that may—or may not!—have been buried with Willa Mae, whose makeshift grave will be plowed up for a supermarket parking lot. Faulknerian access to interior monologues reveals the logic, concerns, and ambitions of each character as they race to exhume Willa Mae in time. What is the significance of revising Faulkner in 2003 for a story about African American experience around the official end of de jure segregation and signal civil rights successes in the 1960s?

For Parks, it is partly a question of what literary model best captures dynamic history. In a 1996 interview, Parks ruminates, "Faulkner has this great thing: he talks about what is and was, or was and is. History is not 'was,' history 'is.' It's present, so if you believe that history is in the present, you can also believe that the present is in the past."[2] By using Faulkner for a contemporary novel about 1960s segregation, Parks gets at how Jim Crow "is," not "was." She thus joins African American traditions that turn to literature, not just legislative reform, to reclaim and signify on an American history with the lives of black people at the center, what John Ernest might describe as "liberating historiography." She revisits not only a modernist classic but also the hallowed ground of civil rights, including the famed 1963 March on Washington for Jobs and Freedom. The novel thereby queries the legacy of civil rights and long-standing promises of black enfranchisement, which remain subjects of vigorous debate. By using a canonical white host text to narrate the lives of black subjects of Jim Crow, Parks raises questions of literary lineage, history's present, and the present's history. Cheryl Wall finds that black women writers tend to construct genealogies that focus on intimate relationships more than alienating encounters across the color line, which she juxtaposes to a black male writer tradition.[3] In this case, Parks taps Faulkner for an integrated American literary tradition that can attend to generational and familial conflicts within a particular black community living under Jim Crow segregation. In doing so, she crosses racial and literary lines to provide a narrative of the past focused on those for whom future legislative reform may fall short, and inclusive of those who may not appear in glossy civil rights coffee-table books.

While the novel takes place during Jim Crow's waning days, Parks's designs are also on the present. Writing from the twenty-first century, Parks returns to civil rights at a moment when many citizens and leaders yearn for—even promise—a break from the nation's past in a reputedly postracial era. Even more so than post–civil rights progress narratives, a postrace narrative has no place for Jim Crow in the present. Deak Nabers tracks in twentieth-century African American literature "a growing skepticism that legislation could meaningfully address America's persistent civil rights problems," prompting writers such as James Baldwin to craft "civil rights politics around the utility of the past rather than the instrumentality of the law."[4] Ultimately for Parks and many post–civil rights writers, the search for black equality and dignity requires that we traverse the nation, especially its rural edges and lower echelons, to tell stories about those largely left out of the spoils of legislative victories and marginalized by overly celebratory narratives of racial progress. This is not to say that Parks creates a divide between literary possibilities and political realities, which would replace one gauzy progress narrative with another. Rather, as her characters light out to get their mother's body, Parks tills the nation's ground to locate those who have been prematurely paved over in celebratory narratives of justice achieved, be they literary or political.

To make this argument, I first examine how Parks's segregation story exhibits post–civil rights ambivalence to integration ideals and exclusively legal versions of justice. Then I consider the ramifications of Faulkner as host text, drawing on adaptation theory to hone my sense of what Parks is doing with literary history. The final two sections suggest that Faulkner's model allows Parks to turn away from Washington and signal legislative gains to explore the legacy and persistence of Jim Crow well after his official death. Parks provides a model of how to narrate a *long civil rights movement* in order to expand a potentially narrow, constricting, and episodic national narrative of black freedom struggles in the twentieth century. The literary realm, Parks suggests from the outer rim of the segregated South, is where we can house the lives, frustrations, and dreams of those far removed from the nation's beltway. From this location, post–civil rights America can better decide who is finally buried for good: Jim Crow or the Beedes.

Contemporary Ambivalence to Civil Rights Integration

Parks sets her story on the eve of the March on Washington, but her characters don't accord much significance to that impending event. In a book that ostentatiously begins, "Where my panties at?" we first learn the year offhandedly.[5] Billy Beede's lover, Snipes (an echo of Faulkner's Snopes family), buys her off after a sleazy sexual encounter: "'What year is it?' Billy asks. 'Sixty-three. And here I got sixty-three dollars in my billfold,' he says smiling" (7). While Parks invites readers to think about 1960s segregation, Billy thinks she's in a romance novel. When that relationship sours, Billy's primary concern is obtaining enough money for an illegal abortion and seeking revenge on her philandering lover, never thinking of her quest as a political parable of black and women's liberation. For readers, though, Parks strews assorted references to signal 1960s political struggles in mundane chatter. Parks's playwriting talents are on full display in her signature dialogue and Faulknerian interior monologues. Unlike her post–civil rights readers, Parks's characters don't distinguish much between events on their porches or the National Mall, between Dill Smiles's latest pig litter and Jim Crow's latest shenanigans.

The novel exudes decided ambivalence toward integration ideals, legislative aims, and formal politics. Riding in Homer Beede Rochfoucault's fancy car bought by the local chapter of the NAACP, Uncle Teddy reports their conversation:

> "Professor Clarke says I could be a congressman or senator one day."
> Homer smiles and sits up straighter thinking of himself behind a big desk. Congressman or Senator Homer Beede Rochfoucault. Then he adds, "I would like to be placed in a position where I can do the most good for my constituents."
> "Your constituents," I says, repeating, and nodding my head. But I'm not sure what the word means. (150)

Parks playfully presents Homer as the clueless beneficiary of a cynical version of civil rights: middle-class uplift without deeper commitments to full citizenship rights and economic justice for all. Still, unlike Toni Morrison's Maureen Peal as civil rights foil, we are not supposed to think ill of Homer. Parks's characters endear even when—especially when—they are wrongheaded. Instead, like Uncle Teddy, we are unsure of the nature of "constituents" and self-elected civil rights leaders.

Parks's ambivalence about integration is especially evident when the Beedes visit their (seemingly) well-to-do relatives while neighbors observe through curtain slits, afraid the full impact of integration has hit their suburb. June notes the trimmed lawns, tidy houses, and peeping neighbors. "'What the hell was they looking at,' Billy says, not asking really cause she knows.

Two Negro women in a truck and a Negro man walked in the nice house where the Negroes live. 'They think we moving in,' I says and we both laugh" (131). These curious neighbors peeking suspiciously through curtains echo Hansberry's screenplay of *A Raisin in the Sun* (1959) when the Youngers first arrive in Clybourne Park, only now black bourgeoisie have joined middle-class whites behind shadowy curtains. And Billy Beede is not nearly as charming as Beneatha. June's laughter is closely akin to "that incongruous juxtaposition of mirth and quaking" (613) that Ralph Ellison identified as a core Jim Crow survival strategy, versus the fatal alternative illustrated by Wesley Brown's character of Jubilee.

Armed with such ambivalence and incongruous laughter, Parks addresses civil rights without directly engaging specific legal struggles. Nabers suggests that literature shifts us from "evaluations of the practical limits of particular civil rights measures like the 1964 Civil Rights Act and the 1965 Voting Rights Acts into assessments of the theoretical limits of the law." Nabers worries, though, that obsession with the past may perpetuate rather than resolve problems, arguing instead that "amnesia might be precisely what we need."[6] However, since the past is a central concern for Parks and contemporary African American literature, amnesia offers an unlikely resolution.[7] Parks provides a more viable approach: looking at the past peripherally. While contemporary readers stand on the other side of the demise of compulsory race segregation, Parks's characters remain ambivalent about integration and its relevance to their daily lives. For instance, uncannily skewering ideas of post–civil rights progress, Uncle Teddy meditates on Billy's fate:

> "It ain't safe out there for a Negro gal. It's 1963 and a Negro life is cheap.
> The life of a Negro man is cheap. The life of a Negro woman is cheaper. The
> price of everything is always going up though, so could be that the price of a
> Negro life too will get high. Maybe the price'll rise to reach the value of the
> cost we brought in slavery times. Not this year though. Not the next. Maybe
> by nineteen hundred and seventy. Maybe by nineteen hundred and eighty
> or nineteen hundred and ninety the price will go up. Maybe by the year two
> thousand, but surely, the world will end by then." (124)

In this deeply serious meditation on the value of black lives, Parks cynically boils everything down to dollars in a human price index tracking inflation since the era of the auction block. The diurnal scope of historiographic fiction renders Uncle Teddy prescient. That is, while *he* cannot imagine the year

2000, Parks's readers are *living* it. Uncle Teddy's apocalyptic cynicism—the world will end before African Americans are fully valued—resonates for readers living four decades after the March on Washington when racial economies still undervalue black life.

Parks eschews overly celebratory narratives of civil rights, going so far as to generate sardonic humor from the movement's greatest icon: Martin Luther King, Jr. While in jail after a dubious traffic stop, Homer relays his encounter with a white sheriff:

> "You look like Martin Luther Coon," he says.
> "My name is Homer Rochfoucault."
> "I wish to God you was Luther Coon. That'd be a good-looking feather in my cap." (167)

Instead of canonizing King, Parks swaps him out for well-meaning but clueless Homer, who is less knowledgeable about black politics than even the stock caricature of the racist sheriff. This irreverent take on a King figure is far removed from the more hagiographic literary portraits of key civil rights figures, such as in Rita Dove's *On the Bus with Rosa Parks* (2000). Through her postmodern experimentation, language play, repetition, and nonlinear meditations on history's present, Parks is well known for incorporating and riffing on historical icons, especially Abraham Lincoln in *The America Play* (1993) and the Venus Hottentot in *Venus* (1996). In Homer's exchange with the white sheriff, Parks switches the script of Jim Crow and civil rights by referencing icons such as King, which simultaneously raises readers' expectations and deflates the icon. Then she quickly diverts our contemporary attention toward daily survival in Jim Crow Texas.

Parks has a reputation for excavating American history, especially through tropes of holes, to find what is buried in America's earth, in this case Willa Mae's grave.[8] Elizabeth Brown-Guillory explains, "Crucial to understanding Parks's plays is the recognition that she concerns herself with reconfiguring American history to include the lives and accomplishments of Black people."[9] In *Getting Mother's Body*, King and various civil rights icons are important reference points, but they aren't terribly riveting and they don't propel the story forward. The most interesting characters are more concerned with Willa Mae's treasure than civil disobedience or federal legislation. In turning toward Faulkner and LaJunta, not King and Washington, we come to appreciate how Jim Crow segregation can be both "was" and "is." Like Willa Mae, Jim Crow delivers a siren song from the grave, dead but not gone.

Faulkner Reinvented

Parks's characters are fascinating windows onto a cultural moment, both then and now. They live up to their Faulknerian forebears, the Bundrens. Parks connects Faulkner's modernist affinity for literary experimentation with a postmodern sense of history as narrative. Parks typically references Faulkner's influence alongside such African American writers as Zora Neale Hurston, Alice Walker, and especially Baldwin, under whom she studied briefly at Mount Holyoke College. Most initial reviews noted the Faulkner connection, calling the novel a "twist on Faulkner," "a cheerful tack across deep Faulknerian waters," or simply an "African American rewrite" of Faulkner; Parks herself describes the novel as a "deep and reverent bow" to Faulkner.[10] The Faulkner connection pushes against more identity-based traditions and markets that might place Parks primarily among black women writers, especially Hurston and Walker, in their shared gifts for spinning a yarn and capturing the cadences of complex rural characters. This may explain why the original dust jacket flags Hurston and Walker as influences, while Faulkner goes unmentioned until the paperback. Faulkner's notoriously questionable racial politics further throws off set ideas about literary and historical kinship in a post–civil rights era. Nevertheless, the use of Faulkner is largely celebrated, though a few critics are less than glowing, including one reviewer who decried Parks's "dumbed-down narration" that unsuccessfully captures the West Texas landscape and feeling.[11]

Faulkner offers Parks not only an aesthetic form but also a model for analyzing race in America while keeping expectations askew about civil rights and the history of race relations. Faulkner's use of the southern gothic to represent tense, ambivalent, and fraught relations between black and white citizens of Jim Crow is well studied, especially in *Light in August*, *The Sound and the Fury*, and *Sanctuary*.[12] That said, Judith Wittenberg notes the dearth of African American characters in Faulkner's work, "but that absence only emphasizes the text's predominant concern with race as a linguistic and social construct rather than a biological given, its focus more on the concept of race than on actual race relations."[13] In her proposal for a new direction for critical race studies, Sharon Holland contemplates the intimacy of quotidian racism and argues, "For Faulkner, the touch 'abrogates'—it nullifies our stubborn insistence upon separation, between races, sexes, or nations, if you will. After all, in Faulkner's modernism, black and white bodies do not always occupy separate spheres. What is at stake here is not presence at all, but the idea of it; the knowledge, no matter how circumscribed—that 'presence' is only . . . half the story."[14] In this way, Faulkner stands as a particularly rich resource to get at how race is present, but also isn't. Parks can suggest that segregation lives on after we bury Jim Crow, even if we can't point to—touch, Holland might say—official race segregation in a post–civil rights era. Still, regarding Faulkner's own race politics, many cite his infamous caution on desegregation, to which Baldwin responded, "But the time Faulkner asks for does not exist—and he is not the only Southerner who knows it. There is never time in the future in which we will work out our salvation. The challenge is in the moment, the time is always now."[15] With a Jim Crow Faulkner, Parks can talk about the now, then, and future of Jim Crow segregation all at once.

Though critical race studies now pervade Faulkner criticism, *As I Lay Dying* remains largely absent from these conversations. Scholars position the intellectually challenged Bundrens as figures of the poor white South by way of rural Yoknapatawpha County, but we haven't yet fully examined the novel's Jim Crow politics.[16] Faulkner doesn't employ the deliberate racial crossings so crucial to many of his other works that are more readily identifiable as segregation narratives. Instead, the novel focuses on the Bundrens' quest to bury Addie, the recently expired and unembalmed matriarch, near her family home in Jefferson County. After eight days of trials under a blazing July sun, we come to know the interior workings (or shortcomings) of each Bundren, but not necessarily cross-racial relations.

Parks turns to Faulkner's novel not only because it finds intricate interiority in surprising places but also because that model allows her to talk about race marginally. For instance, Uncle Teddy thinks, "A car comes up, out-of-towners. White. I give them two dollars worth of gas" (23). Parks approaches this commonplace Jim Crow moment through Faulknerian interiority: we access Roosevelt's mind, not the white patron's, and his thoughts are as mundane as the interaction. Race is omnipresent, but not the core plot. For Uncle Teddy, race is a noun worthy of its own sentence, devoid of adjective, action, or explicit causal relation to anything around it. "White" is a stand-alone signifier not unlike the strange coffin image or Vardaman's fish in Faulkner's novel. All that Uncle Teddy knows about the world is distilled in that one-word sentence. So too, readers can project all they know about Jim Crow and civil rights onto this routine, unremarkable interaction. With Faulkner, Parks addresses race as an experience, a signifier, and a worldview, but without having to tell yet another story about race.

Faulkner's seminal role triggers sharply divergent views of Parks's representation of race and segregation. Many initial critics applaud Parks's "unflinching look at race relations," yet Don Graham detects quite the opposite: "Set in the civil-rights summer of 1963, *Getting Mother's Body* is not overtly-political in nature. Parks, who is black, soft-pedals issues of race in favor of the interior motivations and emotions of her characters."[17] For Graham, Parks's racial identity and her modernist literary sensibilities are incommensurate with justice and race politics. A *Chicago Sun-Times* review notes, "And though Parks offers indicators of what's happening in the broader world around the Beedes, she stays focused on the people, not the times." Parks responds, "We're always taught the only thing that is interesting about black people in literature and film or onstage is when they're dealing with white people. . . . Well, what happens with this family is they do come into contact with white people and they do have to think about the fact that the price of a Negro girl's life is cheap and if she were to travel alone it would be dangerous. But they only think about that when they have to think about it."[18] Channeling Uncle Teddy nearly word for word, Parks underscores how race is both unavoidable and at the same time not the point.

While race is omnipresent and unremarkable in *Getting Mother's Body*, the same is true in crucial moments in Faulkner's novel. To borrow from Toni Morrison's *Playing in the Dark: Whiteness and the Literary Imagination*, blackness haunts the Bundrens' descent into abjection.[19] "The ways in which artists—and the society that bred them—transferred internal conflicts to a 'blank darkness,' to conveniently bound and violently silenced black bodies," Morrison famously argues, "is a major theme in American literature."[20] Such an Africanist presence materializes in two key moments in *As I Lay Dying*. When Darl sets fire to Gillespie's barn, Jewel's back is burned horribly and turns black as he rescues his mother's coffin. Then, when Cash breaks his leg during the barely successful crossing of a flooded river, Anse administers palliative care by encasing Cash's leg in concrete and setting him atop Addie in the glaring southern sun. Despite Cash's contention that "I never noticed it getting hot," the leg boils and chars.[21] Thus the Bundrens slowly, incrementally turn black. Vardaman comments, "'Your back looks like a nigger's Jewel' I said. Cash's foot and leg look like a nigger's. Then they broke it off. Cash's leg bled" (224). These charred bits of rural white bodies uncannily become their own Africanist presence, signaling how the Bundrens' whiteness and its privileges are in jeopardy as they approach the city. That is why Jessica Baldanzi and Kyle Schlabach suggest that the Bundrens' slowly blackening bodies are "a breach of the heavily policed borders that maintain hierarchies of race and class."[22] The pedestrian racism of Vardaman's comparisons further underscores racial caste systems, and therefore the pitiable horror of the Bundrens' quest.

These sites of pain and comparisons to black bodies are strange—even for the Bundrens. The two novels share tropes of broken bodies and dying, but Faulkner's novel divorces blackness from African American history and experience. In fact, Faulkner's black bodies are white. Thus Faulkner places the category of race *in the minds of his characters*, which reminds us that Faulkner's racial politics are as undecidable as Joe Christmas's racial identity. Perhaps with the Beedes, Parks completes the Bundrens' blackening process and brings out Jim Crow politics from the shadows of Faulkner's world, while retaining the host text's sideways approach to race. It follows that Parks places astounding insights about race in characters perceived as obtuse, especially Laz, Parks's own Faulknerian idiot-philosopher in line with Darl. Laz says in a non sequitur to Billy, "'There's more Negro in the world than there is white,' I go but she ain't listening" (15). Laz's comments evoke Marcus Garvey, the Nation of Islam, and Black Power, but Parks does not signal them as such, focusing instead on daily lives rather than grand political ideologies.

Having speculated that Faulkner's model allows Parks to approach race peripherally, I should also note *how* Parks uses her host text. Recognizable events, names, jokes, traits, and objects from *As I Lay Dying* and Faulkner's other work pervade Parks's novel, but not in direct one-to-one relationships. For instance, Parks lends Cash's carpentry skills to Snopes, the cartoonish coffin salesman, and Cash's logic to Laz's financial sophistication. It is as if Parks reshuffles Faulkner's deck, delighting in new combinations as she deals out Faulkner's cards to the various players in her story. For example, Dill Smiles, Willa Mae's lesbian lover who passes—sort of—as a man, evokes

Faulkner's endlessly ambiguous characters such as Joe Christmas. Laz says, "Dill is more of a man than I am. She's had Willa Mae and she's had herself. That's two women more than I've had" (155). This running joke culminates in a one-line chapter that echoes Vardaman's famous line, "My mother is a fish" (84). At a roadside rest stop, Laz remarks, "She pees standing up" (192). As a woman who pees like a man, serves as Billy's surrogate father, and gets called "Miss He-She-It" by June, Laz finds Dill not grotesque, but a heroic model for his own clumsy heterosexuality- and masculinity-in-training in the Jim Crow South.

As Parks brings Faulkner across the color line and out West, she finds lost voices, unmet dreams, and broken bodies not only in Faulkner's world but also in Jim Crow history. Instead of Cash's blackened leg, for instance, Parks offers June, who's been short of one leg for quite awhile before the story even starts. June reports, "When I was sixteen I lost my leg. I'd like a new leg, but even if we could get the money together for it, I ain't yet seen one in my color" (19). Parks surgically removes a figure of blackness from Faulkner's world (Cash's encased leg) and uses that absence to signal Jim Crow's presence and the difficulty of restoring June's broken body. Further, Parks rescues female stories in particular from Faulkner's sidelines. Whereas Dewey Dell's thwarted quest for an abortion remains unresolved in Faulkner's novel, Billy and her pregnancy are central, as is Billy's relationship to her mother. Indeed, while Faulkner devotes one chapter to a dead woman talking (Addie's strange, beautiful, and revealing monologue), Willa Mae speaks throughout. Actually, she mostly sings the blues, further integrating Faulkner's model into vital black cultural traditions.

It is ultimately most accurate to call Parks's use of Faulkner an adaptation, more so than a revision or resignification, which signals how neo–segregation narratives in general reinvent more than revise segregation narratives and Jim Crow scripts. Linda Hutcheon draws on Darwinian evolutionary concepts to explain that adaptations are symbiotic relationships that create richness via "intertextual echoing," but the adaptation must adjust to its new surroundings.[23] For Parks, this requires adapting Faulkner's environment to make room for the Beedes. For her readers, this requires adapting national narratives so that folks like the Beedes may survive, if not thrive. As neo–segregation narratives demonstrate, this is not only a legislative project but also an imaginative one.

The March Away from Washington

If Faulkner's model allows Parks to address race and Jim Crow peripherally, this shapes her use of civil rights historical landmarks. We learn about the March on Washington largely through barber and beauty shop gossip. Dill relays Little Walter's conversation with the local pastor while steaming his face in the communal setting: "'You oughta go to Warshington with us, Pastor Peoples,' he says. Next month there's supposed to be an organizing of some kind up there. Negroes and other civil rights folks will march around Washington and demand justice from President Kennedy. A few folks from here is going. Last time I heard Peoples talk about it he was sitting on the fence" (87). Lincoln's citizens express interest in the event, but without specific legislative plans for strategic federal appeals to support the rights and dignity of African Americans. The townsfolk are well acquainted with civil rights activities, but that is just one aspect of their complex lives in a sleepy one-gas-station town—and certainly not the most important one if the local pastor himself is ambivalent about coming along for the ride. Readers thus view the march with the pastor: in a reclined pose, unhurried and interested more in the talk around the community than the Washington beltway.

The women are excited about the march too, especially its place in Lincoln's social calendar. While relaxing a townswoman's hair, Mrs. Ruthie Montgomery chimes in: "'You all gonna make history' I says. I wish I was going but I don't got no car and Addie and Walter ain't invited me to ride with them" (93). Though she sees the march as another social outing, her remark cues John Reilly's ideas about African American literature's "history-making" ability, as well as Parks's own well-known willingness to make up history in her plays.[24] For Mrs. Ruthie Montgomery, the way to "make history" is to go along for the ride. Her internal worries about exclusion are more attuned to small-town social orders than political demands for first-class citizenship. If Parks begs the question of the march's role in the lives of black people, Lincoln's barber and beauty shops answer with a pleasant, not-so-political, curiosity. Debates about beltway legal reform, civic inclusion, and community organizing pepper the pedestrian chatter of these Hurston-esque townsfolk, but grand civil rights debates are secondary to daily life.

The march's location becomes an issue, but not regarding federal jurisprudence. Rather, the issue is climate and its effect on hair:

"Warshington, D.C., got all that humidity," Addie says.

"They shoulda took that into account when they planned the march," I [Mrs. Ruthie Montgomery] says. "Seems to me, when they planned that March, they shoulda thought about how all that water was gonna be hanging in the air."

"They was thinking about marching to the Capitol," Addie says. "The Capitol's in Warshington."

"Then, when they thought about where they was putting the Capitol, they shoulda thought about the weather too," I says. (93)

Hair is often a trope for racial pride (or its lack) in segregation-minded literature, from Geraldine's postures of racial uplift and related terror of moisture in Morrison's *The Bluest Eye* to Beneatha's decision to go "natural" as an act of racial pride in Hansberry's unexpurgated *A Raisin in the Sun*. In Parks's novel, concerns about humidity and black women's hair is much more subtle, like de facto racial segregation. The scene's humor cuts to the quick of civil rights goals because while Mrs. Ruthie Montgomery assumes that Washington's power brokers share her experiences and concerns, Parks suggests that exclusion is built into the national capital's geography itself. Parks thus delivers a sidelong, yet devastating critique of Washington's near-inherent exclusion of African Americans from locations and practices of representative democracy. For Parks, perhaps a town called LaJunta—literally, a group seizing power after a revolution—is a more honest setting for U.S. democracy than a march in Washington. This may be especially true for black women living under Jim Crow segregation, poverty, and a male-dominated social order. In this story peppered with the voice of a mother who died giving herself a coat hanger abortion, her five-months pregnant daughter need not suffer the same fate. Instead, Billy's path to voice—literary or political—leads not to Washington but Willa Mae's grave.

Parks's rather nonchalant treatment of the march contrasts starkly with its heady ambitions and ensuing grandeur in the historical record. The march brought nearly one quarter million people to the capital, which many cite while ticking off key civil rights successes. Ten years after the march, *The Crisis* convened key organizers of the event and opined, "What, one may ask, became of the euphoria, the harmony, the sense of common cause, the embryonic budding of hope for universal human brotherhood which emerged from the historical March on Washington for Jobs and Justice ten years ago on August 28,

1963?"[25] In a critique uncannily reminiscent of Houston Baker's accusations of betrayal in 2008, Bayard Rustin, one of the march's key architects, confronted the emerging split between integration and self-determination in black leadership and eulogized the march's more elusive goals: widespread economic justice accompanying a moral commitment to black humanity. He explains, "This general agreement over basic goals no longer exists: some have dropped from the struggle, embraced marginal, non-economic issues, or advocated programs which, while they may touch on economic change, are too narrow to reach the great mass of black working people."[26] This critique is particularly poignant since Rustin removed himself from the spotlight fearing his homosexuality, his Communist Party affiliations, and a questionable police surveillance record would threaten the movement's goals.[27] Like King and unlike Rustin, the march has attained iconic status following ensuing civil rights successes. Photographs from the march adorn glossy pages of civil rights commemorative books and retrospective exhibits while King's remarks from that day (the "I Have a Dream" speech) pervade public school curricula and mainstream historical memory. But such progress narratives may confirm Rustin's concern that black working people have been left behind. Parks goes back to Jim Crow to march with the Beedes of the world.

As the Beedes march (well, drive) away from Washington, they remain very cognizant of segregation, both de facto and de jure. At a gas station diner halfway to LaJunta, Billy encounters a benevolent messenger of segregation: the owner's lonely wife. Billy recounts, "The gal pipes up quick, 'Rude don't serve—well, you know, you'd best be getting food someplace else'" (187). Billy knows the subject of the conversation is segregation. The gal knows it too. But Parks leaves the matter unspoken, highlighted by silence. With the quick "piped up" delivery, the use of the em dash to reroute the conversation, and the "you know," Parks ropes her readers into segregation systems without their consent. Amid these unspoken signs of Jim Crow, Billy also encounters a literal sign of Jim Crow at the restrooms: "They got one for ladies and one for gentlemen with a 'Whites Only' sign that's been crossed out, rewrote, and crossed out again" (188). In the middle of nowhere, Parks incorporates a small desegregation struggle between the gal and her husband Rude, a poor white couple far removed from Washington politics and the black community. Signs of segregation struggles past and present hang along the route to LaJunta, but Parks moves along swiftly, barely giving readers time to pause before the next comical escapade.

The bathroom sign directly references Jim Crow, but it is exceptional.

So, we must do as the characters: think about segregation without thinking about it. Uncle Teddy shows us how. He contemplates death and admits, "My parents are buried in the colored section of the Butler County cemetery and my mind had planned, secretly, without me actually thinking about it, to lay Willa Mae alongside them" (47). If we enter the novel like Uncle Teddy, our mind settles on civil rights and Jim Crow secretly, using our own embedded knowledge. As we travel with the Beedes to dig up Willa Mae, we lay her alongside the key successes of civil rights in the cemetery of American history. Parks incorporates casual and often unspoken references to Jim Crow's past without an overall plan for a postsegregation nation. Rather, for instance, Mrs. Faith Jackson rationalizes her decision to indulge Billy and give her a wedding dress for a song: "Seeing as how the Funeral Home is doing so well, and folks is always continuing to die, and Jackson's is the most respected Home, black or white, in the county" (33). For Mrs. Faith Jackson, death and segregation are historical constants. They buttress just enough faith in her husband's business so that she can play a bit part in the soap opera life of Billy and her five-months-gone belly.

Though Uncle Teddy's mind may think about segregation without thinking about it, white characters can't help but think about King, civil rights, and federal power. This is especially true for Officer Masterson, a somewhat dim-witted, thoroughly racist executor of Jim Crow justice. His moniker flags his inheritance of white power. He reports, "I just pulled over a late-model red Mercury convertible going over eighty miles an hour. It's got two Negroes in it. I can hear the people up in New York and Chicago and Washington and Hollywood. I can hear them all talking. Calling me a white supremacist cause I done pulled over two speeding Negroes in what looks like a brand-new car" (162). In his internal monologue, Masterson strikes a defensive pose toward unspoken antisegregation arguments and civil rights rhetoric.

Strangely, Parks positions Officer Masterson as a benevolent, if underinformed, proponent of procedural rights. He ponders, "I tell Shirley back at the station what I caught and she checks through the postings but there ain't no one looking for what I got. . . . I could let them go. Give them a ticket for going too fast and let them go. I pride myself in being fair. I could jest let them on their way with a speeding ticket. But Sheriff wouldn't never let me hear the end of it" (163). Officer Masterson takes pride "in being fair" in his racist fishing expedition. Thus Parks pushes readers toward uncomfortable sympathy for his complicity in the economy of white racism. Lest we too quickly dismiss his bovine self-reflections on race relations, Parks contrasts

Officer Masterson with a cardboard cutout racist in the sheriff, who never gets the luxury of Faulknerian interiority. We learn about his pretty peculiar federal solutions to the race problem: "Sheriff says all niggers should be named Joe Washington. Says we oughta pass a law to make it so. Negroes and Negras both. All Joe Washington" (163). Parks embeds a key irony in this caricature: due to his inability to distinguish between black bodies, the sheriff cedes federal government—all of Washington—to African Americans. "Joe Washington" becomes a generic category not unlike the formal federal citizenship conferred at the national level, even while the sheriff withholds local due process.

As Parks brings Faulkner and Washington-based desegregation concerns to the outer edges of the Jim Crow South, she also ventures beyond a black-and-white Jim Crow world. For instance, at his roadside diner, Uncle Blood Beede describes his two guards: "A man named Joseph and another man, not his brother, who also goes by Joseph. They look Mexican but they say they are Indian. First Joseph says he is Comanche, second Joseph says he is Seminole. The two men, while not claiming to be related, look a lot alike" (195). Uncle Blood, not too unlike Officer Masterson and in line with Jim Crow's Manichean sensibilities, fails to distinguish between the two Josephs even though they hail from very different tribal communities. Readers chuckle at Uncle Blood's imprecision, though its kinship to the racist sheriff is unmistakable. Another good example is when Teddy and June leave the filling station they manage (for a white man) under the command of a Mexican family named Gonzales, who in turn embrace the opportunity.

What must the Beedes' treasure hunt look like to the Josephs and the Gonzales family? Will Willa Mae's jewels, or the March on Washington, do anything for them? Parks raises such questions without fully answering them. Still, she speaks to contemporary multicultural sensibilities since Southwest Texas is both a particularly tenacious area of Jim Crow and decidedly multiracial. Blake Allmendinger notes that Parks chooses "a region that is particularly volatile" and argues that her characters "embark on a more violent and hazardous quest" than the rather peaceful march.[28] In his study of interethnic politics in Austin during Jim Crow, Jason McDonald traces divergent political strategies and finds that African American leaders tended to adopt universalist goals of inclusion, which are akin to civil rights goals, whereas ethnic Mexican leaders preferred strategies of securing rights more attuned to cultural differences.[29]

The perceived simplicity of Jim Crow segregation in the post–civil rights imagination, juxtaposed to the ethnically diverse background along the Beedes' route, holds the promise of speaking to a multicultural present. The abortion-providing white Dr. Parker fancies himself progressive because he crosses multiple lines of segregation: "Throughout the day, my patients come in. Mexicans mostly, coming here for vaccines and stitches. I'm the only doctor around who gives them service. I got three rows of books in my office full of their names. They pay me when they can and I'm pretty much well-liked because I treat them like people and I speak some Spanish" (75). Though he lives outside the law by administering abortions, Dr. Parker is unique in articulating something like the humanism associated with King's dream. However, he does so by allying himself in the most anemic and paternalistic way with characters on the other side of a multiethnic Jim Crow line.

By tempering her narrative with instances of brown-black segregation, Parks eschews the black/white world of Jim Crow and insists on the messiness of multicultural America, a messiness Jim Crow systems sought to contain. In her study of segregation signage, Elizabeth Abel finds, "The further the verbal content [of segregation signs] strayed beyond the standard discursive boundaries, the more essential was the legitimating frame, which was especially salient in border states where segregation signs interpolated immigrant populations into the racial framework of Jim Crow."[30] While Jim Crow's power to contain falters at the South's outer edges and multicultural locations, Parks's novel thrives there. She thereby reframes Jim Crow for post–civil rights America. Parks famously contends, "The Klan does not have to be outside the door for black people to have lives worthy of dramatic literature.... And what happens when we choose a concern other than race to focus on? ... Let's do the math: ... BLACK PEOPLE + x = NEW DRAMATIC CONFLICT (NEW TERRITORY)."[31] By skirting the South's heartland and turning away from Washington for a treasure hunt, Parks brings not only Faulkner but also civil rights racial narratives into "new territory" to speak to a more full register of Jim Crow's citizens and their descendants.

Parks's Post–Jim Crow Ring Trick

While Parks's characters are rather unconcerned about the goings-on in Washington and questions of race are peripheral, overt references to Jim Crow are sprinkled throughout, just not in overt postures of protest. As Billy boards a bus, she reports, "'I don't want no Freedom Riders now,' the Driver says, looking past Uncle Teddy to get a better look at me. . . . 'You best sit towards the back,' Uncle Teddy whispers to me" (56). Uncle Teddy passes along survival strategies (what Richard Wright calls the "ethics of living Jim Crow"), but this moment of generational education is brief. Parks cues contemporary readers to Jim Crow's omnipresence while her characters navigate the terrain matter-of-factly, neither obeisant nor outraged. Like Dill's status as a lesbian passing for a man, Jim Crow is strangely unremarkable. When Precious Blood Beede proudly tells of passing as white under the nose of the local Ku Klux Klan, Billy focuses more on her ring and enlists her in one of Willa Mae's old cons (the Beedes need cash since the sheriff took all their money). In an elaborate ploy called "the ring trick," Billy passes as a rich white woman and swindles a filling station attendant into buying Precious's cheap ring at a big price. Billy could raise her hand in protest of white supremacism, but she's got other things to do.

Parks's characters are acutely aware of the rules of Jim Crow, but they also know how to manipulate them. On finding her truck missing, Dill soliloquizes, "White boys stole my truck. Oh, they ain't gonna get away with this. I'll tell everybody I know. I'll wake up Joe North to get him to take me to Midland and we gonna tell the police. No. The white police ain't gonna do nothing about [it]" (139). Dill acknowledges the limits of Jim Crow law, but she rejects helplessness in the face of white privilege and black second-class citizenship. She ventriloquizes the imagined "white boys": "*Oh, but you shoulda seen what that nigger-lezzy used to sleep with. A white gal. Hells no. The lezzy didn't have no white gal. Sho . . . Well she weren't. If she was white, the bulldagger woulda been hanging from every tree you can see. I never lynched no bulldagger. I ain't neither but I bet it's all right*" (139–40). Dill is *keenly* aware of the danger she faces as a masculine lesbian courting a very light-skinned, beautiful African American woman in the South, an iconic figure of racial and sexual anxiety.[32] Dill also understands the mundane ease with which white citizens of Jim Crow would contemplate lynching someone like her to reinforce their masculinity and white power. Nonetheless, in the minds of the Beedes, Dill roils Jim Crow's highly enforced sexual and racial rules. Homer thinks, "When we were pulled over by that Deputy I was scared. I could see that white man taking my car and lynching me and Uncle Teddy just for sport. When he didn't do any of that, I saw the fingerprints and that picture he took of me as things that would be a bad mark on my career. The white man was doing what he could to keep me down. But Dill tops that white man" (229). In this conspicuously inaccurate reading of social power, Dill "tops" an officer of the law and upsets the social order that lynching practices enforce. In the double meaning of "top" as both hierarchical location and sexual act, Dill repeatedly becomes the unlikely central hero of Parks's irreverent take on the March on Washington, contrary to Bayard Rustin's removed role in the historical record.

Dill even tills the Jim Crow landscape for possible benefits. This leads to a very strange moment in an already curious novel: her soliloquy for lynching and vigilante justice. After shrewd analysis of her status in the white imagination, Dill realizes, "It's Billy Beede stole my truck. Good, cause I'ma kill her for it and the law will not severely punish a colored when a colored woman get kilt" (140–41). With supreme double-consciousness, Dill works *within* Jim Crow justice for her own designs. She acknowledges the lack of value accorded to someone like her—and she exploits it. In doing so, Parks raises questions for contemporary readers about the depth and persistence of inequality after civil rights: Would a "nigger-lezzy" like Dill have a fair shot at justice today, or would her thought experiment still hold water? Further messing with ideas about Jim Crow justice, Parks stages a reverse lynching of Officer Masterson: "'We don't got no colored ho-tel in Tryler,' the policeman says. 'We fine right here,' Billy says. Her voice has a thick strangling sound that loops around the voice of the policeman, his voice trying to be kind, and the sandwiches in his hand, strangling the kindness out of them both" (171–72). Like Faulkner swapping Cash's leg and Jewel's back for black bodies, Parks positions the unwitting cop, armed with good intentions, as metaphorical lynchee. Are we supposed to sympathize with Officer Masterson in this strange reverse lynching? No, but just as Homer places Dill as "top" in the lynching hierarchy, Parks deliberately messes with well-established scripts of racialized violence to instill an off-kilter sense of social order. This way, folks like the Beedes can finally find themselves at the center of a story that values them and their dreams.

By turning away from Washington and heading west to LaJunta, Parks's characters seek deliverance not necessarily steeped in legislative reform and collective organizing. Yet Parks's readers keep the beltway, the movement, and its victories in view. Parks returns to the segregation era by way of literary history and a white modernist host text to reconsider desegregation ideals and cherished civil rights successes. Parks's Jim Crow Faulkner embraces whole hog those sometimes overlooked by celebratory portraits of civil rights struggles, such as we tend to find in contemporary memoirs. I am thinking, for instance, of Carroll Parrott Blue's *The Dawn at My Back* (2003), a memoir about growing up in a middle-class home in Texas with civil rights activist parents to overcome adversity, both political and internalized. Novelistic reimaginings of Jim Crow for a multicultural present, on the other hand, are closer kin to neo–slave narratives. However, whereas Rushdy positions the neo–slave tradition as primarily concerned with Black Power and failures of the New Left, Parks's novel focuses on the more mainstream civil rights movement—especially its belief in legislative politics and national iden-tity—as a way of probing the limits of Black Power and integration to fully enfranchise all African Americans. Parks reclaims the past—political and literary, rural and beltway—so that Mrs. Ruthie Montgomery's assumption about her own centrality to the nation can prove true. In fact, Dill eventually becomes a founding father of sorts, inhabiting the spot left vacant by the Bayard Rustins of history. Near the end of the novel, Willa Mae posthu-mously recalls meeting Old Daddy, who recites the names of his sixteen children: "They named them after presidents and philanthropists, you know, rich folks that like to give money away, and they named them after words they liked saying . . . Washington, Jefferson, Adams, Pierce, Quincy-Adams, Buchanan, Liberty, Freedom, Prosperity, Lincoln, Johnson, Grant, Rocke-feller, Carnegie, Justice, Fortune" (246). With Willa Mae in America's blood-line, Dill as father figure, and Faulkner's model as surrogate, Billy inherits an American (literary) history that may, in its own way, live up to civil rights ideals and national promises in unlikely locations.

Even though the novel remains deeply skeptical of the historical record of civil rights, Parks delivers a strangely happy and abrupt ending, complete with marriage plot. The hidden jewel in Willa Mae's dress seems to finance each character's dream: June's new leg, Uncle Teddy's new church, Dill's new pig litter. But Laz provides the ultimate happy ending when, during his nuptials with Billy, he reveals that he secretly retained Willa Mae's jewel for a wedding ring. The happy ending stands as Parks's own narrative "ring trick": she swaps celebratory stories of the March on Washington with a story about the importance of digging up our past, including hard-living mothers, unwanted babies and relatives, ill-gotten gains, and the daily in-sults and victories of life under Jim Crow. In 1963 King came to the capital to redeem the nation's promissory note of equality in the Declaration of Independence. If America offers an authoritative story of freedom, King counseled, then that story is a political tool. Parks suggests that we need not cash in the past for future gains. Rather, we have the right to demand happy endings—and keep our mothers' rings to boot. Many note that contemporary national conversations about race rarely feature the working class, and certainly not folks like the Beedes. In the introduction I noted that Houston Baker contends, "There is today a monumental divide between black intellectuals and the black majority."[33] Thirty-five years prior, Alice Walker expressed much the same dismay in her essay "Choosing to Stay at Home: Ten Years after the March on Washington" in which she accused, "The very class that owes its new affluence to the Movement now refuses to support the organizations that made its success possible, and has retreated from its concern for black people who are poor."[34] Walker's accusations also echo Rustin's around the same time, as well as many other black intellectuals and writers concerned more with the everyday lives of the black majority than attaining symbolic victories in the halls of power. *Getting Mother's Body* shares their frustrated assessments of civil rights legacies, but Parks offers the literary realm as a repository for the movement's ideals, in all fanciful seriousness.

Parks's ending breaks sharply from her host text. In *As I Lay Dying*, only Anse ends happily, smiling with new false teeth, phonograph, and wife, all leveraged with stolen, sweet-talked, or borrowed currency. The remaining Bundrens end desperate or doomed: Cash is crippled, Jewel has no horse, Darl is committed, Dewey Dell is with unwanted child, Vardaman lacks city-kid privileges, and the new Mrs. Bundren is, well, the new Mrs. Bundren. But in *Getting Mother's Body*, it is not inevitable that patriarchs alone achieve happiness off others' backs. For Parks, we are not bound by a past, be it literary or historical, accurate or fictional, segregated or integrated. Instead, we must dig up the past and assemble our own happy endings from what is buried there. "And if the ending is happier than Faulkner's and implausibly neat," one reviewer remarks, "—if problems evaporate like a mirage retreating from the car's front wheels—it's still a trip well worth taking."[35] The happy ending is far removed from King's integration dream, Uncle Teddy's negro inflation index, and a post–civil rights record that comes up short in achieving socioeconomic equality. Parks may tie up loose ends for the Beedes regarding their personal lives, but she leaves unnarrated their return to Lincoln, Texas, where they will have to reconcile their private treasure hunt with the political treasures other residents sought in Washington, D.C. In this way, Parks's project is both a literary and a historical adaptation, one which is neatly finished in the realm of fiction but remains conspicuously incomplete in the political arena. It is up to her readers to finish the political story. But this fiction delivers as far as the characters are concerned. All of them, this time.

JIM CROW TODAY

When Jim Crow Is but Should Not Be

As racial dynamics have shifted over the course of the post–civil rights era, so too does the work of the neo–segregation narrative. Today, pronouncements of a *postrace era* are increasingly entering mainstream acceptance, especially following the election of Barack Obama as the nation's first (biracial) black president. A postrace era requires a clearly demarcated *race era* to precede it, which is the latest manifestation of the consistent foil of neo–segregation narratives: racial progress narratives that announce clean breaks from a racially tainted past. In Percival Everett's *Erasure* (2001), the unquestionable backwardness of minstrelsy, darkies, and segregation artifacts provides a language to articulate modern-day racial protest. Specifically, the protagonist expresses exasperated rage that marketable depictions of African Americans fail to speak to the full register of his (and others') experiences. The protagonist, writer Thellonius "Monk" Ellison, fumes at the blockbuster success of a novel called *We's Lives in Da Ghetto*: "The reality of popular culture was nothing new. The truth of the world landing on me daily, or hourly, was nothing I did not expect. But this book was a real slap in the face. It was like strolling through an antique mall, feeling good, liking the sunny day and then turning the corner to find a display of watermelon-eating, banjo-playing darkie carvings and a pyramid of Mammy cookie jars. 3 million dollars."[1] For post–Jim Crow subjects such as Thellonius, the obvious ridiculousness of segregation's cardboard caricatures and racist stereotypes can clarify more elusive race politics today. Still, *Erasure* isn't a neo–segregation narrative because Everett imports segregation's artifacts into the contemporary moment. This study, however, concentrates on literature that does the inverse: returns to the Jim Crow era with one eye on the historical record and one on the present.

Neo–segregation narratives consciously induce what I call *temporal dysphoria* because we encounter Jim Crow *today* when we think—and know!—he should be *then*. There is a strange contradiction when contemporary writers return to a Jim Crow period to comment on post–civil rights concerns: the simplicity of Jim Crow thinking is simultaneously absurd and useful. A good parting example of a neo–segregation narrative to pair with Everett's novel is Colson Whitehead's *The Intuitionist* (1999). Whitehead returns to the Jim Crow era in a northern city (probably New York during the Harlem Renaissance) as he playfully delivers an uplift narrative of the most literal sort: a story about elevator inspection. The novel's protagonist, Lila Mae Watson, is the city's second black and first black female elevator inspector. She is an intuitionist, adhering to a philosophy that is on the wane and much derided by the dominant school of elevator inspection, the empiricists. Over the course of the novel, she is drawn into the high-stakes mystery of the two warring camps, ultimately discovering that her chosen philosophy of intuitionism was crafted as a lark. A man passing as white at the prestigious elevator institute invented intuitionism to hoodwink white people.

Whitehead's novel is an exemplary neo–segregation narrative for the postrace era because it addresses race indirectly, inviting readers to map racial schools onto intuitionism and empiricism without confirming that that is the book's underlying subject. More so than Uncle Teddy in *Getting Mother's Body*, Whitehead gets us to think about race by not thinking about it directly. He peppers his novel with just enough references to segregation, uplift, and integration to offer a meditation on the betterment of African Americans that resonates with post–civil rights concerns about the limits of desegregation and the philosophy of integration. The Jim Crow era, and contemporary readers' ideas about it, holds the power to clarify race relations when racism has gone underground. To wit, in another of Whitehead's novels, *John Henry Days*, the black male protagonist insists upon Jim Crow's presence today in a particularly revealing way. "'This isn't Mississippi in the fifties, J.,' One Eye says, cocking his head. 'It's always Mississippi in the fifties,' J. answers."[2] Like Jim Crow, "Mississippi" is overdetermined in the cultural imagination, whether generic, as a shorthand for deep race segregation, or specific, such as the murder of Emmett Till. But the exact referent is effaced in the literary text, probably because "Mississippi" needs no elaboration. As Nina Simone belted in 1963, "Everybody knows about Mississippi. Goddam."

From Toni Morrison to Whitehead, neo–segregation narratives address the strange case of how segregation *is* but *should not be*. Other literary strands are close kin, such as the passing narrative whose resurgence Michelle Elam tracks in twenty-first-century fiction by both black and nonblack writers. This is curious because the genre's concerns—indeed, its very existence—are perceived as quaint and obsolete in an era that likes to think of itself as the "mulatto millennium." Jim Crow's resilience in post–civil rights literature points to a vibrant and ongoing tradition available to contemporary writers who wish to account for racial division in a de facto era, including a reputedly postrace era. They can draw on Lorraine Hansberry as forebear and *The Bluest Eye* as a founding text, sift through the intertwined neo–slave and neo–segregation narrative traditions, and learn from the way neo–segregation narratives evolved to respond to new political debates and needs, from Black Power and black feminism to multiculturalism and sexual diversity. They can draw on iconic moments, tropes, and storylines that a return to Jim Crow allows: Beneatha's audacious "Howdy-do!" to de facto segregation; Lena's ill-fated quest to breach segregated economies in pursuit of better apples and houses; Walter Lee and Asagai's shared spectator position to black nationalist rhetoric in Hansberry's unfilmed screenplay; Claudia's embrace of "funk" culture and her refusal to cross the color line to find beauty in *The Bluest Eye*; John Washington's patrilineal quest to construct a history with black people at the center in *The Chaneysville Incident*; Celie and Sofia's revolutionary indifference to white culture while choosing to stick it out with the black men in their community in *The Color Purple*; Jim Too's radically inclusive separatism in the Jim Crow car in *Darktown Strutters*; the magnet-and-iron-filings orienting power of Jim Crow in the multiethnic literary imagination; and Parks's turn away from the nation's capital toward LaJunta to march with those who didn't make it to Washington and were left out of many ensuing gains of the civil rights movement. They might even take cues from Faulkner's scarred white bodies who become black when they experience suffering, or from how multiethnic-minded writers of varying stripes explore the uses and limits of cross-racial solidarity in the wake of the civil rights movement.

The realm of literature offers unique lessons because literary depictions of Jim Crow have a different purpose than political rhetoric and popular culture, which tend to score quick political points or shoot out brief cultural references from an arsenal of settled ideas. Literature, on the other hand, is well equipped to analyze the narratives and omissions embedded in the American cultural imagination, including Jim Crow's memory. The terrain of literature is also prone more to identification and narrative play than to the taxonomic desires of museums and collector's display cases. For the historical record, writers import contemporary sensibilities of inclusion, identitarian play, and self-conscious multiculturalism, especially to write back into the record outcasts such as Dill Smiles, Jim Too, and Celie. At the same time, for the contemporary moment, writers draw on segregation's stark lines and Jim Crow's notorious reputation in order to address the persistence of racial division and racialist thinking after segregation's official sanction has been revoked.

Nearly a half-century after the civil rights movement's most impressive and celebrated gains, chief among them the Civil Rights Acts of 1964 and 1965, we remain drawn to racial lines, though with new political and philosophical convictions. Racial identity may now be almost universally seen as a malleable construct, yet racial *lines* persist, especially under the banner of multiculturalism and its commitment to diversity and celebrating difference. In response, stories such as *Erasure* increasingly feature characters of all races struggling, both tragically and comically, to become black—at least as popular culture defines authentic blackness. On the flip side, of course, are stories about black characters accused of not being black enough. Paul Beatty's *White Boy Shuffle* (1996) brilliantly features both these narratives.

The very label "neo–segregation narratives" is disorienting because encountering Jim Crow *today* doesn't fit into neat chronologies of Jim Crow's birth and death. That is why Vince Schleitwiler pushes us to ask how to narrate segregation's death when it has a life after Jim Crow. From the other end, studies of the Jim Crow period marvel over how segregation came to be born in the first place. Grace Elizabeth Hale explains how the color line became America's core policy and notes, "But the whiteness that some Americans made through segregation was always contingent, always fragile, always uncertain."[3] Writers of the time concerned themselves with the strangeness, artifice, maintenance, and rules of this newly installed color line. In his innovative study *How Race Is Made*, Mark M. Smith muses, "Segregationists lived an illogical, emotionally powerful lie that relied on gut rather than brain to fix racial identity and order society. Their ability to make solid what was always slippery is annoyingly impressive."[4] In the post–civil rights and postrace literary imagination, that segregationist logic is now identified with an entire era. The "annoyingly impressive" segregationist mentality and its associated cultural and historical practices now stand as useful literary devices. Jim Crow segregation is *now* laughable on a philosophical level in an era that celebrates messy identities as it plays with or even mocks the idea of racial authenticity. The bright line of segregation, however, also allows writers to get us out of the immediacy of the moment to wrestle with contemporary racial concerns with some moral clarity and historical resonance.

Temporal Dysphoria and Feelings of Racial Injustice in a Postrace Era

Jim Crow Jr. is the bugaboo of the postrace era. Contrary to neo–segregation narrative designs, the postrace era has no room for him and his feelings of racial injustice. In a 2008 oration often dubbed "The Speech on Race," presidential candidate Barack Obama delivered a masterful meditation on race in America reminiscent of the complex personal and political reflections of James Baldwin at his best. He explained the underlying logic of the frustrations, humiliations, and crimped dreams that compose Jim Crow's legacy and that inform the fiery sermons of his pastor, the Reverend Jeremiah Wright of Trinity United Church of Christ in Chicago. Yet Obama also cast Reverend Wright as Jim Crow Sr., a spokesperson of a past age largely irrelevant to the present. Thus he participated in the long-standing tradition of announcing the death of Jim Crow, casting the *now* as a clean and enlightened break from the *then*. Still, Obama declared, "I can no more disown him than I can disown the black community."[5] He begged a question: Would he if he could? In any case, Obama broke from Reverend Wright at a press conference six weeks later on April 30, 2008. Jim Crow Sr. was again cast out of postrace America, even though his supposed spokesperson was alive and well—and had voting rights. Year after year leaders ascend national podiums to declare the end of Jim Crow and his irrelevance to the present. These declarations sometimes come doubly wrapped in atonements for slavery, such as the unanimous U.S. Senate declaration in June 2009 that officially "apologizes to African-Americans on behalf of the people of the United States for the wrongs committed against them and their ancestors who suffered under slavery and Jim Crow laws."[6] The apology is tellingly ahistorical because it insists that the subject for which it atones has no place in the present (the matter of reparations is conspicuously absent), which means that feelings of racial injustice today are anachronistic.

In a 2007 editorial in *The Nation*, Gary Younge positions Jim Crow Jr. as the unclaimed orphan of the post–civil rights era: "In the alleyway between de jure and de facto, Jim Crow conceived a son. Even though the deed took place in broad daylight, everybody tried not to notice, and in time some would even try to pretend it hadn't happened."[7] Despite the postrace era's desire for a clean break, Jim Crow symbols appear frequently in contemporary America. The detritus creates what John L. Jackson, Jr., calls "racial Americana," reminders of the salience of race whether we like it or not. Bill Brown discusses the reification and reanimation of Jim Crow objects, leading to the *American uncanny*. He points to Spike Lee's *Bamboozled* as an example of the consumptive economy of negro memorabilia, the Jim Crow merchandise that carries a "residual ontology" or "the historical ontology congealed within objects."[8] For Brown, history becomes visible when its overdetermined objects—say, an Aunt Jemima cookie jar, a mechanical bank in the shape of a cartoonish Negro head, or perhaps a segregation sign—become something else, when they are wrested out of place, reified, and consumed in a historical economy that passes for experience or knowledge. He writes, "We can apprehend the uncanniness of the mechanical bank itself—the very ontological instability expressed by the artifact itself, the oscillation between animate and inanimate, subject and object, human and thing, that has no doubt made it such an iconic emblem of racism within American material culture, that has made it the most despised and most prized object of black memorabilia, simultaneously the object of repulsion and fascination."[9] Brown and other scholars such as Elizabeth Abel propose that collecting such objects might enable control over them and "deanimate" stereotypes of the plantation darky.[10] Yet the awkwardness and politically charged nature of their circulation suggest otherwise: they maintain an uncanny afterlife. Outside the literary realm, the uncanny afterlives of such objects are prime generators of feelings of racial injustice.

The topic of Jim Crow and civil rights legacies is obviously relevant well beyond the realm of literature. This is especially true when the nation celebrates the end, or at least lessening, of racism, while at the same time some versions of liberation adopt segregation's pretty twin, self-segregation or separatism. That is why I end this study by venturing into the political and cultural realms with a few telling examples. When Jim Crow symbols trespass into contemporary America—say, an accusation of a "high-tech lynching" at a U.S. Supreme Court Justice confirmation hearing—the event seems not only wrong per se but also wrong because it belongs in an earlier era. Esther Godfrey considers a notorious Beta Theta Pi Halloween party that featured college kids in blackface and concludes, "Their intent seems to focus on the ability of theatricality to break down racial identities through humor, excess, and exaggeration, though they neglect to consider the performance's power to reaffirm those same racial identities."[11] The jarring appearance of a Jim Crow symbol *today* creates a chronic disorientation, or *temporal dysphoria*, which in turn catalyzes feelings of injustice because it goes against progress narratives associated with Jim Crow *then*.

A good example is the empty lynch noose. The *New York Times* published a graphic illustration with an accompanying op-ed from the Southern Poverty Law Center regarding fifty to sixty noose sightings that pockmarked the nation, primarily the eastern states, in 2006 to 2007 (see fig. 1), after the past decade had witnessed only about a dozen such incidents. The noose is a powerful symbol in post–civil rights America because it simultaneously recalls a Jim Crow past via one of the more horrific means by which the color line was policed and also the corollary history of antilynching activism by leaders from Ida B. Wells to the NAACP. The *empty* noose is particularly powerful because it removes the specific victim and in doing so lays bare the collective message that spectacle lynchings were directed at all African Americans and anyone else who would contemplate crossing the color line. Yet the empty noose also strangely removes actual white violence from the historical record. Historian Jonathan Markovitz suggests that lynching may have faded from material practice after 1880–1930 but looms large as a figure of speech for race relations in the twentieth century and beyond. Noose sightings are potent catalysts when added to current events: the ensuing reaction can set in motion a story about progress in race relations, or rather the lack thereof. In sum, the empty noose *today* creates feelings of racial injustice because it should not be here *now* but rather *then*.

Empty nooses are only one of Jim Crow's overdetermined signs in a post–civil rights era. "Whites Only" signs also often appear in the contemporary arena, be it for playful, reactionary, or progressive means. A good example is the 1996 campaign to defeat California's Proposition 209, which sought to dismantle race-based considerations in college admissions. In her study of the "social life of segregation signs," Elizabeth Abel considers anti–Proposition 209 propaganda featuring a "Whites Only" sign (see fig. 2) at the entrance to the University of California, Berkeley. Abel argues that the campaign effectively "deployed segregation signs in ways that recall and reject the separate but equal formula that has enjoyed a cultural afterlife as a mnemonic aid."[12] I would add that such "mnemonic aids" bring moral

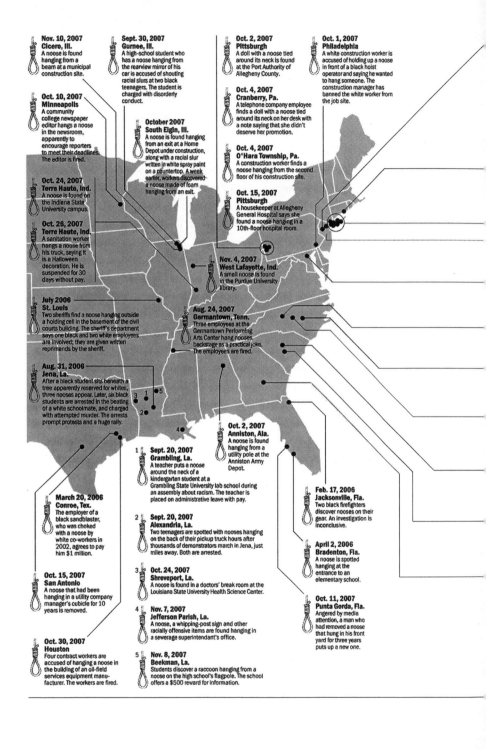

Nov. 10, 2007
Cicero, Ill.
A noose is found hanging from a beam at a municipal construction site.

Sept. 30, 2007
Gurnee, Ill.
A high-school student who has a noose hanging from the rearview mirror of his car is accused of shouting racial slurs at two black teenagers. The student is charged with disorderly conduct.

Oct. 2, 2007
Pittsburgh
A doll with a noose tied around its neck is found at the Port Authority of Allegheny County.

Oct. 1, 2007
Philadelphia
A white construction worker is accused of holding up a noose in front of a black hoist operator and saying he wanted to hang someone. The construction manager has banned the white worker from the job site.

Oct. 10, 2007
Minneapolis
A community college newspaper editor hangs a noose in the newsroom, apparently to encourage reporters to meet their deadlines. The editor is fired.

October 2007
South Elgin, Ill.
A noose is found hanging from an exit at a Home Depot under construction, along with a racial slur written in white spray paint on a countertop. A week earlier, workers discovered a noose made of foam hanging from an exit.

Oct. 4, 2007
Cranberry, Pa.
A telephone company employee finds a doll with a noose tied around its neck on her desk with a note saying that she didn't deserve her promotion.

Oct. 4, 2007
O'Hara Township, Pa.
A construction worker finds a noose hanging from the second floor of his construction site.

Oct. 24, 2007
Terre Haute, Ind.
A noose is found on the Indiana State University campus.

Oct. 15, 2007
Pittsburgh
A housekeeper at Allegheny General Hospital says she found a noose hanging in a 10th-floor hospital room.

Oct. 26, 2007
Terre Haute, Ind.
A sanitation worker hangs a noose from his truck, saying it is a Halloween decoration. He is suspended for 30 days without pay.

Nov. 4, 2007
West Lafayette, Ind.
A small noose is found in the Purdue University library.

July 2006
St. Louis
Two sheriffs find a noose hanging outside a holding cell in the basement of the civil courts building. The sheriff's department says one black and two white employees are involved; they are given written reprimands by the sheriff.

Aug. 24, 2007
Germantown, Tenn.
Three employees at the Germantown Performing Arts Center hang nooses backstage as a practical joke. The employees are fired.

Aug. 31, 2006
Jena, La.
After a black student sits beneath a tree apparently reserved for whites, three nooses appear. Later, six black students are arrested in the beating of a white schoolmate, and charged with attempted murder. The arrests prompt protests and a huge rally.

Oct. 2, 2007
Anniston, Ala.
A noose is found hanging from a utility pole at the Anniston Army Depot.

Feb. 17, 2006
Jacksonville, Fla.
Two black firefighters discover nooses on their gear. An investigation is inconclusive.

March 20, 2006
Conroe, Tex.
The employer of a black sandblaster, who was choked with a noose by white co-workers in 2002, agrees to pay him $1 million.

1 Sept. 20, 2007
Grambling, La.
A teacher puts a noose around the neck of a kindergarten student at a Grambling State University lab school during an assembly about racism. The teacher is placed on administrative leave with pay.

April 2, 2006
Bradenton, Fla.
A noose is spotted hanging at the entrance to an elementary school.

Oct. 15, 2007
San Antonio
A noose that had been hanging in a utility company manager's cubicle for 10 years is removed.

2 Sept. 20, 2007
Alexandria, La.
Two teenagers are spotted with nooses hanging on the back of their pickup truck hours after thousands of demonstrators march in Jena, just miles away. Both are arrested.

Oct. 11, 2007
Punta Gorda, Fla.
Angered by media attention, a man who had removed a noose that hung in his front yard for three years puts up a new one.

3 Oct. 24, 2007
Shreveport, La.
A noose is found in a doctors' break room at the Louisiana State University Health Science Center.

Oct. 30, 2007
Houston
Four contract workers are accused of hanging a noose in the building of an oil-field services equipment manufacturer. The workers are fired.

4 Nov. 7, 2007
Jefferson Parish, La.
A noose, a whipping-post sign and other racially offensive items are found hanging in a sewerage superintendant's office.

5 Nov. 8, 2007
Beekman, La.
Students discover a raccoon hanging from a noose on the high school's flagpole. The school offers a $500 reward for information.

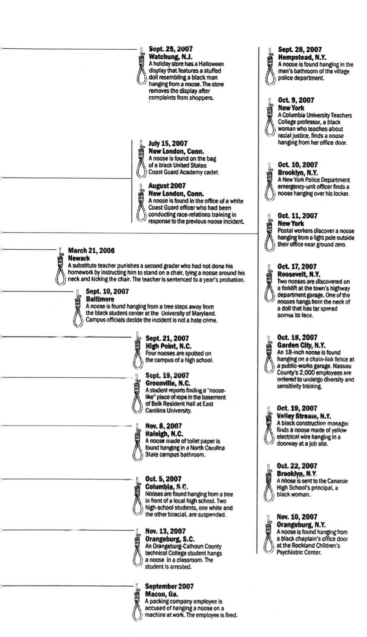

Sept. 25, 2007
Watchung, N.J.
A holiday store has a Halloween display that features a stuffed doll resembling a black man hanging from a noose. The store removes the display after complaints from shoppers.

July 15, 2007
New London, Conn.
A noose is found on the bag of a black United States Coast Guard Academy cadet.

August 2007
New London, Conn.
A noose is found in the office of a white Coast Guard officer who had been conducting race-relations training in response to the previous noose incident.

March 21, 2006
Newark
A substitute teacher punishes a second grader who had not done his homework by instructing him to stand on a chair, tying a noose around his neck and kicking the chair. The teacher is sentenced to a year's probation.

Sept. 10, 2007
Baltimore
A noose is found hanging from a tree steps away from the black student center at the University of Maryland. Campus officials decide the incident is not a hate crime.

Sept. 21, 2007
High Point, N.C.
Four nooses are spotted on the campus of a high school.

Sept. 19, 2007
Greenville, N.C.
A student reports finding a "noose-like" piece of rope in the basement of Belk Resident Hall at East Carolina University.

Nov. 8, 2007
Raleigh, N.C.
A noose made of toilet paper is found hanging in a North Carolina State campus bathroom.

Oct. 5, 2007
Columbia, S.C.
Nooses are found hanging from a tree in front of a local high school. Two high-school students, one white and the other biracial, are suspended.

Nov. 13, 2007
Orangeburg, S.C.
An Orangeburg-Calhoun County technical College student hangs a noose in a classroom. The student is arrested.

September 2007
Macon, Ga.
A packing company employee is accused of hanging a noose on a machine at work. The employee is fired.

Sept. 28, 2007
Hempstead, N.Y.
A noose is found hanging in the men's bathroom of the village police department.

Oct. 9, 2007
New York
A Columbia University Teachers College professor, a black woman who teaches about racial justice, finds a noose hanging from her office door.

Oct. 10, 2007
Brooklyn, N.Y.
A New York Police Department emergency-unit officer finds a noose hanging over his locker.

Oct. 11, 2007
New York
Postal workers discover a noose hanging from a light pole outside their office near ground zero.

Oct. 17, 2007
Roosevelt, N.Y.
Two nooses are discovered on a forklift at the town's highway department garage. One of the nooses hangs from the neck of a doll that has tar spread across its face.

Oct. 18, 2007
Garden City, N.Y.
An 18-inch noose is found hanging on a chain-link fence at a public-works garage. Nassau County's 2,000 employees are ordered to undergo diversity and sensitivity training.

Oct. 19, 2007
Valley Stream, N.Y.
A black construction manager finds a noose made of yellow electrical wire hanging in a doorway at a job site.

Oct. 22, 2007
Brooklyn, N.Y.
A noose is sent to the Canarsie High School's principal, a black woman.

Nov. 10, 2007
Orangeburg, N.Y.
A noose is found hanging from a black chaplain's office door at the Rockland Children's Psychiatric Center.

FIGURE 1. Noose sightings, 2006–7. Mark Potok, Luke Viconti, Barbara Frankel, and Nigel Holmes, graphic for "The Geography of Hate," *New York Times*, November 25, 2007. Image courtesy of Nigel Holmes.

clarity to contemporary issues. Affirmative action is an obviously complex issue, especially because the idea of race-conscious policies for race-neutral ends causes considerable political, moral, and logical concerns across the ideological spectrum. On the other hand, Jim Crow policies are perceived as clearly wrong. Thus Jim Crow symbols are powerful translating engines: feed in the messy details of any current race-related matter and churn out moral or political certitude. In a way, this is how Jim Crow *always* worked in a multicultural and class-stratified society as it translated complex social arrangements into neat black-and-white signs and spaces.

Jim Crow's seemingly settled place in the contemporary imagination is adaptable to any number of vexing issues in a post–civil rights, more multicultural era. This clarifying power holds for conservative political purposes too, such as in a 2007 installment of Chris Muir's political cartoon *Day by Day*, which featured democratic presidential candidate Hillary Rodham Clinton in blackface. In order to lampoon what many detected as Clinton's changed cadence and lexicon on the southern campaign trail, Muir taps the imagery of blackface minstrelsy. Clinton stands behind a podium as a questioner from beyond the frame asks, "Senator Clinton what's your take on 2008?" Clad in blackface, she responds, "Lawdy! I's seen da promised land!" For the cartoon, a candidate in blackface, especially one who speaks in the stereotypical conventions of what an earlier frame identifies as "plantation talk," delivers an artificial, calculated performance in order to connect with southern and African American citizens. Festooned with such Jim Crow iconography, the candidate's efforts to speak across racial lines and voting blocs are clearly suspect.

The contemporary clarifying power of Jim Crow symbolism is so strong that it creates a feeling of moral certitude even when the overall political message is not as clear. A good example is Jam Donaldson's "Hot Ghetto Mess," a successful 2004 website (www.hotghettomess.com) that inspired a DVD in 2005 and a BET reality show in 2007 using the site's tagline "We Got to Do Better." Donaldson solicits and features evidence of what she poses as the sorry state of (black) America, with examples from women clad in downright silly skimpy clothing, neologisms such as "conversate," over-the-top artifacts of "bling" culture, and other evidence of what she paints as "our community's role in and contribution to the bastardization of our images and culture." To whip up feelings of moral disdain, Donaldson admonishes her fellow citizens for participating in a latter-day minstrel show, a stance

FIGURE 2. Anti–Proposition 209 campaign, Berkeley, California, November 2007. Photo originally in *Daily Californian*, November 7, 1997, and featured in Elizabeth Abel, *Signs of the Times: The Visual Politics of Jim Crow* (University of California Press, 2009). Photo courtesy of Jesse Ehrman.

HOT GHETTO MESS
We Got To Do Better

reminiscent of black authority figures speaking from the vantage of a civil rights generation, especially Bill Cosby, and long-standing politics of representation associated with racial uplift ideologies. Still, Donaldson's politics are murky, which is a common fate of moralistic narratives that spend too much time representing—and therefore possibly glamorizing—the very behaviors they seek to condemn. To guard against this possibility, Hot Ghetto Mess tempers its delight in instances of bastardized culture by casting its anti*racist* stance as an anti*minstrelsy* stance. The early website and BET site featured a logo with a blackface minstrel head in a red circle with a line through it (see fig. 3). The success of this strategy, either in general or in particular, is up for debate. Regardless, the historical switcheroo of contemporary debates for condemnation of past practices rests on the assumption that blackface minstrelsy is unanimously offensive. Then, by metonymy, moral condemnation falls on anything associated with blackface minstrelsy today.

Returning to the figure of the empty noose, one of the more infamous appearances crystallized what became known as the "Jena Six." The Jena Six controversy arose when six black high school students were arrested and one was charged with attempted murder (later dropped to aggravated battery and conspiracy) of a white student. This episode culminated a series of racially infused disputes and altercations at the school. According to most accounts, a black student attempted to sit under a schoolyard tree previously

WHITES ONLY

FIGURE 4. Rendition of Jena Six tree as a hang tree, widely used in various grassroots campaigns, 2007. Artist unknown.

and unofficially reserved for white students. In response, students arrived at school the next day to find empty nooses (two or three, depending on the version) dangling from the tree. The incident immediately recalled histories of Jim Crow segregation and the racial terrorism of lynching. The power of Jim Crow imagery today is demonstrated most clearly in the way that the Jena high school tree became an iconic image of a hang tree in materials used and distributed by various activist groups (see fig. 4). In the visual shift from photograph to propaganda, the tree gains what postmodern thinkers might call historicity or what Comedy Central comedian Stephen Colbert might call *historiness*, parallel to his popular neologism *truthiness*. The empty noose provides a clear plan of political action by importing the moral clarity attached to Jim Crow histories: the six arrested African American young men were victims of an unfair legal and cultural process. While many literary and political figures found a morass of political, cultural, and legal issues around the events (including competing interpretations of the nooses themselves), when the Jena Six incident was refracted through the lens of Jim Crow, it served as a bellwether of contemporary race relations and instigated mass demonstrations reminiscent of the civil rights era. In his *Nation* editorial on the controversy, Gary Younge notes, "Paradoxically it has taken the symbolism of the old—complete with nooses and all-white juries—for the nation to engage with the substance of the new: the racial inequalities in

America's penal and judicial system."[13] Contemporary writers, primarily but not exclusively African American, have long known what Younge found: It is useful to draw on the perceived clarity of an earlier era of stark Jim Crow segregation in order to bring some sort of clarity to the perceived messiness of contemporary race relations, especially in a multicultural era, or, conversely, to remind us of the actual messiness of the pre–civil rights era.

Neo–Segregation Narratives in the Postrace Era

What do we gain by juxtaposing these appearances of Jim Crow in popular culture and politics with his appearances in neo–segregation narratives? Some may worry that Jim Crow symbolism does a disservice in the realm of politics by polemicizing and oversimplifying the issue; others might welcome such polarization and call it clarity. In the literary realm, where the metaphorical and figurative are central to meaning making, historiographic fiction writers consciously draw on and influence Jim Crow's continued life in the contemporary imagination, rather than just reflect simplistic ideas about Jim Crow, which in turn simplify the contemporary moment. If Patricia Hill Collins is right that the color line today is absent but its legacy persists, as I discussed in the introduction, then neo–segregation narratives drop Jim Crow into the contemporary imagination to make that absent present visible. And if Houston Baker is also right that many political leaders and academics, both African American and from other backgrounds, have largely abandoned ideals of the civil rights movement, the neo–segregation narrative stands as at least one location where such critical engagement persists, even if this registers a shift from the legislative and grassroots arenas to that of literature and its role in shaping the historical record.

Within a society that likes to think of itself as democratic and just, telling Jim Crow stories raises problems of historical complicity. David Pilgrim considers why he has collected items for his Jim Crow museum since he was a teenager and surmises, "I have long felt that Americans, especially whites, would rather talk about slavery than Jim Crow. All ex-slaves are dead. They do not walk among us, their presence a reminder of that unspeakably cruel system. Their children are dead. Distanced by a century and a half, the modern American sees slavery as a regrettable period when blacks worked without wages. . . . The horrors of Jim Crow are not so easily ignored. The children of Jim Crow walk among us, and they have stories to tell."[14]

The stories that Jim Crow and his children have to tell are both historical and urgent. Keeping alive such historical artifacts and memories is a necessary, delicate, and painful task. Literature, perhaps more so than museums or op-ed pages, is up for the challenge. The postrace era insists on its postness with fervor in direct proportion to its prematurity. Because the "post" in "postness" describes an aspiration rather than a reality, the nation continues to be haunted by a racial past, what John J. Su calls "the ghosts of essentialism" that give rise to racial memory. "Racial memory is invoked," Su argues, "not to provide a fixed or static characterization of individuals but to encourage imaginative explorations of existing portrayals of minority populations from alternative points of view."[15] Neo–segregation narratives deliver these imaginative explorations, especially since their bitemporal designs are equipped to make use of the temporal dysphoria Jim Crow today engenders.

Whether post–Jim Crow, post–civil rights, or postrace, such "post" eras rely on progress narratives that insist—overly so—on a rupture between past and present so that Jim Crow embodies a familiar yet seemingly removed or foreign history. The alluring promise of a postrace era relies on settled historical narratives of Jim Crow, ones that are not terribly accurate or able to account for lived experiences of race. Neo–segregation narratives have challenged and exploited these settled narratives since the civil rights era. They resist siren songs of racial progress because they neither insist on clean breaks from the past nor succumb to sloppy thinking that equivocates between now and then. Pronouncements of a postrace era raise the stakes in the contest over how to narrate Jim Crow today because to even acknowledge his existence in the historical record, let alone today, is to court accusations of being a relic of a race era, an anachronism. Neo–segregation narratives offer new national narratives of a Jim Crow who remains relevant, not locked in an imagined past.

Returning to Whitehead's neo–segregation narrative, *The Intuitionist* is instructive because it presciently casts postrace pronouncements as the latest manifestation of a long-standing tendency to proclaim a new generational innocence for the racial sins of past eras. Lila Mae Watson fancies herself a trailblazing first, doing right by her ancestors and living true to her intuitionist philosophy. She thinks she is in a bootstraps narrative as she attempts to rise up the ranks of elevator inspectors. As she learns the secret history of the intuitionist/empiricist debate, as intricate as it is mundane, she comes to appreciate how embroiled she is in the racial underpinnings of her uplift narrative. Upon uncovering the black origins of both intuitionism and empiricism, Lila Mae declares, "They always take away from our people. I don't know if they know he was colored, but if they do you know they ain't going to tell the truth. They would never admit that. Them downstairs would never say that they worship a nigger."[16] For Lila, the refusal to acknowledge race and the concomitant equivocation between raceless and white is unacceptable, evidence in and of itself of racism.

Eventually, though, Lila Mae learns that in the search for the perfect elevator, racial origins are simultaneously crucial and irrelevant. "'Colored people think two of our presidents were colored. We make noises about it, but nothing ever comes of it,' she explains. 'His color doesn't matter once it gets to that level. The level of commerce. They can put Fulton into one of those colored history calendars if they want—it doesn't change the fact that there's money to be made from his invention'" (250). No matter how high the elevator goes, no matter how perfectly she intuits its proper workings, there is no escaping the fact that she is certified by an elevator institute built on a Jim Crow history of race segregation, exclusion, and petty racial bickering. The desires for a clean break and the desire for a black history to celebrate are twins separated at birth. The dawn of a new era rests on a connection to that from which an era is breaking. The shift from de jure to de facto, like the shift from racial history to modern commerce, are simply different stops on the same elevator. Lila may be a "first," that most enduring of tropes in African American history, but to be the first is also to join a very long line of the excluded, the not-firsts. As Whitehead cheekily demonstrates, buried in plain sight in the moniker *"postrace"* is the undeniable thing that must not be spoken.

► ► ►

Dominant narratives of segregation point to *Plessy v. Ferguson* as ground zero of the color line, and *Brown v. Board of Education of Topeka* as an aftershock. We feel those reverberations in the twenty-first century, though their place in America's racial narrative remains contested. In 2007, the U.S. Supreme Court struck down voluntary school desegregation programs in Seattle, Washington, and Louisville, Kentucky. Race was used as a factor in determining school districts, whether by arbitrary tiebreaker to achieve diversity (Seattle) or to continue components of a court-ordered desegregation program after it was no longer required (Louisville). In his majority opinion,

Chief Justice John Roberts argued that desegregation plans in schools that were never legally segregated (Seattle), or that had "eliminated the vestiges of past segregation" (Louisville), had the same effects as legal segregation before *Brown*. Roberts concluded bluntly, "The way to stop discrimination on the basis of race is to stop discriminating on the basis of race."[17] The Roberts opinion is a sleight of hand that swaps postracism with postrace. In his dissent, Justice Stephen J. Breyer rejected that barstool simplicity. He noted a "cruel irony" in equivocating between acknowledging race and racism. Breyer lamented, "Finally, what of the hope and promise of *Brown*? In the twenty-first century segregation is being repackaged by some as an outcome of the very movements and programs designed to redress histories of racial disenfranchisement and achieve American promises of equal opportunity."[18] Legal scholar Derrick Bell detects a sea change in all this. "In its new guise," Bell surmises, "the standard of strict scrutiny offers little support for black people seeking to challenge racially discriminatory practices that do not overtly mention race. But it enables any white person to challenge policies intended to remedy past discrimination, because those policies are typically couched in racial terms."[19] In the end, Bell explains, this new attitude means that the federal courts need not—must not—consider actual histories of racial inequality, only abstract principles of neutrality and equality.

The scripts of segregationists and antisegregationists have strangely flipped in a post–civil rights era. The civil rights movement sought an end to racism by way of dismantling its legal, and to some extent cultural, apparatus. Race consciousness, a key attribute of progressive post–civil rights politics, is accused of creating the very racial disenfranchisement it is meant to ameliorate. On the other hand, the doctrine of legal neutrality for individual citizens ("color blindness"), once associated with civil rights commitments to integration, is now claimed by apologists for de facto segregation. In a post–Black Power era of multiculturalism and FUBU, the clothing brand For Us By Us, many members of black communities are not even sold on the original ideal of integration, perhaps responding to Baldwin's prophetic question, "Do I really want to be integrated into a burning house?"[20] Self-segregation has returned to favor as an antidote to smug proclamations of postracial equality.

This historical flipping creates a profound urgency to revisit earlier moments of segregation and the stories we tell about them. The neo–segregation narrative is well primed for that task. In his discussion of postmodern slave narratives, Timothy Spaulding emphasizes their work with conceptions of time, both historical and narrative. "In order to emphasize the links between past and present," Spaulding explains, "contemporary African American writers create narratives that undermine conventions of linearity and distinctions between past and present."[21] Spaulding concentrates on speculative, fantastic fiction with time-traveling characters or playful anachronisms, which are stark examples of how "writers of postmodern slave narratives challenge with willful ignorance or abstraction."[22] That task—both aesthetic and political—is also urgent in contemporary depictions of Jim Crow because the link between eras of de jure and de facto is quite slippery, if there is such a distinction to be made at all.

Neo–segregation narratives help us see the difference between postracial desires and the goal of achieving a postracism era. Keith Byerman considers the twin pulls of remembering and forgetting in contemporary African American fiction and concludes, "It is necessary to go through the shame and disruption of remembering in order to begin to forge relationships that can become communities that can make a difference. Constantly working against this is the desire to forget, to create a different history or to reject the past altogether. The possibility for change is in memory, but a memory few want to keep."[23] With their bitemporal designs, neo–segregation narratives incite temporal dysphoria so that the specter of de jure segregation threatens to resurface from its settled place in history, thereby jeopardizing comforting or congratulatory narratives of racial progress. Neo–segregation narratives provoke an anxiety in post–civil rights and postrace eras that the "post" cannot be claimed. Telling stories of how Jim Crow *is* versus how Jim Crow *was* is a simultaneously urgent and wearying prospect. From there, neo–segregation narratives begin the tough work of imagining how Jim Crow *will be no longer.*

NOTES

Introduction. Jim Crow Then

1. Elizabeth Abel and Hortense Spillers worry whether segregation museum displays can bear the burden of representing lived experience (Abel, "American Graffiti," esp. 22; Spillers, Commentary). For more on civil rights memorialization, see Romano and Raiford, *Civil Rights Movement*.

2. Leeming, *James Baldwin*, 354.

3. Regarding Goldberg's collection, Abel writes, "In a calculated shift of context, she and other African American collectors reappropriate segregation signs and other artifacts of discrimination as a burden of proof against their producers. Repossessed, the signs now speak as symptoms; instead of imprinting the bodies they address, they fingerprint the bodies they express" ("American Graffiti," 16).

4. See Morrison, *Remember: The Journey to School Integration*, 2004.

5. Alice Walker, "Choosing to Stay at Home," 165.

6. See Clark, *Black Manhood*, for a discussion of black manhood in this novel and Gaines's work more generally.

7. Romano and Raiford, *Civil Rights Movement*, 1.

8. See especially Lott and Lhamon on Jim Crow's origins.

9. Many scholars are reconsidering civil rights historiography, including the Mellon-funded "Publishing the Long Civil Rights" initiative at University of North Carolina, Chapel Hill.

10. For a particularly good example, see Lowe, *Bridging Southern Cultures*.

11. Wall, Afterword, 163.

12. Ibid., 164.

13. See Dixon's *The Leopard's Spots* (1902), *The Clansman* (1903), and *The Traitor* (1907) collected in *The Reconstruction Trilogy* (1997).

14. My discussion of Wright's essay and key segregation narrative traits draws heavily on the introduction to *Representing Segregation*.

15. Wright, "Ethics of Living Jim Crow," 1418.

16. See Blandón, "'¿Qué Dice?,'" for an analysis of Johnson's transnational segregation narratives.

17. Wright, "Ethics of Living Jim Crow," 1411.

18. Tyner, *War, Violence, and Population*, 36.

19. See Farrah Jasmine Griffin, *"Who Set You Flowin'?"* 15.

20. See Schleitwiler, "Into a Burning House"; Totten, "Embodying Segregation."

21. Fourteen-year-old Emmett Till was tortured and murdered in 1955 while visiting family in Mississippi from his hometown of Chicago. The murderers, J. W. Milam and Roy Bryant, were acquitted by an all-white jury despite considerable incriminating evidence. Till's mother demanded an open-casket funeral and a photograph of Till's mutilated body circulated in national magazines such as *Jet*.

22. Metress, "No Justice, No Peace," 101.

23. Collins, *Black Sexual Politics*, 32.

24. Trudier Harris, "Smacked Upside the Head," 7.

25. See for example Allen, *Without Sanctuary*; Apel, *Imagery of Lynching*; Dray, *At the Hands of Persons Unknown*; Goldsby, *Spectacular Secret*; Gunning, *Race, Rape, and Lynching*; Markovitz, *Legacies of Lynching*; O'Brien, "Cosmopolitanism"; Pfeiffer, *Rough Justice*; Rice, *Witnessing Lynching*; Smith and Apel, *Lynching Photographs*; Stephens, "Racial Violence and Representation"; Waldrep, *Lynching in America*; Wood, *Lynching and Spectacle*.

26. Goldsby, *Spectacular Secret*, 284.

27. Ibid., 290.

28. See Thadious Davis, "Reclaiming the South"; Duck, *Nation's Region*; Peckham, "Segregation/Integration"; Robinson, "Race, Place, and Space"; Thomas, *Civic Myths*. McCaskill and Gebhard, in *Post-Bellum, Pre-Harlem*, provide a terrific overview of African American literature during the emergence of the Jim Crow era (1877–1919) but stop short of identifying a distinct segregation aesthetic.

29. On the other hand, scholars have successfully explored how other eras, group experiences, or geographical locations shape the literary imagination, such as diaspora (e.g., Brent Hayes Edwards and Paul Gilroy), slavery (e.g., DoVeanna Fulton, Venetria Patton, and Jenny Sharpe), and migration (e.g., Farrah Jasmine Griffin and Lawrence Rodgers). These signal experiences influence larger understandings of African American identity in literature (e.g., Keith Byerman and Cheryl Wall), African Americans' relationship to American literature (e.g., Morrison, *Playing in the Dark*; Eric Sundquist), and African American participation in various literary movements such as modernism (e.g., Baker, *Modernism and the Harlem Renaissance*) or genres such as the sermon (e.g., Hubbard, *Sermon and the African American Literary Imagination*).

30. Duck, *Nation's Region*, 25.

31. Ibid., 20.

32. "By approaching this issue through a paradigm of southern apartheid," Duck explains, "I do not mean to suggest that racial inequity has been limited to the South or has been practiced only against African Americans but rather to note that southern anti-black oppression has provided a potent and prominent model for understanding U.S. racial discrimination more generally" (*Nation's Region*, 4).

33. Castronovo, *Beautiful Democracy*, 213.

34. For another study of such crowds in American literature, see Esteve, *The Aesthetics and Politics of the Crowd*, especially her chapter "Vicious Gregariousness: White City, the Nation Form, and the Souls of Lynched Folk," 118–51.

35. Castronovo, *Beautiful Democracy*, 108.

36. Castronovo explains, "In rearticulating 'the beautiful,' the men and women at *The Crisis* walked a dangerous ground, trying to recuperate forms of representation that had done so much injury to black people" (*Beautiful Democracy*, 110).

37. Castronovo, *Beautiful Democracy*, 108.

38. Rushdy, *Neo–Slave Narratives*, 18, 54–95.

39. Jackson, *Science for Segregation*, 200.

40. Belluscio, *To Be Suddenly White*, 18.

41. Ibid.

42. Baker, *Betrayal*, xii.

Chapter One. Jim Crow Jr.

1. Margaret Walker, "How I Told My Child about Race," 496.

2. Hansberry, *To Be Young*, 45.

3. For the most thorough study of these efforts, see Keppel's chapter, "The Dialectical Imagination of Lorraine Hansberry" (*Democracy*, 203–29). See also Ossie Davis's eulogy, "Malcolm X."

4. Bernstein, "Inventing a Fishbowl," 19. Bernstein traces both racist and antiracist strands of the critical reception of the play, which often positioned the play as either particular to black experience or universal. The "fishbowl" sits in the more subtle strand of racist readings of the play's particularity. Bernstein counters, "Obviously, there was an anti-racist project inherent to the demand that white audiences see themselves (i.e., the 'universal') in black characters" (21).

5. Hansberry, *Unfilmed Original Screenplay*, 155. Further citations given parenthetically in text.

6. For more on the unfilmed screenplay genre, see my "Reading a 'Closet Screenplay.'"

7. Bigsby, *Confrontation and Commitment*, 159.

8. Hansberry, *Raisin* (1959), 1.1. Further citations given parenthetically in text.

9. Lipari, "Fearful of the Written Word," 87.

10. Wilkerson, Introduction, xxxv.

11. See Roberts and Klibanoff's *The Race Beat*. For literary and cultural studies of such journalism and media-savvy activism, especially civil rights photography, see Raiford, "Come Let Us Build," and Trodd, "Negative Utopia."

12. Miller, "Measuring Him Right," 138–39.

13. James Baldwin, "Sweet Lorraine," 444.

14. Nemiroff, Introduction, 5.

15. Ibid., 9.

16. James Baldwin, "Sweet Lorraine," 444.

17. Carter, *Hansberry's Drama*, 68. Carter examines two extant film scripts before one version was published by Penguin in 1994.

18. Carter, *Hansberry's Drama*, 76.

19. Their desire to gawk without being seen lends credence to Lipari's view that Hansberry's screenplay, more than the play, pictures a whiteness that tries in vain to pose as innocent.

20. I should note that the Clybourne Park scenes were also open to easy manipulation, as evidenced by the film trailer in which the white producer David Susskind endorses the film, assuring viewers that they have never experienced anything like it. Then bright scenes of the suburban house take up a disproportionate amount of time and visual space.

21. Washington, "Revisited," 113–14.

22. Washington, "Black Women Write," 185. Washington avers, "Contrary to the mainstream image of the award-winning Broadway author of *A Raisin in the Sun*, Lorraine Hansberry of *Freedom* was a militantly left-wing, antiracist, anticolonialist, socialist feminist, whose activities in the 1950s earned her a three-binder FBI file" (194).

23. Wilkerson, Introduction, xl.

24. Lipari, "Fearful of the Written Word," 95.

25. Crowther, "*Raisin in the Sun*," 24; Lee, "Commentary," xlvi; "Listen, Don't Look," 103.

26. For instance, film scholar Mark A. Reid places the Hollywood film in the long tradition of "the modernist black-family melodrama" ("*Take a Giant Step*," 85). Reid traces this film tradition to Theodore Ward's *Big White Fog* (1938) and stresses the importance of a tradition of productions written, directed, and/or produced by African Americans. He explains, "The power to delete certain ideological expressions of black culture highlights the limitations of Hollywood productions for black scenarists and/or black directors who became involved in black commercial productions" (87).

27. Lipari, "Fearful of the Written Word," 83.

28. Keppel, *Work of Democracy*, 202.

29. Lee, "Commentary," xlvi.

30. Wilkerson, Introduction, xxxvi.

31. Hansberry, "What Could Happen," 8.

32. Ibid.

33. Keppel, *Work of Democracy*, 210–11.

34. Wilkerson, Introduction, xxx.

35. Carter, *Hansberry's Drama*, 68.

36. Hansberry, *To Be Young*, 228.

37. Reid, *"Take a Giant Step,"* 86. This is from a letter by Arthur Kramer to fellow production executive David Susskind.

38. Carter, *Hansberry's Drama*, 71.

39. Hansberry, *To Be Young*, 51.

40. See esp. 100–103.

41. Gourdine, *"Drama* of Lynching," 539. Her choice of version is noteworthy: rather than consider the stage play in her argument about Grimké's and Hansberry's drama, Gourdine chooses the unfilmed screenplay.

42. *"A Raisin."*

43. Carter, *Hansberry's Drama*, 75.

44. Abell, "African/American," 468.

45. Ibid., 469.

46. Rich, "Problem with *Lorraine Hansberry*," 247.

47. Keppel, *Work of Democracy*, 233.

48. Baraka, "Sweet Lorraine," 526. For a very similar posthumous reclamation of an author Baraka attacked during his lifetime, see Baraka's reclamation of James Baldwin as forebear of Black Arts, in his *"Jimmy!"*

49. Baraka, "A Wiser Play," 41.

50. Keppel, *Work of Democracy*, 191.

51. Gordon, "Somewhat Like War," 122. She explains, "By offering such stark parallels to the violence of Southern Jim Crow, these comparisons work to demystify Chicago's complex racist power structures. Collapsing the distinctions between racial oppression in the North and South—while attending to the specifics of the local—Hansberry poses the potential for a more unified, national black struggle" (128).

52. Morrison, *Bluest Eye*, 205. Further citations given parenthetically in text.

53. On Claudia MacTeer's resistance, see Grewal, "Laundering the Head of Whitewash," for a recent study; and Klotman, "Dick-and-Jane," for an early study.

54. See Douglas, "What the Bluest Eye Knows," for a recent examination of cross-cultural knowledge in these encounters. On racial introspection of these cross-racial encounters, see Stewart, "Negroes Laughing at Themselves?"

55. Rushdy, *Neo–Slave Narratives*, 5.

56. Margaret Walker, "Southern Black Culture," 83.

57. Morrison, *Beloved*, 251.

58. Ibid., 73. This phrase frames Barnett's examination of history and collective memory in the novel.

59. Butler, *Kindred*, 101. Further citations given parenthetically in text.

60. Margaret Walker, "Southern Black Culture," 83.

Chapter Two. Jim Crow Returns, Jim Crow Remains

1. Lorde, "Afterimages," 339.

2. Ibid.

3. For an examination of the figure of Till in literary and cultural memory, see Metress and Pollack, *Emmett Till*.

4. Bradley, "Novelist Alice Walker," 331.

5. The novel was also adapted for a 2005 Broadway play.

6. Combahee River Collective, "Black Feminist Statement," 280.

7. This is a common observation in feminist criticism. See Thielman, "Alice Walker and the 'Man Question,'" for an overview of this dilemma specific to Walker and *The Color Purple*.

8. Byerman, *Remembering the Past*, 6. Byerman finds that trauma theory best accounts for the presentist designs of such historiographic fictions and "their desire to understand and explain the American past as it has impacted and continues to impact black people" (9).

9. Romine, *Narrative Forms of Southern Community*, 206.

10. Bradley, *Chaneysville Incident*, 2. Further citations given parenthetically in text.

11. Rushdy, *Remembering Generations*, 69.

12. George Henderson, "South of the North," 115.

13. Ibid., 113.

14. When John returns home, he thinks of himself as a "boogeyman" (29), similar to how Old Jack haunts the Hill from his shack out past the cemetery.

15. See Carby, "Ideologies of Black Folk," 139; George Henderson, "South of the North"; Rushdy, *Remembering Generations*.

16. George Henderson, "South of the North," 121.

17. Rushdy, *Remembering Generations*, 5.

18. The term "transgeneration aftereffects" is borrowed from Rushdy, *Remembering Generations*, 83.

19. Rushdy, *Remembering Generations*, 8.

20. On that last point, Thadious Davis considers works about the South by black northerners, including Bradley, and argues, "These are works by black outsiders to the region, who are nonetheless intimately involved in the process of revising not personal or individual history but communal and public history" ("Reclaiming the South," 64). The concern of regionality in the novel is shared by many, including Gourdine, regarding the African diaspora.

21. Byerman, *Remembering the Past*, 8.

22. Hogue, "Problematizing History," 442.

23. Ibid., 443.

24. Ensslen, "Fictionalizing History," 291. See Beardslee, *Literary Legacies,* for a discussion of oral history in the novel (59–98). Matthew Wilson, "African-American Historian," suggests that more than a counternarrative, John's revisionist history combines oral history and African American vernacular traditions with the traditional archive and official historical imagination to come to a synthetic understanding, or what Byerman calls a "coherent reconstruction" (*Remembering the Past,* 133), of both the past and one's present place in it. For a similar point, see Rushdy, *Remembering Generations,* 190–91n26.

25. Byerman, *Remembering the Past,* 126; Rushdy, *Remembering Generations,* 69. For an alternative reading, see Gliserman who reads this moment in psychoanalytic terms of a cold body "under tension" that holds five generations of pain (*Psychoanalysis,* 150), which achieves warmth by novel's end.

26. Rushdy, *Remembering Generations,* 88; Byerman, *Remembering the Past,* 131; Rushdy, *Remembering Generations,* 93.

27. Pavlić, *Crossroads Modernism,* 267–68. Tracking the trope of descent, Pavlić notes that Ellison's invisible man never fully emerges from underground and argues, "John Washington emerges from Afro-modernist seclusion and modern intellectual dissociation into diasporic modernist communion with his audience and ancestors" (xxi).

28. Rushdy, *Remembering Generations,* 84.

29. See George Henderson, "South of the North"; Hogue, "Problematizing History"; Lock, "Building Up from Fragments"; Pavlić, *Crossroads Modernism*; Wilson, "African-American Historian."

30. Pavlić, *Crossroads Modernism,* 272, 277.

31. George Henderson, "South of the North," 116.

32. Ibid., 117.

33. Bradley repeats the trope of stinky, buried history when John says to Judge Scott about Moses's death, "You just wanted to be sure they got him in the ground so you wouldn't have to smell the stink. But I've got news for you—they never bury anybody that deep" (*Chaneysville Incident,* 238).

34. Rushdy, *Remembering Generations,* 87.

35. Byerman, *Remembering the Past,* 134.

36. I am reversing James Baldwin's famed tongue-in-cheek response to miscegenation fears in *The Fire Next Time* (1962) when he questions why he would want to marry a white man's sister.

37. Byerman is also perplexed by the relationship: "Her devotion to the relationship is never at issue; in fact, one question is why she would want to sustain the connection given John's coldness, arrogance, and cynicism" (*Remembering the Past,* 134).

38. Egan, "Unraveling Misogyny," 265.

39. Ibid., 265, 267, 279, 286.

40. Moses, *Dissenting Fictions*, 55.

41. Ibid., 57.

42. Ibid., 76.

43. Alice Walker, "Writing *The Color Purple*," 359.

44. While there are abundant articles and books that feature the novel, in addition to McDowell, "Changing Same," and Jenkins, "Queering Black Patriarchy," some of the most influential feminist readings include Berlant, "Race, Gender, and Nation"; Bobo, "Sifting through the Controversy"; Trudier Harris, "On *The Color Purple*"; Mae Henderson, "*The Color Purple*"; Barbara Smith, "Truth That Never Hurts"; and Warhol, "How Narrative Produces Gender."

45. Watkins, "Sexism, Racism, and Black Women Writers," 1. He places Walker's work alongside literature by Ntozake Shange, Toni Morrison, Toni Cade Bambara, and Gayl Jones, as well as Michelle Wallace's *Black Macho and the Myth of the Superwoman* (1979).

46. Watkins, "Sexism, Racism, and Black Women Writers," 1.

47. Jenkins, "Queering Black Patriarchy," 970.

48. Thadious M. Davis, "Reclaiming the South," 65.

49. Alice Walker, *The Color Purple*, 11. Further citations given parenthetically in text.

50. Early, "Color Purple as Everybody's Protest Art," 266.

51. See Beaulieu, *Black Women Writers*, 140; Lysik, "You Have Seen How a [Wo]Man Was Made a Slave"; Rascher, "Neo–Slave Narratives."

52. Christian, "What Celie Knows," 23.

53. Ibid.

54. Jenkins argues, "By reexamining the ways that Walker's queering of the black patriarch, and disruption of oppositional gender roles within the black family, cast her as a kind of authorial 'cultural infidel,' scholars of her work might better understand how rigid sexual and familial hierarchies upon which the salvific wish is based forces a whole host of alternative familial ad national possibilities" ("Queering Black Patriarchy," 996).

55. Alice Walker, *In Search of Our Mothers' Gardens*, xi.

56. For more on the mirror scene, see Ross, *Manning the Race*.

57. See Rubin's famous essay, "The Traffic in Women: Notes on the 'Political Economy' of Sex."

58. Molly Hite argues that the film version amplifies the conflict between black men and women. She tracks how Steven Spielberg converts "Mister _____" to "Mister" and shifts the emphasis on female voice, reunion, and romance, "not only restoring voice to the father but making paternal words uniquely efficacious" because Mister's activities in D.C., an entirely new plot revision, seem to bring about Nettie and Celie's reunion (*Other Side of the Story*, 115–16).

59. Gilmore, *Gender and Jim Crow*, xxii.

60. Ibid.

61. Byerman, *Remembering the Past*, 136.

62. Bradley, "Novelist Alice Walker," 332.

63. Collins, *Black Sexual Politics*, 63.

Chapter Three. Jim Too

1. Quoted words from James Baldwin, *Blues for Mister Charlie*, xiv.

2. For more on racial polarization in Baldwin's play and its segregation aesthetic, see my "Baldwin's Unifying Polemic."

3. See Metress, "No Justice, No Peace," on recurring tropes in representations of Till.

4. Baraka, "*Jimmy!*," 132.

5. Gubar, *Racechanges*, 112–16; Chude-Sokei, *Last "Darky*," 1; Hale, *Making Whiteness*, 212; Lott, *Love and Theft*, 115.

6. Lhamon, *Raising Cain*, 176.

7. Wesley Brown, *Darktown Strutters*, 12. Further citations given parenthetically in text.

8. Lott, "Blackface and Blackness," 6.

9. Lott, *Love and Theft*, 22; Lhamon, "Who's Who?" 222; Lhamon, *Raising Cain*, 56; Cockrell, *Demons of Disorder*, xi, 15–16. Lott disentangles the stage trickster in minstrelsy from earlier and overlapping trickster slave tales, while also chronicling the influence of southwestern humor and circus traditions (23–25).

10. Southern, "Black Musicians," 43.

11. Ellison, "Change the Joke," 104.

12. Gubar, *Racechanges*, xx.

13. Hale broadens this historical observation in her discussion of representations of slaves and ex-slaves after emancipation: "African Americans were never the first folks to create slave or free images for themselves within either the southern regional context or the larger American culture of which the South was a distinct but vital part" (*Making Whiteness*, 17).

14. Lhamon, "Who's Who?" 223.

15. Gubar, *Racechanges*, 75.

16. Ibid., xiv.

17. Mahar, *Behind the Burnt Cork Mask*, 1.

18. Lott, *Love and Theft*, 30.

19. Chude-Sokei, *Last "Darky*," 8.

20. Ibid., 7.

21. Godfrey, "To Be Real," 13.

22. Abbott and Seroff, *Ragged but Right*, 3.

23. Lott, *Love and Theft*, 113.

24. Ibid., 113, 115, 20.

25. Lhamon, *Raising Cain*, 176, 178.

26. Hale, *Making Whiteness*, 151.

27. Smith and Apel, *Lynching Photographs*, 64.

28. Lhamon, *Raising Cain*, 176–77.

29. Ibid., 191.

30. Ibid.

31. Lott, *Love and Theft*, 27.

32. Lhamon, *Jump Jim Crow*, viii.

33. Herbert, "Bush's Not So Big Tent," A21.

34. Qtd. in Aftab, *Spike Lee*, 258

35. Tucker, *Lockstep and Dance*, 109.

36. Qtd. in Aftab, *Spike Lee*, 269.

37. Godfrey, "To Be Real," 11.

38. Tucker, *Lockstep and Dance*, 99, 109.

39. For another reading of *Bamboozled*'s presentation of the historical distance from blackface minstrelsy, especially around black collectibles, or "negro memorabilia," see Bill Brown, "Reification, Reanimation, and the American Uncanny," esp. 180–91.

40. Gubar, *Racechanges*, 11.

41. Ibid., xv.

42. Ross, *Manning the Race*, 84–85.

43. Abbott and Seroff, *Ragged but Right*, 4.

44. Tucker, *Lockstep and Dance*, 110.

45. Ibid., 115.

46. Lhamon, *Raising Cain*, 179.

47. Gubar, *Racechanges*, 96.

48. Hutcheon, *Poetics of Postmodernism*, 40.

Chapter Four. Jim Crow in Idaho

1. Alexie, *Reservation Blues*, 5. Further citations given parenthetically in text.

2. For more on blues and African American influence in Alexie, see Hafen, "Rock and Roll," and Paquaretta, "African-American Subjectivity."

3. Similar anxieties also reshaped literary studies outside the U.S. context; cf. Charles Bernheimer's *Comparative Literature in the Age of Multiculturalism* and Haun Saussy's *Comparative Literature in an Age of Globalization*.

4. John Howard Griffin, *Black Like Me*, 5. Further citations given parenthetically in text.

5. See, for example, Kate Baldwin, "Black Like Who?"; Lott, "White Like Me"; and Wald, "Most Disagreeable Mirror."

6. Vogel, *ReWriting Race*, 10.

7. Ronald Takaki traces an immigrant history in which "the newcomers from a Pacific shore found that racial qualities previously assigned to blacks had become 'Chinese'" (*Different Mirror*, 205). Takaki also traces how racist systems exploited interminority animosity, such as in the Reconstruction South where "[d]uring the 1870s, Louisiana and Mississippi planters imported several hundred Chinese laborers and pitted them against black workers" (202). See also Jun's discussion of the relation between African Americans and Asian Americans in nineteenth-century citizenship in "Black Orientalism"; and Rogers Smith's *Civic Ideals*, which discusses how post-Emancipation citizenship laws created legal categories of "black" and "white" and necessitated court cases to interpret the law for multiethnic America.

8. For a local multiethnic history of Pocatello, see Marsh, Purce, and Watkins, *"Triangle."*

9. Spanbauer, *Man Who Fell in Love*, 5. Further citations given parenthetically in text.

10. For a study of the foundling and fluid sexuality, see Nealon, *Foundlings*.

11. Allmendinger, *Ten Most Wanted*, 7.

12. Allmendinger, *Imagining the African American West*, 53.

13. Ibid., 130.

14. Gonzales-Day, *Lynching in the West*, 34.

15. Markovitz, *Legacies of Lynching*, xvi, xix, xx.

16. Lipez, "Mavericks of Excellent, Idaho," 4.

17. Huhndorf, *Indians*, 20.

18. Treuer, *Native American Fiction*, 160.

19. A good corollary example is reputedly Navajo writer Nasdijj whose memoir *The Boy and the Dog Are Sleeping* (2003) won a 2004 PEN/Beyond Margins award sponsored by the Open Book Committee to support literature by racial and ethnic minorities. Nasdijj was unmasked as gay white writer Tim Barrus, including an exposé in the *LA Weekly* in which Alexie accused Nasdijj of stealing his stories. See Fleisher, "Navahoax."

20. Belluscio, *To Be Suddenly White*, 1. Belluscio is quoting Elaine K. Ginsberg's *Passing and the Fictions of Identity*.

21. Sherry L. Smith, *Reimagining Indians*, 4.

22. Ifill, *On the Courthouse Lawn*, xii, xvii, xiv.

23. Scanlon, "Ethics and the Lyric," 18. Scanlon draws on work by Martha Nussbaum, Derek Attridge, Wayne Booth, and Michael Eskin, among others, and rescues the lyric genre from Mikhail Bakhtin's marginalization in his theories of dialogic narrative. She further explains, "Hayden's poem, with a subject so very abhorrent as lynching, provides a test case for the dialogic lyric and its participation in the forms and discourses of ethics that is both powerful and deceptively simple. As I anticipate my own reader, I actively hope and even expect that I address those whose outrage at racial violence is profound" (17–18).

24. Frederickson, *Black Image*, 328.

25. Washington reminded her audience, "Somehow, disturbingly, American studies was not part of the amazing renaissance in African-American culture in the 1970s" ("Disturbing the Peace," 3).

26. Washington, "Disturbing the Peace," 7–8.

27. Washington, Commentary, 699.

28. See for example Jonathan Brennan's collection *When Brer Rabbit Meets Coyote*.

29. Kingston, *Woman Warrior*, 49. Further citations given parenthetically in text.

30. Whalen Bridge, "Conversation," 80.

31. For instance, Singh and Schmidt urge more "intra-ethnic or multi-racial comparisons of Asian Americans, Blacks, Latinos, and Whites in ways that will not treat their cultural histories as if they developed autonomously" ("On the Borders," 7).

32. Kim, "Literature as Engagement," 117.

33. Takaki, *Different Mirror*, 7.

34. Wu, "Native Sons and Native Speakers," 1461.

35. Ibid., 1472.

Chapter Five. Jim Crow Faulkner

1. For an overview of Parks as playwright, see Geis, *Suzan-Lori Parks*.

2. Jiggets, "Interview with Suzan-Lori Parks," 317.

3. Drawing on blues traditions and Adrienne Rich's concept of writing as revision, Wall explains, "Whether one perceives texts as responding to their precursors or as signifying on them, tradition constitutes a theoretical line in which texts produce and are produced by other texts" (*Worrying the Line*, 11).

4. Nabers, "Past Using," 221, 222.

5. Parks, *Getting Mother's Body*, 3. Further citations given parenthetically in text.

6. Nabers, "Past Using," 222, 241.

7. In addition to Geis's overview of Parks as playwright, see Baker-White, "Questioning the Ground"; Brown-Guillory, "Reconfiguring History," esp. 191–92; Rayner and Elam, "Unfinished Business"; Ryan, "No Less Human"; and Worthen, "Citing History." Regarding African American literature, see, for example, Byerman, *Remembering the Past*, and Suzanne Jones, *Race Mixing*. Regarding Gaines's *A Lesson before Dying*, Byerman argues, "By situating the novel in the period just before the civil rights movement, he can engage the question of how much conditions have changed in the modern era of race relations" (45).

8. On Parks and holes, see Elam and Rayner, "Echoes from the Black (W)hole."

9. Brown-Guillory, "Reconfiguring History," 184.

10. Armstrong, "Suzan-Lori Parks"; "And Bear in Mind," 3; Rev. of *Getting Mother's Body*; Marshall, "Moment with . . . Suzan-Lori Parks."

11. Graham, "Not-So-Great Plains," 78.

12. Foundational work in this area includes Fowler and Abadie's key collection *Faulkner and Race* (1987) and work by Thadious Davis, Toni Morrison, James Snead, Eric Sundquist, Philip Weisenstein, and Judith Wittenberg, among many others. Wittenberg, "Race in *Light in August*," helpfully overviews such studies (148) and Faulkner's intertextual connections to black writers such as Nella Larsen (149).

13. Wittenberg, "Race in *Light in August*," 148.

14. Holland, "The Last Word on Racism," 416.

15. James Baldwin, "Faulkner and Desegregation," 106.

16. On the Bundrens, see Fabijancic, "Reification, Dereification, Subjectivity," and Leyda, "Reading White Trash." Three telling exceptions on race in *As I Lay Dying* are Towner's comparison, in "Black Matters on the Dixie Limited," of *As I Lay Dying* and Toni Morrison's *The Bluest Eye*; Gold's reading of Cora's whiteness in "A Mammy Callie Legacy" (156); and Baldanzi and Schlabach's discussion of American identity in the novel in the context of the 2002 Georgia crematory scandal ("What Remains?" 47–50).

17. Hughes, "First Fiction," 39; Graham, "Not-So-Great Plains," 78.

18. Weathersbee, Rev. of *Getting Mother's Body*.

19. On the Bundrens' abjection, see Calkins, "Be Careful."

20. Morrison, *Playing in the Dark*, 38.

21. Faulkner, *As I Lay Dying*, 213. Further citations given parenthetically in text.

22. Baldanzi and Schlabach, "What Remains?" 47.

23. Hutcheon, *Theory of Adaptation*, 121. Hutcheon builds on Cowart's work, which explores the multiple versions of symbiosis: parasitism, commensalism, and mutualism. See also Saunders, *Adaptation and Appropriation*.

24. On her *America Play*, Parks famously quips, "I don't see any history out there, so I've made some up" ("Alien Nation," 26). I am grateful to an anonymous reader for this connection.

25. "Day of Hope and Commitment," 221.

26. Rustin, "The Washington March," 226.

27. For more on Rustin, the march, and his role in civil rights memory, see D'Emilio, *Lost Prophet*; Rustin, *Time on Two Crosses*.

28. Allmendinger, *African American West*, 114.

29. McDonald, "Confronting Jim Crow."

30. Abel, "American Graffiti," 13.

31. Quoted in Elam, "Towards a New Territory," 92. Thank you to an anonymous journal reviewer for this reference.

32. For recent work on race, sexuality, and lynching, see Apel, *Imagery of Lynching*.

33. Baker, *Betrayal*, xii.

34. Alice Walker, "Choosing to Stay at Home," 168.

35. Michael Harris, Rev. of *Getting Mother's Body*, 5.

Epilogue. Jim Crow Today

1. Everett, *Erasure*, 29.

2. Whitehead, *John Henry Days*, 127.

3. Hale, *Making Whiteness*, 8.

4. Mark M. Smith, *How Race Is Made*, 66.

5. Obama, "A More Perfect Union."

6. U.S. Senate, "Apologizing."

7. Younge, "Jena Is America," 10.

8. Bill Brown, "Reification," 180.

9. Ibid., 183.

10. Ibid., 181.

11. Godfrey, "To Be Real," 29.

12. Abel, "American Graffiti," 22.

13. Younge, "Jena Is America," 10.

14. Pilgrim, "The Garbage Man."

15. Su, "Ghosts of Essentialism," 380–81.

16. Whitehead, *The Intuitionist*, 139. Further citations given parenthetically in text.

17. *Parents Involved in Community Schools v. Seattle School Dist.*

18. Ibid.

19. Bell, "Desegregation's Demise," B11.

20. James Baldwin, *Fire Next Time*, 94.

21. Spaulding, *Re-forming the Past*, 25.

22. Ibid.

23. Byerman, *Remembering the Past*, 10.

BIBLIOGRAPHY

Abbott, Lynn, and Doug Seroff. *Ragged but Right: Black Traveling Shows, "Coon Songs," and the Dark Pathway to Blues and Jazz.* Jackson: University Press of Mississippi, 2007.

Abel, Elizabeth. "American Graffiti: The Social Life of Segregation Signs." *African American Review* 42, no. 1 (2008): 9–24.

———. *Signs of the Times: The Visual Politics of Jim Crow.* Berkeley: University of California Press, 2010.

Abell, Joy L. "African/American: Lorraine Hansberry's *Les Blancs* and the American Civil Rights Movement." *African American Review* 35, no. 3 (2001): 459–70.

Aftab, Kaleem. *Spike Lee: That's My Story and I'm Sticking to It.* New York: Norton, 2005.

Alexie, Sherman. *Reservation Blues.* New York: Warner Books, 1995.

Allan, Tuzyline Jita. *Womanist and Feminist Aesthetics: A Comparative Review.* Athens: Ohio University Press, 1995.

Allen, James, ed. *Without Sanctuary: Lynching Photography in America.* Santa Fe: Twin Palms, 2000.

Allmendinger, Blake. *Ten Most Wanted: The New Western Literature.* New York: Routledge, 1998.

———. *Imagining the African American West.* Lincoln: University of Nebraska Press, 2005.

"And Bear in Mind." *New York Times Book Review,* May 25, 2003.

Apel, Dora. *Imagery of Lynching: Black Men, White Women, and the Mob.* New Brunswick, N.J.: Rutgers University Press, 2004.

Armstrong, Rhonda Jenkins. "Suzan-Lori Parks." In *Voices from the Gaps: Women Artists and Writers of Color, An International Website.* http://voices.cla.umn.edu/vg/Bios/entries/parks_suzanlori.html (accessed May 17, 2006).

Baker, Houston, Jr. *Modernism and the Harlem Renaissance.* Chicago: University of Chicago Press, 1989.

———. *Betrayal: How Black Intellectuals Have Abandoned the Ideals of the Civil Rights Era.* New York: Columbia University Press, 2008.

Baker-White, Robert. "Questioning the Ground of American Identity: George Pierce Baker's *The Pilgrim Spirit* and Suzan-Lori Parks's *The America Play.*" *Journal of American Drama and Theater* 12, no. 2 (2000): 71–89.

Baldanzi, Jessica, and Kyle Schlabach. "What Remains?: (De)composing and (Re)covering American Identity in *As I Lay Dying* and the Georgia Crematory Scandal." *Journal of the Midwest Modern Language Association* 36, no. 1 (2003): 38–55.

Baldwin, James. *Go Tell It on the Mountain*. 1953. Reprint, New York: Dial, 2000.

———. "Faulkner and Desegregation." In *Nobody Knows My Name*, 100–106. New York: Dial, 1961.

———. *The Fire Next Time*. 1963. Reprint, New York: Vintage, 1991.

———. *Blues for Mister Charlie*. New York: Dial, 1964.

———. "Sweet Lorraine." 1969. In *The Price of the Ticket: Collected Nonfiction, 1948–1985*, 443–47. New York: St. Martin's, 1985.

Baldwin, Kate. "Black Like Who?: Cross-Testing the 'Real' Lines of John Howard Griffin's *Black Like Me*." *Cultural Critique* 40 (1998): 103–43.

Baraka, Amiri. "A Wiser Play Than Some of Us Knew." *Los Angeles Times*, March 22, 1987, 41.

———. "Jimmy!" In *James Baldwin: the Legacy*, edited by Quincy Troupe, 127–34. New York: Simon & Schuster, 1989.

———. "Sweet Lorraine." In *The LeRoi Jones/Amiri Baraka Reader*, edited by William J. Harris, 525–28. New York: Thunder's Mouth, 1991.

Barnett, Pamela E. "Figurations of Rape and the Supernatural in *Beloved*." *PMLA* 112, no. 3 (1997): 418–27.

Beardsley, Karen. *Literary Legacies, Folklore Foundations: Selfhood and Cultural Tradition in Nineteenth and Twentieth-Century American Literature*. Knoxville: University of Tennessee Press, 2001.

Beatty, Paul. *White Boy Shuffle*. New York: Picador, 1996.

Beaulieu, Elizabeth Ann. *Black Women Writers and the American Neo–Slave Narrative*. Westport, Conn.: Greenwood Press, 1999.

Bell, Derrick. "Desegregation's Demise." *The Chronicle of Higher Education*, July 13, 2007: B11.

Belluscio, Steven J. *To Be Suddenly White: Literary Realism and Racial Passing*. Columbia: University of Missouri Press, 2006.

Berlant, Lauren. "Race, Gender, and Nation in *The Color Purple*." *Critical Inquiry* 14, no. 4 (1988): 831–59.

Berlin, Ira, et al., eds. *Remembering Slavery: African Americans Talk about Their Personal Experiences of Slavery and Emancipation*. 1999. Reprint, New York: New Press, 2007.

Bernheimer, Charles, ed. *Comparative Literature in the Age of Multiculturalism*. Baltimore: Johns Hopkins University Press, 1995.

Bernstein, Robin. "Inventing a Fishbowl: White Supremacy and the Critical Reception of Lorraine Hansberry's *A Raisin in the Sun*." *Modern Drama* 42, no. 1 (1999): 16–27.

Bigsby, C. W. E. *Confrontation and Commitment: A Study of Contemporary American Drama, 1959–66*. Columbia: University of Missouri Press, 1968.

Blandón, Ruth. "'¿Qué Dice?': Latin America and the Transnational in James

Weldon Johnson's *Autobiography of an Ex-Colored Man.*" In *Representing Segregation: Toward an Aesthetics of Living Jim Crow, and Other Forms of Racial Division*, edited by Brian Norman and Piper Kendrix Williams, 201–20. Albany, N.Y.: SUNY Press, 2010.

Blue, Carroll Parrott. *The Dawn at My Back: Memoir of a Black Texas Upbringing.* Austin: University of Texas Press, 2003.

Bobo, Jacqueline. "Sifting through the Controversy: Reading *The Color Purple.*" *Callaloo* 12, nos. 2/3 (1989): 332–42.

Bonner, Marita. "The Whipping." 1940. Reprint in *Imagining America: Stories from the Promised Land*, edited by Wesley Brown and Amy Ling, 12–20. New York: Persea, 1991.

Boston Women's Health Collective. *Our Bodies, Ourselves.* New York: Simon and Schuster, 1973.

Bradley, David. *The Chaneysville Incident.* 1981. Reprint, New York: Harper & Row, 1990.

———. "Novelist Alice Walker: Telling the Black Woman's Story." 1984. In *Speech and Power: The African-American Essay and Its Cultural Contents from Polemics to Pulpit*, edited by Gerald Early, 1:325–37. Hopewell, N.J.: Ecco Press, 1992.

Brennan, Jonathan, ed. *When Brer Rabbit Meets Coyote: African-Native American Literature.* Urbana: University of Illinois Press, 2003.

Brooks, Gwendolyn. *Maud Martha.* 1953. Reprint, Chicago: Third World Press, 1992.

———. "A Bronzeville Mother Loiters in Mississippi. Meanwhile, a Mississippi Mother Burns Bacon." 1960. In *Selected Poems*, 75–80. Reprint, New York: HarperPerennial, 1999.

Brown, Bill. "Reification, Reanimation, and the American Uncanny." *Critical Inquiry* 32, no. 2 (2006): 175–207.

Brown, Frank London. *Trumbull Park.* 1959. Reprint, Boston: Northeastern University Press, 2005.

Brown, Wesley. *Tragic Magic.* New York: Random House, 1978.

———. *Darktown Strutters.* New York: Cane Hill, 1994.

Brown-Guillory, Elizabeth. "Reconfiguring History: Migration, Memory, and (Re)Membering in Suzan-Lori Parks's Plays." In *Southern Women Playwrights*, edited by Robert L. McDonald and Linda Rohrer, 183–97. Tuscaloosa: University of Alabama Press, 2002.

Butler, Octavia. *Kindred.* 1979. Reprint, Boston: Beacon, 1988.

Byerman, Keith. *Remembering the Past in Contemporary African American Fiction.* Chapel Hill: University of North Carolina Press, 2005.

Calkins, Paul Luis. "Be Careful What You Wish For: *As I Lay Dying* and the Shaming of Abjection." *Faulkner Journal* 12, no. 1 (1996): 91–109.

Carby, Hazel. "Ideologies of Black Folk: The Historical Novel of Slavery." In *Slavery and the Literary Imagination*, edited by Deborah McDowell and Arnold Rampersad, 125–43. Baltimore: Johns Hopkins University Press, 1989.

Carter, Stephen. *New England White*. New York: Knopf, 2007.

Carter, Steven. *Hansberry's Drama: Commitment and Complexity*. Urbana: University of Illinois Press, 1991.

Caruth, Cathy. "The Claims of the Dead: History, Haunted Property, and the Law." *Critical Inquiry* 28, no. 2 (2002): 419–41.

Castronovo, Russ. *Beautiful Democracy: Aesthetics and Anarchy in a Global Era*. Chicago: University of Chicago Press, 2007.

Chafe, William, Raymond Gavins, and Robert Korstand, eds. *Remembering Jim Crow: African Americans Tell about Life in the Segregated South*. New York: New Press, 2008.

Christian, Barbara. "What Celie Knows That You Should Know." 1990. In *New Black Feminist Criticism, 1985–2000*, edited by Gloria Bowles, M. Giulia Fabi, and Arlene R. Keizer, 20–30. Reprint, Urbana: University of Illinois Press, 2007.

Chude-Sokei, Louis. *The Last "Darky": Bert Williams, Black-on-Black Minstrelsy, and the African Diaspora*. Durham, N.C.: Duke University Press, 2005.

Clark, Keith. *Black Manhood in the Fiction of James Baldwin, Ernest J. Gaines, and August Wilson*. Urbana: University of Illinois Press, 2004.

Cockrell, Dale. *Demons of Disorder: Early Blackface Minstrels and Their World*. Cambridge: Cambridge University Press, 1997.

Collins, Patricia Hill. *Black Sexual Politics: African Americans, Gender, and the New Racism*. New York: Routledge, 2005.

Combahee River Collective. "A Black Feminist Statement." 1977. In *Home Girls: A Black Feminist Anthology*, edited by Barbara Smith, 272–82. Reprint, Latham, N.Y.: Kitchen Table: Women of Color Press, 1983.

Cowart, David. *Literary Symbiosis*. Athens: University of Georgia Press, 1993.

Cox, Elizabeth. *Night Talk*. St. Paul, Minn.: Graywolf, 1997.

Crowther, Bosley. "*A Raisin in the Sun*." *New York Times*, March 30, 1961, 24.

Dailey, Jane, Glenda Elizabeth Gilmore, and Bryant Simon, eds. *Jumpin' Jim Crow: Southern Politics from Civil War to Civil Rights*. Princeton: Princeton University Press, 2000.

Davis, David. "Climbing Out of the 'Briar Patch': Robert Penn Warren and the Divided Conscience of Segregation." *Southern Quarterly* 40, no. 1 (2001): 109–20.

Davis, Ossie. "Malcolm X." In *Lit by Some Larger Vision: Selected Speeches and Writings*, 151–54. New York: Atria, 2006.

Davis, Thadious M. *Faulkner's "Negro": Art and the Southern Context*. Baton Rouge: Louisiana State University Press, 1983.

————. "Reclaiming the South." In *Bridging Southern Cultures: An Interdisciplinary Approach*, edited by John Lowe, 57–76. Baton Rouge: Louisiana State University Press, 2005.

Davis, Thulani. *1959*. New York: Grove Weidenfield, 1992.

"A Day of Hope and Commitment." Editorial. *The Crisis* 80, no. 7 (1973): 221–22.

Deloria, Philip J. *Playing Indian*. New Haven: Yale University Press, 1999.

D'Emilio, John. *Lost Prophet: The Life and Times of Bayard Rustin*. Chicago: University of Chicago Press, 2004.

Dixon, Thomas. *The Reconstruction Trilogy*. Newport Beach, Calif.: Noontide Press, 1997.

Douglas, Christopher. "What the Bluest Eye Knows about Them: Culture, Race, and Identity." *American Literary History* 78, no. 1 (2006): 141–68.

Dove, Rita. *On the Bus with Rosa Parks*. New York: W. W. Norton, 2000.

Dray, Philip. *At the Hands of Persons Unknown: The Lynching of Black America*. New York: Modern Library, 2003.

Du Bois, W. E. B. *The Souls of Black Folk*. 1903. Reprint, New York: Oxford University Press, 2007.

Duck, Leigh Anne. *The Nation's Region: Southern Modernism, Segregation, and U.S. Nationalism*. Athens: University of Georgia Press, 2006.

Dunbar, Eve. "Black Is a Region: Segregation and American Literary Regionalism in Richard Wright's *The Color Curtain*." *African American Review* 42, no. 1 (2008): 109–20.

Early, Gerald. "The Color Purple as Everybody's Protest Art." *Antioch Review* 44, no. 3 (1986): 261–75.

————, ed. *Speech and Power: The African-American Essay and Its Cultural Content from Polemics to Pulpit*. 2 vols. Hopewell, N.J.: Ecco Press, 1993.

Edwards, Brent Hayes. *The Practice of Diaspora*. Cambridge, Mass.: Harvard University Press, 2004.

Egan, Philip J. "Unraveling Misogyny and Forging the New Self: Mother, Lover, and Storyteller in *The Chaneysville Incident*." *Papers on Language and Literature* 33, no. 3 (1997): 265–87.

Ehrenstein, David. "Off-White Like Me." *LA Weekly*, March 26, 2008.

Elam, Harry, Jr. "Towards a New Territory in 'Multicultural' Theater." In *The Color of Theater*, edited by Roberta Uno and Lucy Mae Burns, 91–114. London: Continuum, 2002.

Elam, Harry, and Alice Rayner. "Echoes from the Black (W)hole: An Examination of *The America Play* by Suzan-Lori Parks." In *Performing America: Cultural Nationalism in American Theater*, edited by Jeffrey D. Mason and Ellen J. Gainor, 179–92. Ann Arbor: University of Michigan Press, 1999.

Elam, Michelle. "Passing in the Post-Race Era: Danzy Senna, Philip Roth, and Colson Whitehead." *African American Review* 41, no. 4 (2007): 749–68.

Ellison, Ralph. "Change the Joke, Slip the Yoke." 1958. In *The Collected Essays of Ralph Ellison*, 100–12. Reprint, New York: Modern Library, 1995.

———. "An Extravagance of Laughter." 1985. In *The Collected Essays of Ralph Ellison*, 613–58. Reprint, New York: Modern Library, 1995.

———. *Invisible Man*. 1952. Reprint, New York: Vintage, 1995.

Ensslen, Klaus. "Fictionalizing History: David Bradley's *The Chaneysville Incident*." *Callaloo* 11, no. 2 (1988): 280–96.

Ernest, John. *Liberation Historiography: African American Writers and the Challenge of History, 1794–1861*. Chapel Hill, N.C.: University of North Carolina Press, 2004.

Esteve, Mary. *The Aesthetics and Politics of the Crowd in American Literature*. Cambridge: Cambridge University Press, 2003.

Everett, Percival. *Erasure*. Lebanon, N.H.: University Press of New England, 2001.

Fabijancic, Tony. "Reification, Dereification, Subjectivity: Towards a Marxist Reading of William Faulkner's Poor-White Topography." *The Faulkner Journal* 10, no. 1 (1994): 75–94.

Faulkner, William. *As I Lay Dying*. 1930. Reprint, New York: Vintage, 1985.

———. *Light in August*. 1932. Reprint, New York: Vintage, 1991.

Fleisher, Matthew. "Navahoax." *LA Weekly*, January 26, 2006.

Fowler, Doreen, and Ann J. Abadie, eds. *Faulkner and Race*. Jackson: University Press of Mississippi, 1987.

Frederickson, George M. *The Black Image in the White Mind: The Debate on Afro-American Character and Destiny, 1817–1914*. New York: Harper and Row, 1971.

Fulton, DoVeanna S. *Speaking Power: Black Feminist Orality in Women's Narratives of Slavery*. Albany: SUNY Press, 2005.

Gaines, Ernest J. *The Autobiography of Miss Jane Pittman*. 1971. Reprint, New York: Dial, 2009.

———. *A Lesson before Dying*. New York: Knopf, 1997.

Gates, Henry Louis, Jr. *The Signifying Monkey: A Theory of African-American Literary Criticism*. New York: Oxford University Press, 1989.

Geis, Deborah. *Suzan-Lori Parks*. Ann Arbor: University of Michigan Press, 2008.

Gilmore, Glenda. *Gender and Jim Crow*. Chapel Hill: University of North Carolina Press, 1996.

Gilroy, Paul. *Against Race: Imagining Political Culture beyond the Color Line*. Cambridge, Mass.: Belknap, 2000.

———. *The Black Atlantic: Modernity and Double Consciousness*. 1993. Cambridge: Harvard University Press, 2003.

Ginsberg, Elaine K. *Passing and the Fictions of Identity*. Durham, N.C.: Duke University Press, 1996.

Gliserman, Martin. *Psychoanalysis, Language, and the Body of the Text.* Gainesville: University Press of Florida, 1996.

Godfrey, Esther. "'To Be Real': Drag, Minstrelsy, and Identity in the New Millennium." *Genders* 41 (2005). http://www.genders.org.

Goings, Kenneth. *Mammy and Uncle Mose: Black Collectibles and American Stereotyping.* Bloomington: Indiana University Press, 1994.

Gold, Lael. "A Mammy Callie Legacy." *Faulkner's Inheritance, edited by* Joseph R. Urgo and Ann J. Abadie, 141–59. Jackson: University of Mississippi Press, 2007.

Goldsby, Jacqueline. *A Spectacular Secret: Lynching in American Life and Literature.* Chicago: University of Chicago Press, 2006.

Gonzales-Day, Ken. *Lynching in the West: 1850–1935.* Durham, N.C.: Duke University Press, 2006.

Gordon, Michelle. "'Somewhat Like War': The Aesthetics of Segregation and *A Raisin in the Sun.*" *African American Review* 42, no. 1 (2008):121–34.

Gourdine, Angelletta K. M. "The *Drama* of Lynching in Two Blackwomen's Drama, or Relating Grimké's *Rachel* to Hansberry's *A Raisin in the Sun.*" *Modern Drama* 41, no. 4 (1998): 533–45.

———. *The Difference Place Makes: Gender, Sexuality, and Diaspora Identity.* Columbus: Ohio State University Press, 2002.

Graham, Don. "Not-So-Great Plains. *Texas Monthly* 31, no. 1 (2003): 74–80.

Gresham-Nemiroff, Jewell Handy. Foreword. In *A Raisin in the Sun: The Unfilmed Original Screenplay*, by Lorraine Hansberry, ix–xxii. New York: Penguin, 1994.

Grewal, Gurleen. "'Laundering the Head of Whitewash': Mimicry and Resistance in *The Bluest Eye.*" In *Approaches to Teaching the Novels of Toni Morrison*, edited by Nellie Y. McKay and Kathryn Earle, 118–26. New York: Modern Language Association of America, 1997.

Griffin, Farrah Jasmine. *"Who Set You Flowin'?": The African-American Migration Narrative.* New York: Oxford, 1995.

Griffin, John Howard. *Black Like Me.* 1961. Reprint, New York: Signet, 1996.

Grimké, Angelina Weld. *Rachel.* 1916. Reprint, Ann Arbor: University of Michigan Library, 2009.

Gubar, Susan. *Racechanges: White Skin, Black Face in American Culture.* New York: Oxford University Press, 1997.

Gunning, Sandra. *Race, Rape, and Lynching: The Red Record of American Literature, 1890–1912.* New York: Oxford University Press, 1996.

Hafen, P. Jane. "Rock and Roll, Redskins, and Blues in Sherman Alexie's Work." *Studies in American Indian Literature* 9, no. 4 (1997): 71–78.

Hale, Grace Elizabeth. *Making Whiteness: The Culture of Segregation in the South, 1890–1940.* New York: Pantheon, 1998.

Haley, Alex. *Roots.* New York: Doubleday, 1976.

Hall, Jacquelyn Dowd. "The Long Civil Rights Movement and the Political Uses of the Past." *Journal of American History* 91, no. 4 (2005): 1233–63.

Hammonds, Evelyn. "Black (W)holes and the Geometry of Black Female Sexuality." 1994. In *Feminism and Race*, edited by Kum-Kum Bhavnani, 379–93. New York: Oxford University Press, 2000.

Hansberry, Lorraine. *A Raisin in the Sun*. 1959. Reprint, New York: Random House, 1986.

———. "The Negro Writer and His Roots: Toward a New Romanticism." 1959. In *Speech and Power: The African-American Essay and Its Cultural Contents from Polemics to Pulpit*, edited by Gerald Early, 1:129–141. Hopewell, N.J.: Ecco Press, 1992.

———. "What Could Happen Didn't." *New York Herald Tribune*, March 26, 1961, 8.

———. *To Be Young, Gifted, and Black*, edited by Robert Nemiroff. New York: Penguin, 1970.

———. *A Raisin in the Sun: The Unfilmed Original Screenplay*. New York: Penguin, 1994.

Harris, Michael. Rev. of *Getting Mother's Body* by Suzan-Lori Parks. *Los Angles Times Book Review*, June 1, 2003: R5.

Harris, Trudier. "On *The Color Purple*, Stereotypes, and Silence." *Black American Literature Forum* 18, no. 4 (1984):155–61.

———. "Smacked Upside the Head—Again." Back Talk. *African American Review* 42, no. 1 (2008): 7–8.

Henderson, Carol E. *Scarring the Black Body: Race and Representation in African American Literature*. Columbia: University of Missouri Press, 2002.

Henderson, George L. "South of the North, North of the South: Spatial Practices in David Bradley's *The Chaneysville Incident*." In *Keep Your Head to the Sky: Cosmology, Ethics and the Making of African American Home Ground*, edited by Grey Gundaker, 113–43. Charlottesville: University Press of Virginia, 1998.

Henderson, Mae. "*The Color Purple*: Revisions and Redefinitions." *SAGE* 2, no. 1 (1985): 14–18.

Herbert, Bob. "Bush's Not So Big Tent." *New York Times*, July 16, 2004, A21.

Hite, Molly. *The Other Side of the Story: Structures and Strategies of Contemporary Feminist Narrative*. Ithaca, N.Y.: Cornell University Press, 1989.

Hogue, W. Lawrence. "Problematizing History: David Bradley's *The Chaneysville Incident*." *CLA Journal* 38, no. 4 (1995): 441–60.

Holland, Sharon P. "The Last Word on Racism: New Directions for a Critical Race Theory." *South Atlantic Quarterly* 104, no. 3 (2005): 403–23.

Hopkins, Pauline. *Winona*. 1902. Reprint in *The Magazine Novels of Pauline Hopkins*, 285–438. New York: Oxford University Press, 1990.

————. *Of One Blood*. 1903. Reprint in *The Magazine Novels of Pauline Hopkins*, 439–621. New York: Oxford University Press, 1990.

Hubbard, Dolan. *The Sermon and the African American Literary Imagination*. Columbia: University of Missouri Press, 1994.

Hughes, Carolyn. "First Fiction." *Poets & Writers* 31, no. 4 (2003): 36–46.

Hughes, Langston. *Not without Laughter*. 1930. Reprint, New York: Dover, 2008.

Huhndorf, Shari. *Indians in the American Cultural Imagination*. Ithaca: Cornell University Press, 2001.

Hurston, Zora Neale. *Their Eyes Were Watching God*. 1937. Reprint, New York: HarperPerennial, 1990.

Hutcheon, Linda. *A Poetics of Postmodernism: History, Theory, Fiction*. New York: Routledge, 1988.

————. *A Theory of Adaptation*. New York: Routledge, 2006.

Ifill, Sherrilynn. *On the Courthouse Lawn: Confronting the Legacy of Lynching in the Twenty-first Century*. Boston: Beacon, 2007.

Jackson, John L., Jr. "Little Black Magic." *Racial Americana*. Special issue of *South Atlantic Quarterly* 104, no. 3 (2005): 393–402.

Jackson, John P., Jr. *Science for Segregation: Race, Law, and the Case against Brown v. Board of Education*. New York: New York University Press, 2005.

Jenkins, Candice M. "Queering Black Patriarchy: The Salvific Wish and Masculine Possibility in Alice Walker's *The Color Purple*." *Modern Fiction Studies* 38, no. 4 (2002): 969–1000.

Jiggetts, Shelby. "Interview with Suzan-Lori Parks." *Callaloo* 19, no. 2 (1996): 309–17.

Johnson, Charles. *Middle Passage*. New York: Plume, 1990.

Johnson, James Weldon. *The Autobiography of an Ex-Colored Man*. 1912. Reprint, New York: Hill and Wang, 1991.

————. *Along the Way*. 1933. Reprint, New York: Penguin, 2008.

Jones, Edward P. *The Known World*. New York: Amistad, 2003.

Jones, Gayl. *Corregidora*. New York: Random House, 1975.

Jones, Suzanne. *Race Mixing: Southern Fiction since the Sixties*. Baltimore: Johns Hopkins University Press, 2004.

Jun, Helen H. "Black Orientalism: Nineteenth-Century Narratives of Race and U.S. Citizenship." *American Quarterly* 58, no. 4 (2006): 1048–66.

Kenan, Randall. "This Far; Or, A Body in Motion." In *Let the Dead Bury Their Dead*, 140–62. San Diego: Harcourt Brace, 1992.

Keppel, Ben. *The Work of Democracy: Ralph Bunche, Kenneth B. Clark, Lorraine Hansberry and the Cultural Politics of Race*. Cambridge, Mass.: Harvard University Press, 1995.

Kim, Myung Ja. "Literature as Engagement: Teaching African American Literature to Korean Students." *MELUS* 29, nos. 3–4 (2004): 103–20.

Kincaid, Nanci. *Crossing Blood*. New York: Putnam, 1992.

Kingston, Maxine Hong. *The Woman Warrior*. 1975. Reprint, New York: Vintage, 1989.

Klotman, Phyllis R. "Dick-and-Jane and the Shirley Temple Sensibility in *The Bluest Eye*." *Black American Literature Forum* 13, no. 4 (1979): 123–25.

Kubitsche, Missy Dehn. "'So You Want a History Do You?': Epistemologies and *The Chaneysville Incident*." *Mississippi Quarterly* 49, no. 4 (1996): 755–74.

Kushner, Tony. *Caroline, Or Change*. New York: Theater Communications Group, 2004.

Larsen, Nella. *Passing*, 1929. Reprint, New York: W. W. Norton, 2007.

Leak, Jeffrey. *Racial Myths and Masculinity in African American Literature*. Knoxville: University of Tennessee Press, 2005.

Lee, Chang-Rae. *Native Speaker*. New York: Riverhead, 1995.

Lee, Spike. "Commentary: Thoughts on the Screenplay." In *A Raisin in the Sun: The Unfilmed Original Screenplay*, by Lorraine Hansberry, xlv–xlvii. New York: Penguin, 1994.

———. *Bamboozled*. New Line Cinema, 2000.

Leeming, David. *James Baldwin: A Biography*. New York: Knopf, 1994.

Lester, Cheryl. "Racial Awareness and Arrested Development: *The Sound and the Fury* and the Great Migration (1915–1928)." In *The Cambridge Companion to William Faulkner*, edited by Philip M. Weinstein, 123–45. New York: Cambridge University Press, 1995.

Leyda, Julia. "Reading White Trash: Class, Race, and Mobility in Faulkner and Le Sueur." *Arizona Quarterly* 56, no. 2 (2000): 37–64.

Lhamon, W. T., Jr. *Raising Cain: Blackface Performance from Jim Crow to Hip Hop*. Cambridge, Mass.: Harvard University Press, 1998.

———. "Who's Who." Afterword. In *Darktown Strutters*, by Wesley Brown, 221–30. Amherst: University of Massachusetts Press, 2000.

———. *Jump Jim Crow: Lost Plays, Lyrics, and Street Prose of the First Atlantic Popular Culture*. Cambridge, Mass.: Harvard University Press, 2003.

Lipari, Lisbeth. "'Fearful of the Written Word': White Fear, Black Writing, and Lorraine Hansberry's *A Raisin in the Sun* Screenplay." *Quarterly Journal of Speech* 90, no. 1 (2004): 81–102.

Lipez, Richard. "The Mavericks of Excellent, Idaho." Review of *The Man Who Fell in Love with the Moon*, by Tom Spanbauer. *Washington Post Book World*, October 6, 1991, 4.

"Listen, Don't Look." *Newsweek*, April 10, 1961, 103.

Lock, Helen. "'Building Up from Fragments': The Oral Memory Process in Some Recent African-American Written Narratives." *College Literature* 22, no. 3 (1995): 109–20.

Locke, Alain, ed. *The New Negro*. 1925. Reprint, New York: Touchstone, 1999.

Lorde, Audre. "Afterimages." 1982. *The Collected Poems of Audre Lorde, 339*. Reprint, New York: W. W. Norton, 1997.

Lott, Eric. *Love and Theft: Blackface Minstrelsy and the American Working Class.* New York: Oxford University Press, 1993.

———. "White Like Me: Racial Cross-Dressing and the Construction of American Whiteness." In *Cultures of United States Imperialism*, edited by Amy Kaplan and Donald Pease, 474–95. Durham, N.C.: Duke University Press, 1993.

———. "Blackface and Blackness: The Minstrel Show in American Culture." In *Inside the Minstrel Mask: Readings in Nineteenth-Century Blackface*, edited by Annemarie Bean and James Hatch, 3–32. Middletown, Conn.: Wesleyan University Press, 1996.

Love, Nat. *The Life and Adventures of Nat Love; Better Known in the Cattle Country as "Deadwood Dick."* 1907. Reprint, Charleston, S.C.: BiblioBazaar, 2007.

Lowe, John, ed. *Bridging Southern Cultures: An Interdisciplinary Approach.* Baton Rouge: Louisiana State University Press, 2005.

Lysik, Marta. "'You Have Seen How a [Wo]Man Was Made a Slave; You Shall See How a Slave Was Made a [Wo]Man': Alice Walker's *The Color Purple* as Neo–Slave Narrative." *American Studies* (Warsaw, Poland) 21 (2004): 17–34.

Mahar, William J. *Behind the Burnt Cork Mask: Early Blackface Minstrelsy and Antebellum American Popular Culture.* Urbana: University of Illinois Press, 1999.

Malcolm X, as told to Alex Haley. *The Autobiography of Malcolm X.* 1965. Reprint, New York: Ballantine, 1992.

Maly, Michael T. *Beyond Segregation: Multiracial and Multiethnic Neighborhoods in the United States.* Philadelphia: Temple University Press, 2005.

Markovitz, Jonathan. *Legacies of Lynching: Racial Violence and Memory.* Minneapolis: University of Minnesota Press, 2004.

Marouan, Maha. "Interpolating Harriet Tubman: Representation of Gender and Heroism in David Bradley's *The Chaneysville Incident*." *Columbia Journal of American Studies*. http://www.cjasmonthly.com/chaneysville1.html (accessed March 12, 2008).

Marsh, Kevin, Thompson Purce, and Mary Sanders Watkins. *The "Triangle": A Slice of America.* Pocatello: City of Pocatello Planning and Development Services, 2006.

Marshall, John. "A Moment with . . . Suzan-Lori Parks, Playwright." *Seattle Post-Intelligencer*, May 26, 2003.

Martin, Michael E. *Residential Segregation Patterns of Latinos in the United States, 1990–2000: Testing the Ethnic Enclave and Inequality Theories.* New York: Routledge, 2007.

McBride, James. *Song yet Sung.* New York: Riverhead, 2008.

McCaskill, Barbara, and Caroline Gebhard. *Post-Bellum, Pre-Harlem: African American Literature and Culture, 1877–1919*. New York: New York University Press, 2006.

McDonald, Jason. "Confronting Jim Crow in the 'Lone Star' Capital: The Contrasting Strategies of African-American and Ethnic-Mexican Political Leaders in Austin, Texas, 1910–1930." *Continuity and Change* 22, no. 1 (2007): 143–69.

McDowell, Deborah. "'The Changing Same': Black Women's Literature, Criticism, and Theory." *New Literary History* 18, no. 2 (1987): 281–302.

McDowell, Deborah, and Arnold Rampersad, eds. *Slavery and the Literary Imagination*. Baltimore: Johns Hopkins University Press, 1989.

McKittrick, Katherine, and Clyde Woods. *Black Geographies and the Politics of Place*. Cambridge, Mass.: South End Press, 2007.

Metress, Christopher. "'No Justice, No Peace': The Figure of Emmett Till in African American Literature." *MELUS* 28, no. 1 (2003): 87–103.

Metress, Christopher, and Harriet Pollack, eds. *Emmett Till in Literary Memory and Imagination*. Baton Rouge: Louisiana State University Press, 2008.

Miller, Jeanne-Marie A. "'Measuring Him Right': An Analysis of Lorraine Hansberry's *A Raisin in the Sun*." In *Teaching American Ethnic Literatures*, edited by John R. Maitino and David R. Peck, 133–45. Albuquerque: University of New Mexico Press, 1996.

Morrison, Toni. *The Bluest Eye*. 1970. Reprint, New York: Penguin, 1994.

———. *Beloved*. 1987. Reprint, New York: Plume, 1988.

———. *Playing in the Dark: Whiteness and the Literary Imagination*. New York: Vintage, 1992.

———. *Paradise*. New York: Knopf, 1997.

———. *Remember: The Journey to School Integration*. Boston: Houghton Mifflin, 2004.

———. *A Mercy*. New York: Knopf, 2008.

Moses, Cathy. *Dissenting Fictions: Identity and Resistance in the Contemporary American Novel*. New York: Garland, 2000.

Muir, Chris. *Day by Day*. April 26, 2007, www.daybydaycartoon.com.

Nabers, Deak. "Past Using: James Baldwin and Civil Rights Law in the 1960s." *Yale Journal of Criticism* 18, no. 2 (2005): 221–42.

Nealon, Christopher. *Foundlings: Lesbian and Gay Historical Emotion Before Stonewall*. Durham, N.C.: Duke University Press, 2001.

Nemiroff, Robert. Introduction. In *A Raisin in the Sun*, by Lorraine Hansberry, 5–14. New York: Random House, 1986.

Norman, Brian. "Reading a 'Closet Screenplay': Hollywood, James Baldwin's Malcolms, and the Threat of Historical Irrelevance." *African American Review* 39, nos. 1–2 (2005): 103–18.

———. "Baldwin's Unifying Polemic: Racial Segregation, Moral Integration, and the Polarizing Figure of Emmett Till." In *Emmett Till in Literary Memory and Imagination*, edited by Christopher Metress and Harriet Pollack, 75–97. Baton Rouge: Louisiana State University Press, 2008.

Norman, Brian, and Piper Kendrix Williams, eds. "Representing Segregation." Special issue, *African American Review* 42, no. 1 (2008): 1–178.

———. *Representing Segregation: Toward an Aesthetics of Living Jim Crow, and Other Forms of Racial Division*. Albany, N.Y.: SUNY Press, 2010.

North, Michael. *The Dialect of Modernism: Race, Language, and Twentieth-Century Literature*. New York: Oxford University Press, 1998.

Obama, Barack. "A More Perfect Union." Speech. Philadelphia, Pennsylvania, March 18, 2008. http://www.whitehouse.gov.

O'Brien, C. C. "Cosmopolitanism in Georgia Douglas Johnson's Anti-Lynching Literature." *African American Review* 38, no. 4 (2004): 571–88.

Okada, John. *No-No Boy*. 1957. Reprint, Seattle: University of Washington Press, 1978.

Palliser, Charles. "Predestination and Freedom in *As I Lay Dying*." *American Literature* 58, no. 4 (1986): 557–73.

Paquaretta, Patricia. "African-American Subjectivity and the Blues Voice in the Writings of Toni Morrison and Sherman Alexie." In *When Brer Rabbit Meets Coyote: African-Native American Literature*, edited by Jonathan Brennan, 278–91. Urbana: University of Illinois Press, 2003.

Parents Involved in Community Schools v. Seattle School Dist. No. 1. No. 05 908; No. 05–915. Sup. Ct. of the U.S. 28 June 2007.

Parks, Suzan-Lori. "Alien Nation: An Interview with the Playwright by Michele Pearce." *American Theatre* 13 (1994): 26

———. *Getting Mother's Body*. New York: Random House, 2003.

Patton, Venetria K. *Women in Chains: The Legacy of Slavery in Black Women's Fiction*. Albany, N.Y.: SUNY Press, 2000.

Pavlić, Ed. *Crossroads Modernism: Descent and Emergence in African-American Literary Culture*. Minneapolis: University of Minnesota Press, 2002.

Peckham, Joel. "Segregation/Integration: Race, History, and Theoretical Practice in the American South." *Southern Quarterly* 40, no. 1 (2001): 28–38.

Pemberton, Gayle. "Black Women Writers." *New York Times*, July 17, 1986, 21.

Petry, Ann. *The Street*. 1946. Reprint, Boston: Mariner Books, 1998.

Pfeifer, Michael J. *Rough Justice: Lynching and American Society, 1874–1947*. Urbana: University of Illinois Press, 2004.

Pilgrim, David. "The Garbage Man: Why I Collect Racist Objects." *Jim Crow Museum of Racist Memorabilia*. http://www.ferris.edu/jimcrow/.

Posnock, Ross. *Color and Culture: Black Writers and the Making of the Modern Intellectual.* Cambridge, Mass.: Harvard University Press, 1998.

Raiford, Leigh. "'Come Let Us Build a New World Together': SNCC and Photography of the Civil Rights Movement." *American Quarterly* 59, no. 4 (2007): 1129–57.

"*A Raisin in the Sun.*" *Time,* March 31, 1961.

Randall, Alice. *The Wind Done Gone.* Boston: Mariner, 2002.

Rascher, Stephen Robert. "The Neo–Slave Narratives of Hurston, Walker, and Morrison: Rewriting the Black Woman's Slave Narrative." PhD diss., University of Connecticut, 1998.

Rayner, Alice, and Harry Elam. "Unfinished Business: Reconfiguring History in Suzan-Lori Parks's *The Death of the Last Black Man in the Whole Entire World.*" *Theater Journal* 46 (1994): 448–61.

Reed, Ishmael. *Flight to Canada.* New York: Random House, 1976.

———. *Reckless Eyeballing.* New York: St. Martin's, 1986.

Reid, Mark A. "*Take a Giant Step, A Raisin in the Sun*: The U.S. Black Family Film." *Jump Cut* 36 (1991): 81–88.

Reilly, John M. "History-Making Literature." In *Belief vs. Theory in Black American Literary Criticism,* edited by Joe Weixlmann, 85–120. Greenwood, Fla.: Penkevill, 1986.

Rev. of *Getting Mother's Body. Kirkus Reviews* 71, no. 6 (2003): 422.

Rice, Anne P. *Witnessing Lynching: American Writers Respond.* New Brunswick: Rutgers University Press, 2003.

Rich, Adrienne. "The Problem with *Lorraine Hansberry.*" *Freedomways* 19 (1979): 247–55.

Roberts, Gene, and Hank Klibanoff. *The Race Beat: The Press, the Civil Rights Struggle, and the Awakening of a Nation.* New York: Vintage, 2007.

Robinson, Angelo. "Race, Place, and Space Re-Making Whiteness in the Post-Reconstruction South." *Southern Literary Journal* 35, no. 1 (2002): 97–107.

Rodgers, Lawrence. *Canaan Bound: The African American Great Migration Novel.* Chicago: University of Illinois Press, 1997.

Rogin, Michael. *Blackface, White Noise: Jewish Immigrants in the Hollywood Melting Pot.* Berkeley: University of California Press, 1998.

Romano, Renee, and Leigh Raiford, eds. *The Civil Rights Movement in American Memory.* Athens: University of Georgia Press, 2006.

Romine, Scott. *The Narrative Forms of Southern Community.* Baton Rouge: Louisiana State University Press, 1999.

Ross, Daniel W. "Celie in the Looking Glass: The Desire for Selfhood in *The Color Purple.*" *Modern Fiction Studies* 34, no. 1 (1988): 69–84.

Ross, Marlon B. *Manning the Race: Reforming Black Men in the Jim Crow Era.* New York: New York University Press, 2004.

Roth, Philip. *The Human Stain.* New York: Houghton Mifflin, 2000.

Rubin, Gayle. "The Traffic in Women: Notes on the 'Political Economy' of Sex." 1976. In *The Second Wave: A Reader in Feminist Theory,* edited by Linda Nicholson, 27–62. New York: Routledge, 1997.

Rushdy, Ashraf. *Neo–Slave Narratives: Studies in the Social Logic of a Literary Form.* New York: Oxford University Press, 1999.

———. *Remembering Generations: Race and Family in Contemporary African American Fiction.* Chapel Hill: University of North Carolina Press, 2001.

Rustin, Bayard. "The Washington March: A Ten-Year Perspective." *The Crisis* 80, no. 7 (1973): 224–27.

———. *Time on Two Crosses: The Collected Writings of Bayard Rustin.* San Francisco: Cleis, 2003.

Ryan, Katy. "'No Less Human': Making History in Suzan-Lori Parks' *The America Play.*" *Journal of Dramatic Theory and Criticism* 13, no. 2 (1999): 81–94.

Saunders, Julie. *Adaptation and Appropriation.* New York: Routledge, 2005.

Saussy, Haun. *Comparative Literature in an Age of Globalization.* Baltimore: Johns Hopkins University Press, 2006.

Scanlon, Mara. "Ethics and the Lyric: Form, Dialogue, Answerability." *College Literature* 34, no. 1 (2007): 1–22.

Schleitwiler, Vince. "Into a Burning House: Representing Segregation's Death." *African American Review* 42, no. 1 (2008): 149–62.

Shange, Ntozake. *For Colored Girls Who Have Considered Suicide / When the Rainbow Is Enuf.* 1975. New York: Scribner and Sons, 1977.

Sharpe, Jenny. *Ghosts of Slavery: A Literary Archaeology of Black Women's Lives.* Minneapolis: University of Minnesota Press, 2003.

Singh, Amritjit, and Peter Schmidt. "On the Borders between U.S. Studies and Postcolonial Theory." In *Postcolonial Theory and the United States: Race, Ethnicity, and Literature,* 3–69. Jackson: University Press of Mississippi, 2002.

Smith, Barbara. "The Truth That Never Hurts: Black Lesbians in Fiction in the 1980s." In *Feminisms: An Anthology of Literary Theory and Criticism,* edited by Robyn Warhol, 784–806. New Brunswick, N.J.: Rutgers University Press, 1997.

Smith, Mark M. *How Race Is Made: Slavery, Segregation, and the Senses.* Chapel Hill: University of North Carolina Press, 2006.

Smith, Rogers M. *Civic Ideals: Conflicting Visions of Citizenship in U.S. History.* New Haven: Yale University Press, 1999.

Smith, Shawn Michelle, and Dora Apel. *Lynching Photographs.* Berkeley: University of California Press, 2008.

Smith, Sherry L. *Reimagining Indians: Native Americans through Anglo Eyes, 1880–1940*. New York: Oxford University Press, 2000.

Smith, Wendy. "Words as Crossroads." *Publisher's Weekly*, May 12, 2003, 37–38.

Snead, James. *Figures of Division: William Faulkner's Major Novels*. New York: Methuen, 1986.

Sollors, Werner. *Neither Black nor White yet Both*. New York: Oxford University Press, 1997.

Southern, Eileen, ed. "Black Musicians and Early Ethiopian Minstrelsy." In *Inside the Minstrel Mask: Readings in Nineteenth-Century Blackface Minstrelsy*, edited by Annemarie Bean, James V. Hatch, and Brooks McNamara, 43–63. Hanover, N.H.: Wesleyan University Press, 1996.

Spanbauer, Tom. *The Man Who Fell in Love with the Moon*. New York: Atlantic Monthly, 1991.

Spaulding, Timothy. *Re-forming the Past: History, the Fantastic, and the Postmodern Slave Narrative*. Columbus: Ohio State University Press, 2005.

Spillers, Hortense. Commentary. Panel on "Psychoanalysis, Segregation, and the Sign." Paper presented at annual meeting of the Modern Language Association, San Francisco, December 27, 2008.

Stephens, Judith. "Racial Violence and Representation: Performance Strategies in Lynching Dramas of the 1920s." *African American Review* 33, no. 4 (1999): 655–71.

Stewart, Jacqueline. "'Negroes Laughing at Themselves?' Black Spectatorship and the Performance of Urban Modernity." *Critical Inquiry* 29, no. 4 (2003): 650–77.

Stowe, Harriet Beecher. *Uncle Tom's Cabin, or, Life Among the Lowly*. 1853. Reprint, New York: Modern Library, 2001.

Strasbaugh, John. *Black Like You: Blackface, Whiteface, Insult, and Imitation in American Popular Culture*. New York: Tarcher, 2006.

Styron, William. *The Confessions of Nat Turner*. New York: New American Library, 1967.

Su, John J. "Ghosts of Essentialism: Racial Memory as Epistemological Claim." *American Literature* 81, no. 2 (2009): 361–86.

Sundquist, Eric. *Faulkner: The House Divided*. Baltimore: Johns Hopkins University Press, 1983.

———, ed. *To Wake the Nations: Race in the Making of American Literature*. Cambridge: Harvard University Press, 1993.

Takaki, Ronald. *A Different Mirror: A History of Multiracial America*. Boston: Little, Brown, 1993.

Terkel, Studs. *The Spectator: Talk about Movies and Plays with the People Who Make Them*. New York: New Press, 1999.

Thielmann, Pia. "Alice Walker and the 'Man Question.'" In *Critical Essays on Alice*

Walker, edited by Ikenna Dieke, 67–82. Westport, Conn.: Greenwood Press, 1999.

Thomas, Brook. "Plessy v. Ferguson and the Literary Imagination." *Cardoza Studies* 9, no. 1 (1997): 45–65.

———. *Civic Myths: A Law-and-Literature Approach to Citizenship*. Chapel Hill: University of North Carolina Press, 2007.

Totten, Gary. "Embodying Segregation: Ida B. Wells and the Cultural Work of Travel." *African American Review* 42, no. 1 (2008): 47–60.

Towner, Theresa M. "Black Matters on the Dixie Limited: *As I Lay Dying* and *The Bluest Eye*." In *Unflinching Gaze: Morrison and Faulkner Re-Envisioned*, edited by Carol A. Kolmerten, 115–27. Jackson: University Press of Mississippi, 1997.

Treuer, David. *Native American Fiction: A User's Manual*. Saint Paul, Minn.: Graywolf, 2006.

Trodd, Zoe. "A Negative Utopia: Protest Memory and Spatio-Symbolism of Civil Rights Literature and Photography." *African American Review* 42, no. 1 (2008): 25–40.

Tucker, Linda G. *Lockstep and Dance: Images of Black Men in Popular Culture*. Jackson: University Press of Mississippi, 2007.

Tyner, James. *War, Violence, and Population: Making the Body Count*. New York: Guilford, 2009.

U.S. Senate. "Apologizing for the Enslavement and Segregation of African-Americans." Resolution 26. 111th Cong., 1st sess. 11 June 2009. Passed 18 June 2009. www.senate.gov.

Vogel, Todd. *ReWriting White: Race, Class, and Cultural Capital in Nineteenth-Century America*. New Brunswick, N.J.: Rutgers University Press, 2004.

Wald, Gayle. "'A Most Disagreeable Mirror': Reflections on White Identity in *Black Like Me*." In *Crossing the Color Line: Racial Passing in Twentieth-Century U.S. Literature and Culture*, 152–81. Durham, N.C.: Duke University Press, 2000.

Waldrep, Christopher, ed. *Lynching in America: A History in Documents*. New York: New York University Press, 2006.

Walker, Alice. "Choosing to Stay at Home: Ten Years after the March on Washington." 1973. In *In Search of Our Mothers' Gardens*, 158–70.

———. *The Color Purple*. 1982. New York: Simon & Schuster, 1985.

———. "Writing *The Color Purple*." 1982. In *In Search of Our Mothers' Gardens*, 355–60.

———. *In Search of Our Mothers' Gardens*. New York: Harcourt Brace, 1983.

Walker, Margaret. "How I Told My Child about Race." 1951. In *Speech and Power: The African-American Essay and Its Cultural Contents from Polemics to Pulpit*, edited by Gerald Early, 2:495–98. Hopewell, N.J.: Ecco Press, 1992.

———. *Jubilee*. Boston: Houghton Mifflin, 1976.

———. "Southern Black Culture." 1976. In *On Being Female, Black, and Free: Essays by Margaret Walker, 1932–1992*, 79–85. Knoxville: University of Tennessee Press, 1997.

Wall, Cheryl. *Worrying the Line: Black Women Writers, Lineage, and Literary Tradition*. Chapel Hill: University of North Carolina Press, 2005.

———. Afterword. "Representing Segregation." Special Issue, *African American Review* 42, no. 1 (2008): 163–64.

Wallace-Sanders, Kimberly. *Mammy: A Century of Race, Gender, and Southern Memory*. Ann Arbor: University of Michigan Press, 2008.

Warhol, Robyn. "How Narrative Produces Gender: Femininity as Affect and Effect in Alice Walker's *The Color Purple*." *Narrative* 9, no. 2 (2001): 182–87.

Washington, J. Charles. "*A Raisin in the Sun* Revisited." *Black American Literature Forum* 22, no. 1 (1988): 109–24.

Washington, Mary Helen. "Disturbing the Peace: What Happens to American Studies If You Put African American Studies at the Center?" *American Quarterly* 50, no. 1 (1998): 1–23.

———. "Alice Childress, Lorraine Hansberry, and Claudia Jones: Black Women Write the Popular Front." In *Left of the Color Line: Race, Radicalism, and Twentieth-Century Literature of the United States*, edited by Bill Mullen and James Smethurst, 183–204. Chapel Hill: University of North Carolina Press, 2003.

———. Commentary. *American Quarterly* 55, no. 4 (2003): 697–702.

Watkins, Mel. "Sexism, Racism, and Black Women Writers." *New York Times*, June 15, 1986, 1.

———. *On the Real Side: A History of African American Comedy from Slavery to Chris Rock*. Chicago: Lawrence Hill, 1999.

Weathersbee, Avis. Rev. of *Getting Mother's Body* by Suzan-Lori Parks. *Chicago Sun-Times*, June 24, 2003.

Weaver, Jace, Craig Womack, and Robert Warrior. *American Indian Literary Nationalism*. Albuquerque: University of New Mexico Press, 2006.

Weisenstein, Philip. *What Else but Love?: The Ordeal of Race in Faulkner and Morrison*. New York: Columbia University Press, 1996.

Whalen Bridge, John. "A Conversation with Charles Johnson and Maxine Hong Kingston." *MELUS* 31, no. 2 (2006): 69–94.

Whitehead, Colson. *The Intuitionist*. 1999. New York: Anchor, 2000.

———. *John Henry Days*. New York: Doubleday, 2001.

Wilkerson, Margaret. Introduction. *A Raisin in the Sun: The Unfilmed Original Screenplay*, by Lorraine Hansberry, xxix–xiiv. New York: Penguin, 1994.

Williams, Sherley Anne. *Dessa Rose*. New York: Morrow, 1986.

Wilson, Matthew. "The African-American Historian: David Bradley's *The Chaneysville Incident.*" *African American Review* 29, no. 2 (1995): 97–107.

Wise, Tim. *White Like Me: Reflections on Race from a Privileged Son.* New York: Soft Skull, 2004.

Wittenberg, Judith Bryant. "Race in *Light in August*: Wordsymbols and Obverse Reflections." In *The Cambridge Companion to William Faulkner*, edited by Philip M. Weinstein, 146–67. New York: Cambridge University Press, 1995.

Wolfe, George C. *The Colored Museum.* 1985. Reprint, New York: Grove, 1994.

Wood, Amy Louise. *Lynching and Spectacle: Witnessing Racial Violence in America, 1890–1940.* Chapel Hill: University of North Carolina Press, 2009.

Worthen, W. B. "Citing History: Textuality and the Performativity of Suzan-Lori Parks." *Essays in Theater* 18, no. 1 (1999): 3–22.

Wright, Richard. "Big Boy Leaves Home." 1936. Reprint in *Uncle Tom's Children*, 16–62. New York: HarperPerennial, 1993.

———. "The Ethics of Living Jim Crow." 1937. In *The Norton Anthology of African American Literature*, edited by Henry Louis Gates and Nellie McKay, 1411–19. New York: Norton, 2004.

Wu, Yung-Hsing. "Native Sons and Native Speakers: On the Eth(n)ics of Comparison." *PMLA* 121, no. 5 (2006): 1460–73.

Younge, Gary. "Jena Is America." *The Nation*, October 8, 2007, 10.

INDEX

Breinigsville, PA USA
27 December 2010
252129BV00003B/39/P